DISCARD 1/16

D1597612

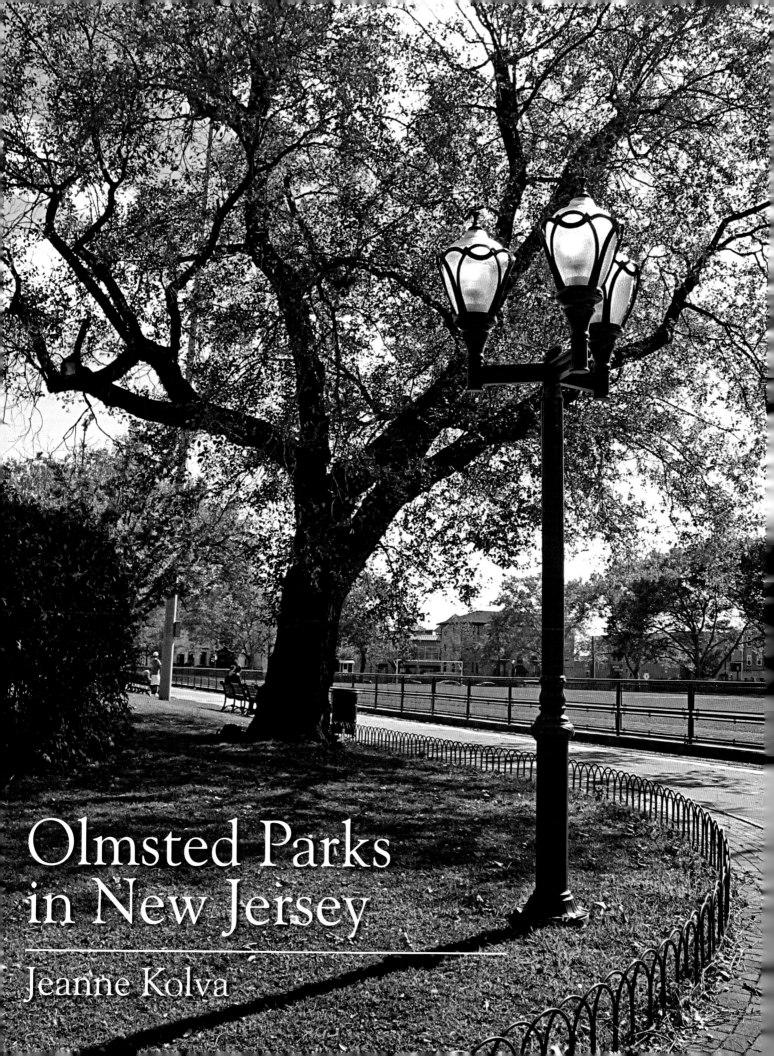

Olmsted Parks
in New Jersey

Jeanne Kolva

Designed by John P. Cheek
Cover design by Bruce Waters
Type set in Goudy OlSt BT/Myriad Pro

ISBN: 978-0-7643-3872-4
Printed in China

Schiffer Books are available at special discounts for bulk purchases for sales promotions or premiums. Special editions, including personalized covers, corporate imprints, and excerpts can be created in large quantities for special needs. For more information contact the publisher:

Published by Schiffer Publishing Ltd.
4880 Lower Valley Road
Atglen, PA 19310
Phone: (610) 593-1777; Fax: (610) 593-2002
E-mail: Info@schifferbooks.com

For the largest selection of fine reference books on this and related subjects, please visit our website at
www.schifferbooks.com
We are always looking for people to write books on new and related subjects. If you have an idea for a book, please contact us at proposals@schifferbooks.com

This book may be purchased from the publisher.
Include $5.00 for shipping.
Please try your bookstore first.
You may write for a free catalog.

In Europe, Schiffer books are distributed by
Bushwood Books
6 Marksbury Ave.
Kew Gardens
Surrey TW9 4JF England
Phone: 44 (0) 20 8392 8585; Fax: 44 (0) 20 8392 9876
E-mail: info@bushwoodbooks.co.uk
Website: www.bushwoodbooks.co.uk

*To my parents
Mary and Karl Kolva
for passing along their
love of the outdoors to all of us.*

Contents

Acknowledgments

Growing up in Rochester, New York, I never knew what it was that made that city's parks so special. It was long after I had become an adult that I learned that the parks I visited as a child, including Highland Park, and Seneca Park, had been designed by the same landscape architects as New York City's famous Central Park. My parents took me to Rochester's parks when I was young and as a return favor, I invited them to accompany me on my first visit to Cadwalader Park, an Olmsted designed park in Trenton. I'd like to thank my parents for taking the family to parks all over the country.

I would like to acknowledge the many other people who helped me with this book. The idea for a survey of all of New Jersey's Olmsted parks was born when I was taking Marta McDowell's class on Historic Landscapes at Drew University's Historic Preservation Certificate program. Preservationist Kathleen Galop gave a presentation on Newark's Branch Brook Park and it set me wondering about the Olmsted legacy in all of New Jersey.

The staff members of the Frederick Law Olmsted Historic Site in Brookline, Massachusetts, were of great help instructing me how to conduct research from afar, due to the fact that their facility was undergoing a major expansion and was closed to the public during 2009 and 2010. The writings available from Olmsted scholars, local historians, and the National Association for Olmsted Parks have been invaluable for setting the stage for my investigation and understanding. All are listed in the bibliography.

I would also like to commend the staff at the libraries of Rutgers University, Plainfield, Trenton, and Montclair, for maintaining great archives of local and regional history. I thank Jessica Myers at Plainfield Public Library; Joseph Lanzara and Kathryn Kauhl at the Archives of the Essex County Park Commission; Vatche Aslanian and Bill Magna at the Passaic County Engineer's Office; Landscape Architect Sean Ryan with the Union County Division of Park Planning and Maintenance; Landscape Architect April M. Stefel; and Wendy M. Nardi and Matthew Metcalf of the Trenton Public Library for their valuable assistance.

I would also like to thank my dear friends for their support and encouragement at the small company where I worked. Without hesitation, the president of the company and Sussex County Historian, Wayne McCabe, shared his important archive regarding Sussex County's High Point State Park. My friends in the Soup group cheered me on through the second year of the project.

And lastly, I would like to thank all the other members of my extended family, Eugene Rice, Daniel Rice, Rebecca Rice, Louise Rice, Judy Kolva, and Gaetano Montelione for encouraging me in many different ways helping sustain this effort. For all your support, I am truly grateful.

Chapter 1
Introduction

In the state of New Jersey, there are just under forty municipal, county, and state-owned parks designed by the landscape architects with the last name of Olmsted. Frederick Law Olmsted, Sr., had input on two of the earliest, but it was primarily the landscape architectural firm Olmsted Brothers, run by his son and stepson that designed the rest. This book showcases the work of the Olmsted Brothers firm run by son Frederick Law Olmsted, Jr., and stepson John Charles Olmsted. Seamlessly, the Olmsted Brothers firm took over the practice started by Senior before his retirement in 1897. The Olmsted Brothers' companies continued designing parks into the 1960s.

The Olmsted designed parks are located as far north as Sussex County (High Point State Park) and as far south as Salem County (Parvin State Park) but are largely found in three counties; Essex, Union, and Passaic. The parks range in size from small neighborhood parks, for example, Wheeler Park in Linden, to large parcels, such as the 2,000-acre South Mountain Reservation, straddling Millburn, South Orange, and Maplewood. The earliest parks in New Jersey designed with input by Frederick Law Olmsted, Sr., are Cadwalader Park in Trenton and Branch Brook Park in Newark. The youngest park designed by the Olmsted Brothers firm is Lenape Park located in Kenilworth. The Olmsted designed parks are a small percentage of the large number of the state's public parks.

View of the pond in the western section of Cadwalader Park, Trenton, New Jersey. *June 17, 2009.*

My goal was to visit all the Olmsted parks in an attempt to portray the characteristics that are in an Olmsted design. So how did I accomplish that? I started by compiling a list of all the parks in New Jersey using *The Master List of Design Projects of the Olmsted Firm 1857-1979,* limiting the list to the section entitled "Parks, Parkways, Recreation Areas, and Scenic Reservations."[1] I then used the internet-based Olmsted Research Guide Online (ORGO) database to further refine the number of parks on my list. ORGO is a database that is a compilation of all the Olmsted companies records. Developed by the Frederick Law Olmsted National Historic Site and the National Association for Olmsted Parks, the database includes descriptions of the holdings at the Frederick Law Olmsted Historic Site in Brookline, Massachusetts, and the Library of Congress in Washington, D.C.

The Olmsted Brothers organized their busy office by assigning individual numbers to all projects, both potential projects and contracted ones. These project numbers identified all the plans, photographs, planting lists, correspondence, and anything else related to a specific project. The company archives is quite enormous as this firm designed over 5,000 parks, campuses, and grounds for private estates throughout the United States and other countries.

My list of New Jersey parks changed several times, first growing then shrinking as I dropped several parks from the list. For example, two parks, including Preakness Valley Park in Passaic County and White Oak Ridge Park in Essex County, were originally public parks that were converted into limited-access golf courses. Casual visitors are prohibited. I determined that golf courses fell outside one of my parameters for defining what is a park, that of being open to all visitors, not just a selected few. Other parks were dropped due to the lack of documentation showing that the Olmsted firm had actually done work on the park, even though there were documents in the archives. The firm was often asked to submit proposals for jobs or consult on others and, even if they had assigned a project number and had items in their files, those were not sure-fire indications of actual design work. A good example is job number 7125 for the Palisades Park along the Hudson River. The six plans listed in the Olmsted archives are topographical maps drawn by State topographer Cornelius C. Vermeule. The Olmsted Brothers did not play an active role in the design of Palisades Park and I had to cross it off my list.

The next part of the process was to visit all the parks, which I did primarily on the weekends beginning in January 2009 and continuing through November 2009. Throughout most of the year 2009, weekends were typically rainy or cloudy with brief patches of sunshine. Nevertheless, I walked through the parks from one end to the other on asphalt covered trails, paths through woods, and on cobble-stoned and crushed stone walkways. I walked along waterways and roadways taking hundreds of photographs using both a digital camera (Canon Powershot A690) and a Single Lens Reflex camera (Canon A-1) loaded with slide film. I visited each park at least once and the majority of them more than once. Needless to say, the more adverse the weather, the fewer people I saw at each park. My photography was selectively turned toward the natural elements rather than depicting the human guests. In the course of conducting the park visits, I was struck by how many sections in the Olmsted parks reminded me of landscapes I've seen along rural roads in the countryside.

The third element of my project was conducting research. I acquired and borrowed as many books as I could that have information about New Jersey's Olmsted parks. These include town pictorials, histories written in the 1910s, and biographies regarding the Olmsteds. I began collecting vintage postcards of the many parks. I also used the Internet extensively locating the websites of several Parks Commissions, conservancy groups, and the American Society of Landscape Architects, as well as sites with historic maps, aerial photographs, New York Times articles, and scanned magazines and books. I visited local libraries to find articles in vertical files and old photographs and maps. These books, articles, and websites are all listed in the bibliography. Lastly, I went to utilize the archives of the three counties that have parks designed by the Olmsteds.

There are only a few parameters for my definition of an Olmsted-designed park.

1. The park must be named either a park or a reservation;

2. The locations of the features imposed upon the lands were to have been designed primarily by the Olmsted company; and,

3. The parks must be open to the general public either for free or for a small fee, such as those charged by state parks.

Public parks typically are not simple creations. They come about through a complicated process that includes land acquisition, planning, development, and management. Land acquisition involves identifying property owners and creating surveys. Ownership and boundary issues often arise as the documentation of undeveloped land has a unique set of variables and mysteries. Purchases can initially be expensive due to the large size of most parcels involved. The work of developing vacant land into a park involves complex interactions between engineers, designers, county and municipal officials, contractors, and laborers. Due to the fact that this work is done outside, the climate and weather become important factors. But the overall drive to finance the creation and maintenance of a public park is the most important factor of all. The developmental history of each park follows its own unique path and I tried to give details of each to show how complicated a process it is.

The book is organized in roughly chronological order beginning with the oldest parks and continuing through to the youngest. If documented, the individual employees responsible for each park are included. Employee biographies are to be found in a chapter at the end. Several employees had long careers with the Olmsted Brothers firm and others were there for short periods. Collectively, their work established the legacy of parks with Olmsted designs in the Garden State.

Circa 1910 postcard view of canoes on the lake in Branch Brook Park, Newark, New Jersey.

Characteristics of Olmsted Parks

According to the New York City Landmarks Preservation Commission there are classifiable elements that typically characterize an Olmsted designed park. Many of these can be seen in the parks the Olmsted Brothers designed in New Jersey.[2]

1. *They are works of art*. This means that the parks use forms that appear natural but which are designed, engineered, and physically created in an artistic way.

2. *They have their roots in English romantic style of landscape design.* This includes a mix of naturalized waterways, open spaces bordered by varieties of vegetation, and natural woodlands with meandering walkways.

3. *They provide a strong contrast to an urban environment*. Natural characteristics include a wide range of colors, shapes, and forms that are opposite to the blocky, angular, brown and gray seen in urban areas. Many parks provide a green oasis for wildlife and people.

4. *They are characterized by the use of bold forms.* Individual trees, winding walkways, walls with staircases, ponds, and large open fields all create individual forms that are unmistakably that of Olmsted design and planning.

5. *They contain artistically composed plantings.* The skillful arrangements of groves of trees, individual trees, bushes, flower beds, and woodlands is the most common characteristic of all the parks.

6. *Vistas create aesthetic organizing elements.* In many of New Jersey's parks and reservations, the high viewpoints are the main attractions.

7. *Each might have a provision for a formal element.* A small number of New Jersey's parks have formal promenades or gardens laid out in more geometric patterns.

8. *They provide for the separation of traffic.* Pedestrian walkways and drives with parking areas are kept as far apart as possible.

9. *They provide visitor services*. The majority of parks in New Jersey have picnic grounds, and visitor centers that include bathrooms, concession stands, and a variety of recreational facilities.

10. *They integrate the architecture into the landscape*. The buildings seen in each park were designed by local architects in the architectural style at the time. The buildings are small and were typically placed near the outer sections of the parks. This was planned to keep heavy vehicular traffic to a minimum in the inner reaches of the parks.

11. *They were built to provide for recreation.* Most of New Jersey's parks have large, open, multi-use fields and smaller, specialized playing fields for a variety of sports.

In 1986, eminent Olmsted scholar Charles E. Beveridge wrote a guide to Olmsted's stylistic traits and called it the "Seven S's of Olmsted's Design." They include Scenery, Suitability, Style, Subordination, Separation, Sanitation, and Service.[3]

1. Scenery: The designs for "passages of scenery" were made for small spaces and in areas intended for active use. The Olmsteds designed the topography and planting plans in each park to give an enhanced sense of the landscape. Through the development of hills, winding paths, and curving roadways, they created indefinite boundaries and opened up new views. The Olmsted plans avoided hard edges and singular specimen planting, creating instead designs that had a broad mix of colors, textures, and forms.

2. Suitability: The designs were always suited to the natural scenery and topography of each specific site. There was a concerted effort to enhance the "genius of the place" whether a mountaintop woodland or a park along the shore of a lake. The plans for parks were always based on topographical maps created by local surveyors. The use of plantings native to the location is also a key element in Olmsted parks.

3. Style: The Olmsteds designed sections of parks in specific styles, each for a particular effect. Most of New Jersey's parks have sections both in the "Pastoral" style, which includes open greenswards with waterways, scattered specimen trees, and groves of trees, and in the "Picturesque" style, which is characterized by profuse plantings, especially with shrubs, creepers, and ground cover on steep and broken terrain. Both offer a sense of nature's rich bounty.

Circa 1906 postcard of the Northern Division, Branch Brook Park in Newark showing the Olmsted design separating winding walkways and waterways from roads with the use of vegetation borders.

4. Subordination: Each individual feature was to be coordinated with the overall naturalistic design scheme and not to stand out. This was the Olmsteds' art to conceal Art.

5. Separation: There was a separation of areas designed in different styles, so that the mixture of styles would not dilute the intended effect of each. There was also a conscientious separation of travelways in order to insure safety of use and reduce distractions for those using each space.

6. Sanitation: The designs always included proper drainage and other engineering considerations. The planning centered on promoting both the physical and mental health of park users.

7. Service: The Olmsteds were very aware of planning parks to serve a purpose of direct utility or service and that would meet fundamental social and psychological needs.

Memorial Park, Maplewood, New Jersey. View of the pastoral landscape designed for the north side of the park. *May 23, 2009.*

The Olmsteds

Frederick Law Olmsted, Sr. (1822-1903) was called an artist "who paints with lakes and wooded slopes, with lawns and banks and forest-covered hills, and with mountainsides and ocean views."[4] He is the founder of American landscape architecture. He is best known as the designer of New York City's Central Park with co-designer Calvert Vaux. Olmsted, Sr., also designed the park systems in Boston, Massachusetts, and Buffalo, New York. The designs of his parks embody Olmsted's social consciousness and commitment to egalitarian ideals. In a time of an extreme divide between the rich and the poor, he hoped that from the shared use of parks by both, a common humanity would arise. He considered his designs to be both works of art and social experiments that would have a civilizing influence upon crowded urbanites.[5]

Olmsted was born in Hartford, Connecticut, in 1822. His father, John Olmsted, was a prosperous merchant and nature lover. Frederick had a younger brother, John Hull Olmsted. His mother, Charlotte Law Olmsted, nee Hull, died when he was scarcely four years old. His father remarried in 1827 to Mary Ann Bull, who shared her husband's strong love of nature and had perhaps a more cultivated taste. Frederick Law Olmsted was a graduate of Phillips Academy in 1838 and he contracted sumac poisoning, which weakened his eyes. He gave up his plans to attend college. After moving to New York City in 1840, he worked as a seaman, merchant, and journalist. Through the support of his father, Olmsted settled on a farm on the south shore of Staten Island in 1848, where he lived until 1854. This farm became the locus of his experiments with horticulture. In 1859, Olmsted married Mary Cleveland Perkins Olmsted, the widow of his brother John, who had died in 1857. He adopted her three sons (Olmsted's nephews), among them John Charles Olmsted. Frederick and Mary had two children together who survived infancy: a daughter and a son, Frederick Law Olmsted, Jr.

Olmsted became best known for his work as a landscape architect when he, along with Calvert Vaux, designed Central Park and Riverside Park in Manhattan, and Prospect Park in Brooklyn. In 1865, the two formed a company, Olmsted, Vaux and Company. Olmsted's career in New York was hindered by politics and he was dismissed from the New York Park Commission in 1878. He moved to Brookline, Massachusetts, in 1882. He would retire in 1895 and live his remaining years at McLean Hospital in Belmont, Massachusetts.[6] His retirement came just at the time when New Jersey was just beginning to develop its parks and park systems.

The next generation of Olmsteds began to be more involved with the company beginning in the late 1870s. Frederick Law Olmsted, Sr.'s stepson John Charles Olmsted had been an active participant in the administrative affairs of the office and in 1884, the firm was renamed F. L. & J. C. Olmsted Company when John Charles became a full partner. This continued to operate until 1894 when the company was changed to F. L. Olmsted and Company (1889-1893). In 1893, Charles Eliot joined the firm and it became Olmsted, Olmsted, and Eliot. The name lasted until 1897, when Eliot died and son Frederick Law Olmsted, Jr., joined the firm. Once again the name of the company became F. L. and J. C. Olmsted, however this time the F. L. stood for the son. A year later, the company name was standardized as the Olmsted Brothers. It would continue to be known by that name from 1898 to 1961.[7]

John Charles Olmsted (1852-1920)

When John Charles was a seven year old, he came to live in the house of his uncle and new stepfather, Frederick

Law Olmsted, Sr. He grew up various places as his new father moved the family when his occupation changed. After graduating from Yale's Sheffield Scientific School, John Charles began his professional career as an apprentice in his stepfather's firm. Making full partner by 1884, John Charles continued as a full partner in the company (through all the name changes) until his death in 1920. In addition to his extensive design and planning work, John Charles also was responsible for creating a productive and efficient office and a training program for employees. He introduced modern office methods, such as using typewriters, and he oversaw the training of apprentices, clerks, and draftsmen in the busy office. Like his stepfather, John Charles was committed to the development of landscape art and comprehensive planning as a profession. He was a founding member of the American Society of Landscape Architects. His professionalism spanned from the "City Beautiful" era into modern "City Efficient" times. His progressive and pragmatic approach led many municipal and county planners to advocate for comprehensive park systems.[8] His ideals and guidance were instrumental in establishing the Essex County park system.

John Charles Olmsted, circa 1909. *Courtesy National Park Service, Frederick Law Olmsted National Historic Site*.

Frederick Law Olmsted, Jr. (1870-1957)

The younger Frederick Law Olmsted was born on Staten Island. After graduating from the Roxbury Latin School in 1890 and earning his bachelor's degree at Harvard University in 1894, he began his career as an apprentice to his famous father after whom he was named. Upon his father's retirement in 1897, Frederick Law Olmsted Jr. (known as Rick) became a full partner along with his stepbrother John Charles Olmsted in the family business. For the next half-century, the Olmsted brothers' firm completed thousands of landscape projects nationwide. In 1899, he became one of the founding members of the American Society of Landscape Architects and maintained himself a firm advocate of the City Beautiful movement, which called for comprehensive planning and civic improvements. In 1910, he offered crucial advice on the creation of a new bureau of national parks. His best contribution was the simple words that would guide conservation in America for generations to come (National Park Service Organic Act, 1916):

> To conserve the scenery and the natural and historic objects and the wild life therein and to provide for the enjoyment of the same in such manner and by such means as will leave them unimpaired for the enjoyment of future generations.

His long career included consultations on state and metropolitan park systems, and greenways across the country. In 1928, while working for California State Park Commission, Olmsted completed a statewide survey of potential parklands that defined basic long-range goals and provided guidance for the acquisition and development of state parks. Under the leadership of John Charles Olmsted and Frederick Law Olmsted, Jr., the Olmsted Brothers firm employed nearly 60 staff members at its peak in the 1920s. As the last surviving family member in the firm, Frederick Law Olmsted, Jr. retired in 1949, eight years before his death.[9]

The Olmsteds were significant participants in what has been dubbed the "City Beautiful Movement." This was an idea brought out by progressive thinkers of the importance of beautifying urban environments for the civilizing effect it would have. It emerged from the 1893 Columbian Exposition in Chicago. The Exposition provided a prominent American example of a great group of buildings designed in relation to each other and in relation to open spaces. This resulted in large-scale and comprehensive urban planning incorporating aesthetics and design. Parks and park systems were included as vital parts of this movement for their intrinsically restorative qualities. Consistent with the comprehensive vision of the City Beautiful Movement, county park systems were designed as master plans with

James F. Dawson, Frederick Law Olmsted, Jr., and Percival Gallagher at work. Date unknown. *Courtesy National Park Service, Frederick Law Olmsted National Historic Site.*

small neighborhood parks, larger scenic parks within cities, and suburban reservations. Supporters of the movement called for the installation of public art and removal of visual pollutants, such as billboards.[10]

This movement would be altered in the early 20th century with the advent of automobiles and their impact on land use. Advocates for park systems would now have them linked by parkways (roads lined with trees and plantings). The City Efficient Movement followed with new laws and court cases relative to land use, zoning, subdivision control, and administrative planning regulation. Civil engineers, attorneys, and public administrators began to play a larger role in city planning with an increase in demand for modern public services, such as highways and sanitary sewers. Scientific methods would now be used to address the social needs of city dwellers throughout the country. In New Jersey, the Olmsted parks stand as a testament to the progressive thinkers and planners who embraced the ideals of both the City Beautiful and City Efficient movements.

From the large-scale ideals of park systems to the smallest details of benches and arbors, the Olmsteds consistently provided expert landscape architectural planning to their clients. The Olmsted legacy in New Jersey is manifest in several ways. The neighborhood parks are oases of engineered natural beauty in urban neighborhoods and the reservations are regional wilderness havens. The county park systems are comprehensive in scope and used democratically. In particular, the Union County system stands as the only instance where the Olmsted Brothers firm was successful in convincing a Park Commission to acquire all the land necessary to establish linked parks.[11] The Union County parkways and greenways established precious connected public spaces. This can act as a grand example of public-minded planning for counties that previously had land use planning focused solely on the interests of private development. The Olmsted name continues to play an important role for this collection of parks, now each between fifty and 120 years old, as they are coming to be recognized as historic sites and eligible for listing in the New Jersey and National Registers of Historic Places. The Olmsted parks in New Jersey are magnificent historic landscapes and worthy of preservation.

Endnotes Chapter 1: Introduction

[1]National Association for Olmsted Parks. *The Master List of Design Projects of the Olmsted Firm 1857-1979*. Lucy Lawliss, Caroline Loughlin, Lauren Meier, eds. Second Edition. (Washington, D.C.: National Association for Olmsted Parks, 2008); 66-70.
[2]William A. Mann. *Landscape Architecture: An Illustrated History in Timelines, Site Plans, and Biography*. (New York: John Wiley & Sons, Inc., 1993); 358.
[3]Charles E. Beveridge, "The Seven S's of Olmsted Design," January 1986 posted on the National Association of Olmsted Park's website at www.olmsted.org/ht/d/sp/i/1168/pid/1168
[4]Elizabeth Stevenson. *Parkmaker: A Life of Frederick Law Olmsted*. (New Brunswick, N. J.: Transaction Publishers, 2000); p. 399.
[5]Elizabeth Stevenson. *Parkmaker: A Life of Frederick Law Olmsted*; p. 377.
[6]Wikipedia entry on Frederick Law Olmsted, Sr. at the website: http://en.wikipedia.org/wiki/Frederick_Law_Olmsted.

[7]David Grayson Allen. *The Olmsted National Historic Site and the Growth of Historic Landscape Preservation*. (Hanover, N. H.: University Press of New England, 2007); p. 8.
[8]Arleyn Levee. "John Charles Olmsted," in Charles A. Birnbaum and Robin Karson. *Pioneers of American Landscape Design*. (New York: McGraw-Hill, 2000); p. 283.
[9]Susan L. Klaus. "Frederick Law Olmsted, Jr.", in Charles A. Birnbaum and Robin Karson. *Pioneers of American Landscape Design*. (New York: McGraw-Hill, 2000); pp. 273-276.
[10]Ulana D. Zakalak. National Register Nomination for Weequahic Park Historic District, March 29, 2002. On file with the National Park Service, Washington, D.C.
[11]My thanks to Sean Ryan Landscape Architect in the Union County Division of Parks and to April M. Stefel, Landscape Architect in the Plainfield Planning Department for pointing out the significance of the Olmsted Brothers' overall design in Union County.

Chapter 2
Cadwalader Park: Trenton (1891)

Before it became Cadwalader Park, the acreage that was just outside the older boundary of the city of Trenton was a landscaped, 80-acre, private estate owned by George Farlee. The estate included "Ellarslie," an Italianate mansion designed in 1848 by John Notman and built by Henry McCall, Sr. Now the Trenton City Museum, the mansion is listed in the State and National Registers of Historic Places.

In 1881, McCall's son had sold the property to George Farlee and Farlee offered it for sale seven years later. On May 15, 1888, after many months of vigorous lobbying by Trenton businessman Edmund C. Hill (1855-1936), Trenton's Common Council voted to purchase the George Farlee estate with the expressed purpose that it would become a public park. The 1893 Manual of the Park Commission of the City of Trenton states;

> The $69,600 purchase included the Farlee property, embracing about 90 acres, also a strip of eight acres belonging to the adjoining Cadwalader estate, and the Atterbury river frontage of one-quarter of a mile. The river frontage was secured with a view to a river drive in the future, the boulevard to extend from either the lower or upper Delaware bridge.[1]

Hill was a baker by trade and a developer by avocation, and also a member of the Common Council. He chaired the Parks Committee and was principal advocate for the idea of creating city parks in Trenton. His obituary in the New York Times on April 17, 1936, honored him as the "Father" of Trenton's park system. Soon after purchase by the City, the formerly private estate lands were open to the public. The landscaped estate lands included "27 acres of well-kept lawns, two ravines with towering forests on both sides, and babbling brooks making music along their dark depths." Park Committee furnished a bandstand, prairie dog farm, and bear pit, as well as benches and picnic tables. By August 1888, the Trenton Horse Railroad provided transportation to the throngs of visitors going to the new park. In December 1888, the name of the park was changed to Cadwalader Park in an effort to entice the Cadwalader descendents to sell their adjacent estate lands for development.[2] The land of the park would change a few years later. Frederick Law Olmsted, Sr. landed the job of redesigning Cadwalader Park in 1890 after interviewing with committee members Lewis Lawton and Edmund C Hill.

Circa 1910 postcard showing the main drive in Cadwalader Park, Trenton, New Jersey. Pre-existing trees were always incorporated into the Olmsteds' park designs.

Recently, Glenn R. Modica wrote an excellent book about the nearby Cadwalader Heights neighborhood titled, *Cadwalader Heights: The History of an Olmsted Neighborhood, Trenton, New Jersey.* He includes a very detailed chapter on Cadwalader Park. The park is bounded by Stuyvesant Avenue to the northeast, Parkside Avenue to the southeast, the Delaware and Raritan Canal to the southwest, and Cadwalader Drive to the northwest. The one existing Olmsted plan of the park, which experts have determined is the final plan, shows the curvilinear drives, perimeter plantings, the pond, a shelter, and a large open space of the boys playground in the northern section.[3] The 1896 report from the Park Commission states:

A thorough landscape survey of the park was made by Frederick L. Olmsted of Boston and his plans have been generally followed in the improvements. There is nearly a mile of macadam drive along which 200 young trees have been set out. In addition to the numerous paths existing in the old property, others have been laid out for pleasant strolls through the grove and ravines, and the Commission has still further additions in contemplation. Hundreds of flowering plants lend embellishment to the lawns in the summertime. Fields are set apart for baseball, cricket and football, and the tennis and croquet players have numerous courts. In the near future a lake will be formed by damming a perpetual stream which flows on the west side, so that there can be boating and skating, according to season.[4]

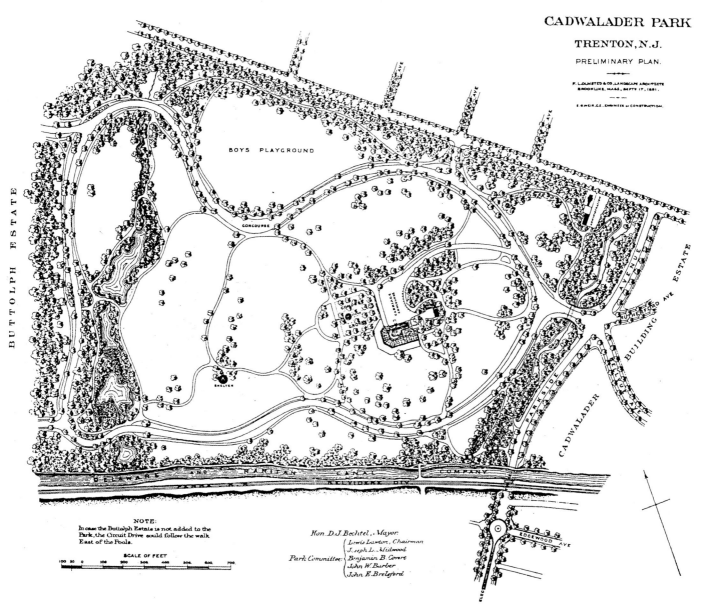

F. L. Olmsted & Company, Landscape Architects. Preliminary plan of Cadwalader Park, Trenton dated September 17, 1891. *Courtesy of the Trenton Public Library.*

Except in the northwestern part of the park, the roadways in place roughly follow Olmsted's plan. A note on the plan states that if the neighboring property to the northwest was not purchased to become part of the park, the drive could then follow the path to the east of the ponds. The drive is positioned east of the pond as the neighboring property of the Buttolph Estate never became part of Cadwalader Park.

In general, Olmsted's naturalistic plan was followed. Purchase orders show native plantings were purchased from local nurseries and exotic specimens came from larger nurseries in Pennsylvania and Massachusetts. Over the ensuing years many other elements found in public parks have been added. The 1901 Report of the Park Commission indicated that the park had a new aviary and the original deer paddock had been expanded into a zoo that included such animals as four alligators, an ostrich, two black bears, eight monkeys, and one bull.

Three important public sculptures were erected in the park; one of George Washington, the second of John Roebling, and the third, Mercer County's Civil War monument. The statue of Washington standing in the prow of a small boat had been carved in Italy, exhibited in Philadelphia at the 1876 Centennial Exhibition, and purchased at auction by councilmen Whitaker and Hill. It was erected in the park on April 18, 1892, located on a slight rise approximately 500 feet west of Ellarslie. The statue remained there until 1976, when it was moved to South Montgomery Street in downtown Trenton.[5]

The statue of industrial engineer John A. Roebling, designed by sculptor William Couper, was erected on June 30, 1908. It stands approximately 600 feet northwest of the Museum, now with a backdrop made from a grove of beech trees. The statue pays tribute to the engineer who was first in the country to make wire rope that was used in suspension bridges. The bronze statue of Roebling seated in an armchair with his legs crossed is atop a base of red Swedish granite. Commemorative tablets with bas-reliefs of the Brooklyn Bridge and a railroad bridge over the Niagara River are affixed to either side.[6]

This historic photograph taken circa 1910 shows the section of Cadwalader Park with the newly erected memorial to John A. Roebling. *Courtesy of the Trenton Public Library.*

Now surrounded by mature trees, the Roebling memorial is located in a pastoral section of Cadwalader Park, Trenton, New Jersey. *October 20, 2009.*

The third monument is the Mercer County Soldiers and Sailors monument created by sculptor Charles P. Owen and architect Alfred R. Baxter. Dedicated on June 19, 1909, it commemorated those who served in the United States Army and Navy during the Civil War from 1861-1866. The fifty-foot memorial consists of a granite base and tall column, two Civil War figures, a soldier and a sailor in bronze flanking the base, and a Civil War Color Guard figure atop the column. The soldier is standing erect holding a gun that rests vertically before him and the sailor stands holding a telescope in his crossed arms and his right leg is upon a coil of heavy rope. The color guard holds an American flag on a pole in his left hand and reaches for the hilt of his sword with his right.[7] This monument is located east of the Museum near the Parkside Avenue entrance.

Olmsted applied his design philosophy to the nearly one hundred acres of the former McCall estate, resulting in what is now Cadwalader Park. Both the pastoral and the picturesque elements of Frederick Law Olmsted's design work are included. There are natural rolling hills and hillocks, a managed waterway, native and exotic plantings, subspecies of trees and shrubs, and meandering footpaths that rarely intersect the roadway. The park had a deer paddock next to the pond, and hundreds of trees planted in groves and as individual specimens, including some that are rare at this

latitude.[8] The picturesque heavily wooded perimeter along Parkside Avenue includes a rustic stone bridge that carries the entrance off Parkside Avenue over a small brook. The park acts as a centerpiece of the Cadwalader Heights neighborhood that surrounds it.

The Mercer County Soldiers and Sailors Memorial was created by sculptor Charles P. Owen and architect Alfred R. Baxter. It was erected in 1909 to commemorate Civil War veterans. Cadwalader Park, Trenton, New Jersey. *February 15, 2009.*

The autumn colors on display at Cadwalader Park, Trenton, New Jersey. *October 20, 2009.*

Red-tailed hawk on the wing at Cadwalader Park, Trenton, New Jersey. *February 15, 2009.*

The plantings in Cadwalader Park in Trenton include trees native to New Jersey as well as selected exotic species. *October 20, 2009.*

Endnotes Chapter 2: Cadwalader Park

[1]Manual of the Park Commission of the City of Trenton. Trenton, N. J.: Naar, Day & Naar, Printers, 1893.

[2]Glenn R. Modica. *Cadwalader Heights; The History of an Olmsted Neighborhood, Trenton, New Jersey.* (Newtown, Pennsylvania: Bucks Digital Printing, 2007): 25-31.

[3]Glenn R. Modica. *Cadwalader Heights; The History of an Olmsted Neighborhood, Trenton, New Jersey.* (Newtown, Pennsylvania: Bucks Digital Printing, 2007): 29.

[4]Manual of the Park Commission of the City of Trenton. Trenton, N. J.: Naar, Day & Naar, Printers, 1893.

[5]The Trenton Historical Society has a web page with many newspaper articles about the statue from the time it was purchased in 1889 to the time it was moved in 1976. The web site address is: www.trentonhistory.org/records/statue.html.

[6]Alfred N. Barber. *John A. Roebling: An Account of the Ceremonies at the Unveiling of a Monument to His Memory.* (Trenton, New Jersey: Roebling Press, 1908): 1-5.

[7]Save Outdoor Sculpture! database on the Smithsonian Institution Research Information System (SIRIS) at the Smithsonian American Art Museum. The website is www.americanart.si.edu/research/programs/sos.

[8]Information about Cadwalader Park and the Trenton City Museum and located on the Museum's website at: http://www.ellarslie.org/index.htm.

Chapter 3
Essex County Parks System

Essex County contains twenty-two municipalities and is located in the northeastern part of the state bounded by Passaic, Bergen, Hudson, Union, and Morris counties. The eastern section is low and relatively flat. Newark is located in the eastern section. It is the county seat of Essex County and an old and historic city. Suburban towns covering the twin ridges of the Watchung Mountains define the central section of the county. Waterways include rivers such as the Second, the Hackensack, and the Passaic. The source of the Passaic River is in the broad flat valley in the western section of the county. Four areas in the three municipalities of Verona, North Caldwell, and Essex Fells have the highest elevation of 660 feet above sea level. The lowest point is sea level at Newark Bay and the mouth of the Passaic River.

Plaque at the Ballantine entrance to Branch Brook Park, Newark, New Jersey. *April 18, 2009.*

21

Throughout the eighteenth and nineteenth centuries, Essex County's land was used primarily for agriculture. In 1800, the county population was approximately 20,000. By 1860, as much as 75% of the land remained as farmland. By the 1870s, the population had risen to over 143,000 people with over 100,000 residing in Newark. The growth of Newark as an industrial center began with the construction of the turnpike roads in the first decade of the nineteenth century and the construction of the Morris Canal and railroads in the 1830s. All had a terminus in Newark. Many hatters, leather tanners, and shoemakers moved to Newark and the smaller nearby city of Orange. After the Civil War, shoes and leather remained important industries and were joined by factories producing carriages and machinery. Contributing to the industrial growth, Thomas Edison relocated his laboratories to West Orange in 1887.[1] Industry attracted workers and the need for housing rose swiftly resulting in overcrowded urban conditions. In civic-minded efforts to combat the negative qualities of living in dense urban conditions, the City Beautiful movement arose during the late nineteenth century.

Reflecting the times and complementing the City Beautiful movement, the Essex County Park Commission was established in 1895 and Frederick W. Kelsey of Orange, New Jersey, was one of its key participants. In 1905 he published a history of the first ten years of the Park Commission's activities. His book, *The First County Park System; A Complete History of the Inception and Development of the Essex County Parks of New Jersey*, details the negotiations, problems, successes, and progress of the park system's early development.

Prior attempts to establish a public park in Newark in the 1860s failed as a committee of twenty-six residents could not agree upon a universally accepted location for it. In 1889, the Newark Aqueduct Board dedicated the city reservoir property for use as a park, but no further action was taken and the condition of the area precluded such use. Frederick W. Kelsey was an early advocate of creating a county-wide park system taking localized municipal politics out of the planning process. He spoke at meetings of the Board of Trade of the Oranges and at the Newark Board of Trade. Park Committees of both groups met to begin the cooperative planning that would lead to the establishment of a two-year Essex County Park Commission by legislative act in Trenton in April 1894. The public response to the formation of a Commission with the power to spend $10,000 for initial planning was singularly favorable. Editorials expressed confidence that the first commissioners would "do their work faithfully and well." One commissioner was quoted as saying "public parks are a common possession in which the poor and the rich share and share alike."[2]

1889 map of Essex County, New Jersey by Scarlett & Scarlett, Surveyors and Civil Engineers.
Courtesy of Special Collections and University Archives, Rutgers University Libraries.

In the first year, the Commission sought expert advise through a competition and visited possible locations for parks based on the responses from several landscape architect firms including Olmsted, Olmsted & Eliot, and Messrs. John Bogart and Nathan F. Barrett Landscape Architects and Engineers. The commissioners wrote a charter and petitioned to have a permanent Commission established deciding that its members should be appointed by a judge rather than chosen by voters in elections. The commissioners also discussed how best to finance the parks by studying how other countries and states paid for theirs. The decision was to institute a financing system based on the county issuing bonds and a special tax levy.

In March 1895, a bill for the creation of a permanent Park Commission went before Governor Werts for his signature. On the 9th of April, with a substantial majority, voters approved the Essex County Park act and gave the Commission the authority to spend over $2,500,000. On April 18, 1895, the new Essex County Park Commission was announced and on April 20, 1895, the newly-appointed commissioners, Messrs. Peck, Meeker, Shepard, Kelsey, and Murphy, took the prescribed oath of office and the same afternoon met in the rooms of the former commission for organization.[3] By July, 1895, bonds had been produced and the negotiations for land began. The area that would become Branch Brook Park was purchased by the end of 1896. Negotiations for land that would become Eagle Rock and South Mountain Reservations, East Side Park (now Independence Park), Weequahic Park, and West Side Park were also underway. At one point, the Commission discussed setting a required minimum wage for laborers at $1.25 per day, but it was not accepted and contractors paying market wages prevailed.[4]

The first Essex County park to be finished in 1897, was a small park in the Ironbound section of Newark. The term "Ironbound" refers to the neighborhood's physical boundaries of heavy industry and several railroads. It was originally named East Side Park and it was designed by John Bogart and Nathan F. Barrett, Landscape Architects and Engineers. The12.69 acre-park, now named Independence Park, is bordered by Walnut Street on the north, Adams Street on the west, Oliver Street on the south, and Van Buren Street on the east.

In his 1905 book, Frederick W. Kelsey stated that in 1895, the first Commission made the selection of this area for a park. He described East Side Park as a "level tract and the landscape treatment with trees on the border, walks, and lawn is similar to most city squares or parks of small acreage. The park contains little more than twelve acres and cost upward of $160,000."[5] Beginning in 1899, the Olmsted Brothers firm was commissioned to draw up plans for several modifications and additions to the park. In the *Fourth Annual Report of the Park Commission 1898-1899*, the Olmsted Brothers wrote the following short summary of East Side Park.

> This small park, containing only about twelve and one-half acres, had already been completed in a simple semi-formal style, but, with the idea of making it more useful, we made plans for two outdoor gymnasia with dressing and toilet houses, after the manner of Charles bank in Boston. It is doubtful, however, whether the Board will feel justified in incurring the necessary expense, considering the limited funds at its disposal. The borders of this small park have recently been planted with shrubbery in addition to the trees previously planted. The object is to afford an interesting decoration at moderate expense and to render the park more enjoyable to visitors in it by screening out somewhat more fully the surrounding streets and houses.[6]

On the Swings. East Side Park, NEWARK, N. J.

In 1909, Paul Davis' grandmother sent him a postcard of East Side Park in Newark. She wrote, "Dear Grandson, I am having a nice time but it is warm here. From Grandma." The postcard shows a posed group of children and behind them, the border vegetation that the Olmsted Brothers firm designed to separate the park from its urban surrounding.

By 1913, the park had no roads but 1.5 miles of paths, athletic fields for both boys and girls, a sand court, and a bandstand.[7] Later on in the 1920s, the Olmsted Brothers firm was commissioned to oversee several construction projects in this park including a music court, the men's recreation hall, and children's field house. They contracted with local firms such as Goodwille and Moran, Architects to provide plans. Eastside Park would be renamed Independence Park in 1923 accompanied by a fanfare held on July Fourth of that year. Although the Olmsted Brothers firm had some involvement in this small urban park, their role producing designs was minimal. Independence Park cannot be considered to be an Olmsted designed park.

The young Essex County park system was given a favorable review in the April 6, 1902 edition of the New York Times. It was part travel guide and part critique. Cromwell Childe raved about the parks, which included East Side Park, Westside Park, Branch Brook Park, Orange Park, Weequahic Park, Eagle Rock Reservation, and South Mountain Reservation.[8] By 1913, the Essex County park system had been expanded to include the new parks of Riverbank Park in Newark, Watsessing Park in East Orange, Irvington Park in Irvington, Glenfield Park in Montclair, and Yantacaw Park in Nutley.[9] These were all designed by the Olmsted Brothers, Landscape Architects. Once the Essex County Park Commission started working with the Olmsted Brothers in 1897, the firm became the landscape architects of choice.

The Essex County Park Commission wrote annual reports and provided a yearly summary of the parks development. In 1920, the Commission summarized its activities from the previous years.

pre-war conditions, the Board found itself unable to carry out the mandate of the people. Owing to the greatly increased prices of labor and material, the improvements could not be finished with the money on hand. The Commission, therefore, applied to the last Legislature, which passed an act authorizing the Board of Freeholders of Essex County to issue bonds to the amount of $500,000 to carry on the work. This appropriation also includes money for the purchase of two additional parcels of land at South Mountain Reservation, which will bring the total area of this splendid park up to 2,056 acres. The property was needed to carry the reservation to Glen Avenue, a boundary street, and prevent the erection of structures which would appear to the casual observer to be within the reservation itself and thus greatly detract from its sylvan beauty.[10]

The playgrounds throughout the Park System are increasing in popularity each year and more than justifying the cost of their establishment. Their most notable accomplishment during the year was the development of a spirit of helpful service among the children. The ideal community playground is one of the best developers of true Americanism. The Essex County Park playgrounds are attractive children's community centers. They encourage a high quality of activities, which encourage loyalty and public spirit among the children. Every year since the opening of the playgrounds, in 1906, noticeable improvement has been made. The games, dances and plays have changed very little and are used in new and attractive ways. From the first friendly

Before the commencement of the world war the Legislature authorized park bond issues for an addition to West Side Park in Newark, the construction of Vailsburg Park in Newark, and for parks in Belleville, Caldwell and Verona. These issues were approved by the voters on referendum at various elections. The Board deemed these additions highly desirable as extensions to the County Park System.

During the war no construction work was attempted, and as the estimates in each case were based on

The canopy formed by the mature trees in this park offers a shady respite on a very warm day in late spring. Independence Park, Newark, New Jersey. *May 23, 2009.*

competition was stressed, the inter-park athletic contest created intense interest and friendly rivalry, the baseball and basketball leagues developed community spirit. The park playground field days attracted public interest and afforded each playground group an opportunity to exhibit its work and to entertain the children of the other county park playgrounds. "The Essex County Park Playground Song," written by one of the teachers, became very popular on the playgrounds.

The field day exercises and the special feature programs developed a strong friendship among the groups. Under the direction of the teachers, picnics to the county playgrounds were held. The field day exercises gradually gave way to the picnics and parties. The first general playground picnic was held at Eagle Rock Reservation. The next year it was held at South Mountain Reservation. Special cars were chartered to take the children to the reservations. Each group prepared special feature programs. The children spent the day in the reservation and enjoyed the entertainment, songs, games and dances. Ice cream was served after

luncheon. The aims and purposes of the Essex County Park Commission were explained to the children and the natural beauty spots of the reservations were pointed out to them. Several petitions to have a picnic each week during the summer were received.[11]

Essex County would continue to use the Olmsted Brothers' service into the 1950s. As a result, the majority of the county parks would be designed by the Olmsted firms. The Olmsted-designed, Essex County-run parks include: Belleville Park in Belleville; Branch Brook Park, Riverbank Park, Vailsburg Park, Weequahic Park, and Westside Park in Newark; Anderson Park, Brookdale Park, Eagle Rock Reservation, and Glenfield Park in Montclair; Grover Cleveland Park in Essex Fells; Irvington Park in Irvington; Mills Reservation in Cedar Grove; Orange Park in Orange; South Mountain Reservation, which straddles the four municipalities of West Orange, South Orange, Millburn, and Maplewood; Verona Park in Verona; Watsessing Park in East Orange and Bloomfield; and Yantacaw Park in Nutley. These are all discussed in greater detail on the following pages.

PLAYGROUNDS, WEST SIDE PARK. NEWARK, N.J.

Circa 1910 postcard view of a girl's volleyball game at the playground at West Side Park, Newark, New Jersey.

Endnotes Chapter 3: Essex County Parks System

[1]Augustine J. Curley. "Essex County." *Encyclopedia of New Jersey.* Maxine N. Lurie and Marc Mappen, eds. (New Brunswick, New Jersey: Rutgers University Press, 2004): 258-259.
[2]Frederick W. Kelsey. *The First County Park System; A Complete History of the Inception and Development of the Essex County Parks of New Jersey.* (New York, New York: J. S. Ogilvie Publishing Company, 1905): 29.
[3]*Ibid:* 49-59.
[4]*Ibid:* 108.
[5]*Ibid:* 115.
[6]Essex County Department of Parks. *Fourth Annual Report of the Board of Commissioners, 1898-99.* (Newark, New Jersey: Grover Bros., 1900).
[7]Frank John Urquhart. *A History of The City of Newark, New Jersey Embracing Practically Two and A Half Centuries 1666-1913.* (New York,

New York: Lewis Historical Publishing Company, 1915): 858-863.
[8]Cromwell Childe. "A Chain of Beautiful Parks" *New York Times*, 6 April, 1902.
[9]Frank John Urquhart. *A History of The City of Newark, New Jersey Embracing Practically Two and A Half Centuries 1666-1913.* (New York, New York: Lewis Historical Publishing Company, 1915): 858-863.
[10]Essex County Department of Parks. *Twenty-fifth Annual Report of the Board of Commissioners, 1920.* (Newark, New Jersey: The W. H. Shurts Co., Printers, 1921): 9.
[11]Essex County Department of Parks. *Twenty-fifth Annual Report of the Board of Commissioners, 1920.* (Newark, New Jersey: The W. H. Shurts Co., Printers, 1921): 13-14.

Chapter 4

West Side Park: Newark (1898)

Unlike Eastside Park, which arose from direct planning in 1895 by the first Parks Commission, West Side Park came to be as a result of neighborhood advocacy. The Parks Commission had not considered creating a park in this section of Newark. The residents of the west side insisted and actively participated in a lobbying effort throughout 1896. Early in February 1897, the Commission authorized the requisite maps, land options and purchases.[1] This 31-acre park is located in the Central Ward near the western boundary of the City of Newark. It is one block north of Springfield Avenue and bounded by 16th Avenue on the north, South 13th Street on the east, 18th Avenue on the south, and South 17th Street on the west. The name seems to be interchangeable between "West Side Park" and "Westside Park."

In the Fourth annual Report of the Essex County Park Commission in 1899, the following entry summarized the progress made on West Side Park:

> No more land remains to be purchased at Westside Park, and the contract for its development, amounting to $41,842, is in progress. It includes a lake and wading-pool, a series of terraces leading up from this to a long vine-covered walk, a running track, an outdoor gymnasium and a concourse, where concerts can be held. This plan was determined upon after consultation with the residents of that section of Newark, and was made to conform to their wishes in every respect compatible with proper landscape considerations. There is a deep deposit of muck in the southeastern corner of this park, which was formerly Magnolia Swamp, and its proper excavation is a somewhat difficult problem. It is, in some places, thirty feet deep. As it is taken out it is used to reinforce the soil at Branch Brook Park and Eastside Park, which is poor and scant.[2]

The Olmsted Brothers also contributed a more detailed description of their plans for West Side Park the same Annual Report:

> Westside Park belongs to a distinct class of medium-sized pleasure grounds, which we designate as a "local park." It is larger and more varied in its topography than a city square, yet too small to afford the complete degree of seclusion and the sense of expansiveness and rurality important in a large park, and too contracted to warrant the introduction of a drive.
>
> In its west border there is a ridge about ten feet above the adjoining street, and at the foot of the east slope of the ridge, and thirty-one feet below its summit there was a swamp, narrow at the northeast corner of the park and widening out to about one-third of the width of the park at its south end. The ridge is correspondingly broad at its north end. The land has been heretofore used as a farm and is almost destitute of trees. The landscape design is to excavate the marsh and form a small lake along the base of the ridge. The hillside will be a pleasing grassy slope, with a few single trees and groups of trees and some shrubbery on the steeper bank toward the north.
>
> The whole length of the ridge will be occupied by a straight, shaded promenade. In the northern part this will be a single broad walk shaded by a row of trees on each side. The southern portion will comprise three wide parallel straight walks ending at the south in a square court, to be decorated in the middle by a fountain, which may eventually be made more imposing by the aid of architecture and sculpture. The middle and widest walk will be shaded by a row of trees on each side. The two outer walks it is proposed to cover with vine-clad arbors and these arbors will also surround the square court. Abutting upon the northern portion of this arbor it is planned to have a large shelter building with a bandstand either attached in the form of a projecting balcony or separate. A hard gravel terrace, with trees regularly disposed, will surround the shelter creating a formal concert grove overlooking the lake.
>
> From the square court at the south end of the promenade there will be a series of terraces supported by stone retaining walls, with flights of steps, extending down the hill eastward to a water terrace at the lake. The latter will have a central fountain. The other terraces above will be decorated with flowerbeds. All formal flowerbeds will be concentrated in the formal parts of the design. There may be an abundance of perennial flowers in the margins of the irregular shrubberies, and there may be water plants in the margins of the lake.

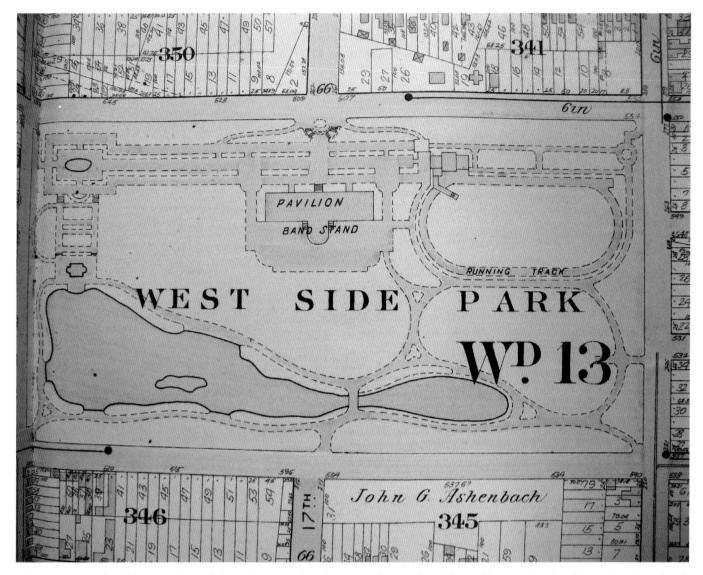

Robinson's 1901 *Atlas of the City of Newark* shows the original configuration of West Side Park located between South 17th Street (on the top) and South 14th Street (on the bottom). Located in Ward 13, it was one of the first parks developed by the Essex County Park Commission. *Courtesy of Special Collections and University Archives, Rutgers University Libraries.*

The remainder of the top of the ridge, north of the concert grove and east of the straight promenade, will be occupied by a hard gravel playground or outdoor gymnasium, surrounded by a running track (five laps to the mile) and outside of this again, on three sides, there will be a walk separated from the running track by an iron picket fence to prevent interference with the runners. The west side will have a grandstand facing east, so the afternoon sun will be behind the spectators. This hard gravel playground will necessarily be ugly in itself, but from the irregular or landscape portion of the park, which is nearly all below it, it will be invisible. It will also be nearly screened out by shrubbery and trees.

Between the outdoor gymnasium and the northern portion of the lake there is planned to be a comparatively level lawn for very little children to play upon under the eye of their parents or nurses. This lawn will be cut into the hillside on the west and filled out in the east. A low vine-covered fence will prevent the children from straying, thus reducing the fear and anxiety of the parents, who may sit in the small shelters. The north end of the lake will be surrounded by a sandy beach and will be only sixteen inches deep. Thus little children may safely wade in it, or play in the sand or sail toy boats without danger. A stone bridge with a fence under it will separate this wading-pool from the deeper part of the lake, which will be treated as naturally as possible.[3]

The Frederick Law Olmsted Historic Site has the plans and sketches created by the Olmsted Brothers employees who worked on this park between 1899 and 1921. They included; John Charles Olmsted, James Frederick Dawson, Arthur H. Vinal, Percy R. Jones, William H. Munroe, Wilber David Cook, Jr., William C. Woolner, Edward Sturgis, H. P. Richmond, Edward A. Douglas, Emanuel Tillman Mische, Herbert E. Millard, Mr. Hemboldt, P.W. Dorr, Edward L. Keeling, Hubert M. Canning, Stanley White, C. R. Wait, Percival Gallagher, Thomas E. Carpenter, and Henry Pree.

The majority of the plans are unsigned; however, there are a few identified with initials or names. Percy R. Jones designed the wading pool and produced the grading plan for the site for a pavilion in 1899. Edward A. Douglas designed the footbridge over the lake and developed the planting plan in February 1900. Architect Arthur H. Vinal designed the arbors, the park benches, and all of the sets of steps in the years 1899 and 1900. James A. Dawson drew plans showing the locations of the existing trees. William H. Munroe drew the general plan of the park. In March 1912, Herbert E. Millard designed the planting plan for the Terrace Gardens. Thomas E. Carpenter drew up a planting plan for the athletic field in 1921 as the park was enlarged along its eastern edge to 13th Street.[4]

In the early twentieth century, Westside Park was described as providing a breathing space for the western portion of Newark. It provided a running track and athletic grounds, a playground and sand court for little children, tennis courts, a bandstand, and a wading pool. The western heights kept some of the highest land in the city from being developed, and a broad esplanade along the western border commanded fine views of the east and west. There were almost two miles of paths.[5]

This postcard view of the lake in West Side Park, Newark, New Jersey shows the plantings designed to encircle the small lake separating it from the playing fields.

C. 1915 postcard view of the Terrace Gardens in West Side Park designed by Olmsted Brothers employee Herbert E. Millard.

The 25th Annual Report of the Essex County Park Commission in 1920 detailed the planned expansion and alterations the park would soon undergo.

West Side Park is in a very thickly settled section of Newark and the increase in population in this locality rendered the original area of the park inadequate. The addition was a block between 13th and 14th Streets and 16th and 18th Avenues adjoining the park, and was connected with it by the closing of 14th Street by the authorities of the City of Newark. It is a part of what was known as Magnolia Swamp and the character of the ground is so wet and boggy that it is almost impossible to erect thereon buildings, which would stand without putting in foundations more expensive than improvements in that vicinity would warrant. It is the intention of the Commission to furnish additional playground facilities in this area.

The plans for improvement of the land have been practically agreed upon. They contemplate the moving of the running track and open-air gymnasium from their present location near the corner of 17th Street and 16th Avenue to a location near the corner of 13th Street and 18th Avenue, where there will be more room. The ground now used for running track and open-air gymnasium will be converted into tennis courts, giving twelve additional courts. The plans also provide for an adequate field house, with lockers and showers, east of 14th Street opposite 17th Avenue. This location may have to be shifted to the 18th Avenue end on account of the difficulty of getting a satisfactory foundation. A baseball field is provided for north of the field house and a concrete wading pool, sand court and shelter near 18th Avenue.[6]

A field house and children's shelter were designed by Frank A. Wright in the Mission style and built by 1923. The following year's plans called for the relocation of the playground to enable the construction of clay tennis courts. The Commission praised the European linden trees in the older section of the park as splendid specimens.

As community needs changed over the ensuing decades, the Parks Commission altered the neighborhood park. Aerial photographs from 1954 and 1966 show that an additional play area was formed when the lake was filled with earth. This is the open area west of the football field. In the 1970s, the County determined that there was a great need for recreation in the inner city and made the rehabilitation of West Side Park a high priority. Completed by 1987, the park underwent a major $2.8 million dollar rehabilitation that included the construction of the large community center complete with gymnasium.[7]

Several areas with the original Olmsted directed plantings remain in West Side Park. This area is located north of the football field and south of the baseball field. *June 27, 2009.*

In the first decade of the 21st century, another round of improvements were funded with grants from Green Acres and the Essex County Open Space Trust Fund. They were completed in November 2004. This phase included replacing eight dilapidated tennis courts with four brand new tennis courts and two new basketball courts. Restroom facilities next to the tennis and basketball courts were renovated and upgraded with new equipment. A new parking lot with twenty-two regular spaces and two handicapped spaces was constructed in front of the Community Center, and pathways throughout the park were repaved. The main park entrance on 17th Street was refurbished with a decorative retaining wall and wrought iron fence. Two other park entrances along 17th Street were upgraded with new steps leading into the park, new paving, signage, and landscaping.

Further alterations were made in a $4 million campaign during 2005 and 2006. Working together, the County, several conservancy and neighborhood groups, and the Amelior and MCJ Foundations collaborated to sponsor two construction projects; one an aesthetic upgrade and the second, recreational. Sheila Pitts of the West Side Park Conservancy affirmed the importance of the collaboration between the public and private sectors and neighborhood groups. The first project was called Center Oval and Perimeter Renovations. This project, designed by the Virginian landscape architecture firm of Rhodeside & Harwell, Inc., followed green construction practices and enhanced the park's aesthetics. It included the installation of new perimeter fencing, ornamental lighting, entrance enhancements, pathway upgrades, tree pruning and planting, and landscaping. The second project was the transformation of the West Side Park Athletic Facility. Now a state-of-the-art recreation complex, it includes a synthetic grass surface that meets NCAA standards and a 400-meter six-lane rubberized running track that replaced an asphalt track. New sports lighting, a scoreboard, spectator bleachers and player benches complement the improvements to the football/soccer field and new long jump and pole vault areas were added at one end of the track. Drainage, walking paths and handicap accessibility were improved, the existing sports lighting at the baseball field was repaired, water fountains were upgraded, and new signs, benches and trash receptacles were added.[8]

Over the past half-century the overall character of West Side Park has changed more than any other Essex County park and today the park would be virtually unrecognizable to its creators. Back in its prime it was the showcase of the Park System, when the lake provided local kids with wading in the summertime and the arboretum was second to none in the city. Terrace gardens in the southwest corner were an architectural highlight, and the stately mall reflected the influence of formal European park design. The stone wall terraces have since been removed and replaced with a bandshell, the current orientation of the park being exclusively towards active recreation.

Endnotes Chapter 4: West Side Park

[1]Frederick W. Kelsey. *The First County Park System; A Complete History of the Inception and Development of the Essex County Parks of New Jersey.* (New York, New York: J.S. Ogilvie Publishing Company, 1905): 115-118.
[2]Essex County Department of Parks. *Fourth Annual Report of the Board of Commissioners, 1898-99.* (Newark, New Jersey: Grover Bros., 1900).
[3]Essex County Department of Parks. *Fourth Annual Report of the Board of Commissioners, 1898-99.* (Newark, New Jersey: Grover Bros., 1900).
[4]My information about individual employees is based on the list of employees found in the Olmsted Papers at the Library of Congress. I added missing first names, middle initials, and dates of service found in other sources of information including, but not limited to, the New York Times, the American Society of Landscape Architects, and books including *Pioneers of American Landscape Design*. My list is more comprehensive than the one found in the Library of Congress and should be most helpful in determining the employee names when only the initials are used on the plans.
[5]Frank John Urquhart. *A History of the City of Newark, New Jersey Embracing Practically Two and A Half Centuries 1666-1913.* (New York, New York: Lewis Historical Publishing Company, 1915): 858-863.
[6]Essex County Department of Parks. *Twenty-fifth Annual Report of the Board of Commissioners, 1920.* (Newark, New Jersey: The W. H. Shurts Co., Printers, 1921): 3.
[7]From Essex County Department of Parks website at www.essex-countynj.org/p/index.php?section/sites/west&ImgLoc=images/west
[8]These two paragraphs are condensed from a press release of 13 December 2006 this is posted on the Essex County Department of Parks website: www.essex-countynj.org/p/index.php?section=pr/print/121306

Chapter 5
Branch Brook Park: Newark (1898)

Branch Brook Park is distinguished by being the first county park to be opened for public use in the United States. It has been placed on both the New Jersey Register of Historic Places in 1980 and the National Register in 1981. Located in the City of Newark and bordered at the southern end by U.S. Route 280, the park crosses Park Avenue, Bloomfield Avenue, and Heller Parkway, terminating near the Newark-Belleville boundary further north. The park runs roughly north and south for nearly 4 miles and it averages 1/4 mile in width. At 359 acres, it is the largest developed park in Essex County. Its features include a combination of gently rolling terrain, open meadowland, small patches of woodland, and several waterways. Named for a branch of a brook that flowed into the Passaic River, the park is best known for its 2,000 cherry trees that blossom during April. These are greater both in variety and number than the famed Washington, D.C., display. The initial cherry tree plantings were a gift in 1927 from the Bamberger family and Mrs. Felix Fuld.

The Southern Division of Branch Brook Park in Newark, New Jersey is the oldest part of the park. The bridge seen in the background was built in 1899 and it carries Park Avenue over the Lake. *October 31, 2009.*

The land was formerly used as Army training grounds during the Civil War. A large part of the land was a marsh known as Old Blue Jay Swamp. To add to the dismal air of the swamp, tenements crowded parts of the surrounding area. Swamp water was used for both drinking and sewage disposal. In sharp contrast, the southern portion of the proposed park contained a circular reservoir basin that supplied clean, fresh water to a "private" association of Newark citizens. In July 1895, the City of Newark transferred approximately 60 acres of this land to the Essex County Park Commission, at a cost of $350,687. The reservoir became the nucleus of Branch Brook Park.[1] Old Blue Jay Swamp was transformed into a lake, flower gardens, and expanses of lawns by 1900. The firm of John Bogart and Nathan F. Barrett had been hired in 1895, to provide plans and advise for development of the park. Their design was romantic in style, and was dominated by geometrical patterned gardens and arbors. It covered the areas of the Southern Division and Middle Division.

The real work in grading and for the surface embellishments of Branch Brook Park was begun the morning of June 15, 1896. No special ceremony graced the occasion. Three of the Essex County Park Commissioners were present. Promptly at 8:30 am, the Commission president turned the first sod with a new spade. The contractors had a large force of men and teams ready.[2]

In 1898, the Olmsted Brothers firm was hired to revise the park's formal design. The public further secured the park's development by approving a $1.5 million dollar allotment. Under the skillful direction of the Olmsted Brothers firm over the next two decades, the park would become more naturalistic. The firm would plant native species of vegetation and create curving paths and roadways, keeping them separated for reasons of safety and aesthetics.[3]

The long, linear park was initially bounded on the west by the Morris Canal and on the east by Lake Street. It was

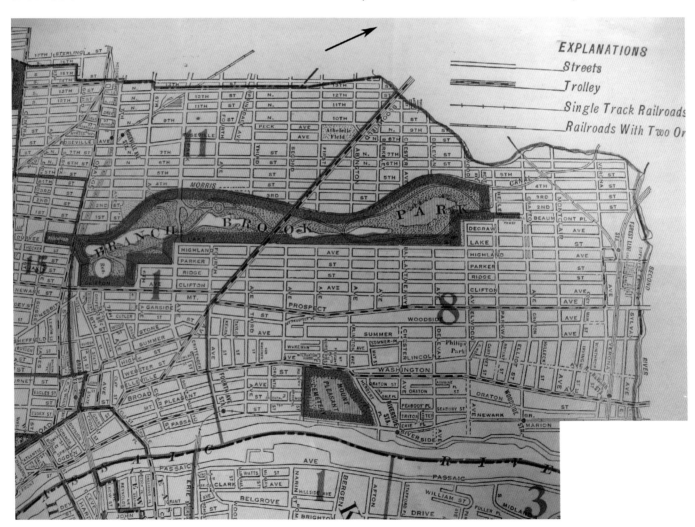

The Interstate Map Company's 1915 *New Map of Newark, New Jersey* shows the Southern, Middle, and Northern Divisions of Branch Brook Park. *Courtesy of Special Collections and University Archives, Rutgers University Libraries.*

divided into four sections. The Southern Division is located between Route 280 and Park Avenue (formerly Fifth Avenue). The Middle Division encompasses the area between Park Avenue and Bloomfield Avenue. The Northern Division runs between Bloomfield Avenue and Heller Parkway. The Extension is an L-shaped piece of the park located north of Heller Parkway along Mill Street and the Second River. This section merges with Belleville Park in Belleville.

Initially, a small and slender portion of the park was treated as an entryway as it extended down to Sussex Avenue. Branch Brook Park grew northward from its nucleus around the reservoir due in part to land acquisitions from several generous and public-spirited Newark families including the family of Robert F. Ballantine, who donated 32 acres of their property. Another 50 acres were given by Z. M. Keene, William A. Righter, and Messrs. Heller. The park doubled in size through acquisitions and purchases between 1924 and 1929.

The Ballantine Gateway at the corner of Lake Street and Ballantine Parkway, (formerly Chester Avenue) is a reminder of that family's generous gift of land. Working in collaboration with the architects, in February 1899, Percy R. Jones made a study for the entranceway and C. R. Wait drew up a preliminary landscaping plan. The architectural firm of Carrère and Hastings designed the buildings, which were described in the 1899 annual report from the Essex County Park Commission.

The Ballantine Gateway consists of two, one-story buildings either side of the entrance, and between these two buildings is a heavy wrought iron entrance gate eleven feet high and forty feet wide. On either side of this gate are massive stone posts with short wingwalls extending from them to the two small buildings. These wingwalls each contain a wrought iron entrance grille for pedestrians. Beyond the buildings on either side is an iron fence eight feet high, with stone piers forming a curved wing-wall along one side of an elliptical plaza. The two buildings are fourteen feet high with steep, tiled roofs. The foundations are local, red sandstone with a Bedford granite base course. This granite is also used for the chain-posts, which extend around the plaza. The walls are of a Lorillard brick, laid in Flemish bond with dark headers, giving interest and color variety to the brickwork and the trim is Indiana limestone. The Commission has decided, in appreciation of the public spirit and generosity shown in the gift, to name it the "Robert F. Ballantine Gateway." Work on the structure is well advanced, and will be completed by next spring. The Board also desires also to acknowledge the gift of a quarter of an acre of land from the Prospect Heights Land and Improvement Company. This land surrounds the Ballantine Gateway, and was needed to give it a proper landscape setting.[4]

Postmarked in February 1907, this picture postcard shows a snowy view of the Ballantine Gateway to Branch Brook Park. This grand entranceway was designed by the New York architects Carrère and Hastings and built in 1899.

In September 1898, the first plans the Olmsted Brothers received were the topographical maps of the middle and northern sections from Fifth (now Park Avenue) to Bloomfield Avenue. John Charles Olmsted made notes and extensive changes to them. Percy R. Jones produced the earliest grading studies, profiles, and sections for portions between Fifth and Bloomfield Avenues. He also prepared a study for an entrance from Sixth Avenue and a grading plan showing the locations of cherry, maple, and poplar trees with a sketch of stairs and walls. Jones also prepared the study for a concert grove, drafted the plan showing proposed revisions to the southern portion from Sussex Avenue to Fifth Avenue, and made sketches for the area east of the lake. One of the outstanding aspects of the design was his concert area in the southern portion bordering Branch Brook Lake.

Arthur H. Vinal drew the preliminary plans for an entrance from Sixth Avenue and an alternative course of the parkway. Wilbur David Cook, Jr. made a 30 x 124-inch plan of the park and a grading plan for portion between Fifth and Bloomfield Avenues. Robert Fuller Jackson created a boundary street from Elmwood Avenue and Degraw Avenue to the junction of Heller Parkway. At the end of November 1898, architects Carrère and Hastings presented their very detailed sketch of a bridge and ornamentation to the Park Commissioners. In December 1898, Percy R. Jones created a revised study for a portion between Orange Street and Ravine Path showing the promenade, boathouse, and skating pavilion and a sketch plan and profile for an entrance from Sussex Avenue. Arthur H. Vinal worked on a preliminary plan for proposed bordering street from the junction of Elmwood Avenue and Degraw Avenue to the junction of Heller Parkway and First Hill Parkway. Mr. Reed produced the grading plan and accompanying cross sections for the concert grove.

The principals in the firm maintained oversight directly over the design work. John Charles Olmsted wrote the following note on Mr. Reed's plan: "I do not see how we can grade to save any of the trees marked thus [Circle x] / and those marked thus [Circle] it seems doubtful if we can save permanently, especially if we grade Fifth Ave. as you suggested some time ago, i.e. with a straight step from the new bridge to the canal. The only way that I can see would be to build a wall in the south side of Fifth Avenue."

The former concert area was the flat land on the west side of the lake in Branch Brook Park's southern section. Its has mature trees such as this hickory tree in its full autumn regalia. *October 31, 2009.*

The Olmsted firm designed an octagonal gazebo to be located directly across the lake on a projection of land known as Meeker Mound. This pavilion became the popular destination for many a visitor. The historic Octagon Shelter was replicated in 2007 at a cost of $353,510. In January 1899, C. R. Wait drew an outline of the area in the Northern Division to be excavated for a waterway. Percy R. Jones drew profiles of the roads and walks in the Northern Division. Planting plans with notes by James Frederick Dawson were made this month and he drew up a sketch showing trees to be moved and others planted. Apparently, the trees in the field were given copper number tags and the tag numbers were shown on the plans. Arthur H. Vinal designed the iron fence, made a preliminary plan for the Southern Division, and sketched elevations and cross section for the Orange Street Bridge. John Charles Olmsted made extensive grading notes on the topographical plan of the Southern Division drives and walks. In February 1899, the firm conducted a tree inventory in the Northern Division. John Charles Olmsted also created a print of that section of the park.

Design work continued throughout 1899. In April, James Frederick Dawson produced a planting study for the concert grove and Mr. Reed created a planting plan for the Middle Division. In July, John Charles Olmsted and Dawson designed the grading plan for the area between Sussex and Sixth Avenues and made a planting plan for planting bulbs in the Southern Division. In August, architectural draftsman H. P. Richmond designed the caps and beams for some arbors. William C. Woolner worked on the Southern Division's Clifton Avenue entrance based on Carrère and Hasting's plans for the bridge there. Mr. Reed drew the details of the steps at the arbor near Eighth and Clifton Avenues and created details of the steps to the shelter on the axis of Sixth Avenue. Emanuel T. Mische added planting notes to the grading plan for the Northern Division. H. P. Richmond produced plans and elevation of a shelter and sand court. Edward A. Douglas drew a plan and elevation for an arbor at the concert grove and rendered details of the steps at the north and south ends of the wall east of the Lotus Garden.

Postmarked in 1906, this postcard view shows the octagonal shelter constructed on Meeker Mound. The former Barringer High School seen in the background was built in 1898. The modern high school presently in the same location opened in 1964. The pavilion on Meeker Mound was carefully reconstructed in 2007.

This photograph was taken by Branch Brook Park visitor K. B. Ward in the early 1900s. The naturalistic, meandering roadways and walkways are an indication of an Olmsted designed park.

In September 1899, Wilbur David Cook, Jr., made revisions to the plan for location and grading for the Eighth Avenue Terrace in the Southern Division and H. P. Richmond and Edward A. Douglas created the details of the steps designed by Carrère and Hastings for that location. Richmond also drew the plan and elevation of an arbor at the Garside addition, a detail of the steps to the shelter at Parker Street and Fifth Avenue, and a detail of steps leading from the concert grove to the bridge over the canal. Douglas developed several planting plans for a portion along Bloomfield Avenue and Lake Street. Arthur H. Vinal drew details of fences at the junction of Eighth and Clifton Avenues and made the grading plan for a temporary connection north of Subway No. 1. Percy R. Jones made sketches for an iron bridge and footbridges over the canal in the Middle and Northern Divisions. At the end of the month, John Charles Olmsted created a plan for the walls and banks along the east shore of lake north of the first bridge in the Southern Division.

This photograph shows another one of the six stone footbridges in the Northern Division of Branch Brook Park. Autumn leaves have fallen onto the carved sandstone seats. *October 31, 2009.*

One of the loveliest areas in Branch Brook Park is in the Northern Division. There, stone bridges of different designs cross a series of shallow meandering "minnow pools." One of Percy R. Jones' stone bridges can be seen in the background. *April 18, 2009.*

In October 1899, Wilbur David Cook, Jr., worked on the planting plan for the Southern Division in the vicinity of Subway No.1. William C. Woolner worked out the planting plan of a portion from Eighth Avenue north to the reservoir and along the canal bank to Subway No. 2. James Frederick Dawson developed the Southern Division planting study along Parker Street and Fifth Avenue. Arthur H. Vinal created details for steps at the boat landing near Bloomfield Avenue as well as rendering a detail for steps on the axis of Delavan Avenue in the Northern Division. In November 1899, Woolner worked on a planting study for the area from Bloomfield Avenue to Abbington Avenue and a planting plan for Clark's Island, both areas in the Northern Division. Percy R. Jones revised a grading plan for the westside of the lake between Seventh Avenue and Subway No. 2. William C. Woolner created the planting plan for trees on Lake Street from Fifth Avenue to Bloomfield Avenue in the Middle Division.

The Olmsteds had very good writers on staff who could summarize complex projects into concise reports. One such report was included in the 1899 Annual Report of the Essex County Park Commission. The Olmsted report stated that they planned border mounds around the perimeter with both trees and shrubbery. It was not practicable to make the border plantings as wide and dense as they should be, however they were created nevertheless. In the informal parts of the Southern Division and in the whole of the Middle Division they planted both native and exotic trees, shrubs, creepers and perennials suited to the accomplishment of somewhat marked landscape gardening effects. In the Northern Division the planting was designed to be quiet in tone but interesting in detail. In the Southern Division the Olmsteds changed the plans of their predecessor, mainly in the interest of lessening the cost of completing the park. They lowered the drive east of the south end of the lake so as to do away with the subway originally contemplated. They incorporated play spaces for children into the designs. This was a sandcourt, which was to be shaded by an awning, as well as a shelter for those in charge of children. Their experience had shown that a sidewalk must accompany every important drive in a city park. Many paths were created.

Newark, N. J.   Winter Scene, Branch Brook Park

This early 20th-century postcard view of Branch Brook Park in winter shows the outline of the Olmsted Brothers overall planting design. The mix of curving walkways, open spaces, and groves of trees develops over time into a landscape that has interest at every turn in the path.

Formal elements including gardens and a concert grove were designed for the Southern Division. The waterways were designed to connect via a wide waterway under Park Avenue. With this, the lake was lengthened for boaters and skaters. By narrowing the lake in the Middle Division and keeping it well over to the west side they secured a fine unbroken body of level land of thirteen acres inside the surrounding walk. This was on the side nearest the dense population, and was used by hundreds of children as a playfield. The lengthening of the lake and broadening of the meadow also added considerably to their value as landscape features. Numerous views from the drive and its accompanying walk over the lake were created with picturesquely planted margins as a foreground, across the meadow, and to the margin of woods in the background. At the time of writing in 1899, the entire Middle Division had scarcely a tree or bush upon it. The plan was to plant broad-leaved evergreens and dark-foliaged deciduous trees and shrubs at the south end and further north, unusually broad-leaved trees that would gradually merge into masses of small-leafed and generally light green trees. At the north end would be concentrated trees and shrubs having notably gray or grayish-green foliage. The design was intended to be an exaggeration of what one would expect to happen under a state of nature.

The bank along Lake Street was to be covered with bushes, many of which will be striking when in flower, but excluding such sorts as are known to tempt people to pick them. Shade trees in ample number were to be provided for the benefit of those not wishing to stroll or play in the open. A wading pool and a sandy beach for little children to play in and a fieldhouse for shelter, refreshments and toilets, and for winter ice skaters, completed the equipment.

Entrance to the Middle Division of Branch Brook Park off Park Avenue. *October 31, 2009.*

BRANCH BROOK PARK

The rustic stone bridges of the Northern Division blend into the pastoral scene the Olmsted Brothers firm designed in Branch Brook Park.

In 1899, the Northern Division of Branch Brook Park was covered with a dense, neglected "wood-lot" growth of trees which caused the flat land to remain extremely swampy. This latter defect was remedied by under-drainage. The forked drive was established around a pond and Clark's Island was modified with more naturalistic banks. A lawn and open groves surrounded this pond. The shallow was deepened and widened irregularly among the trees, and dammed into a series of narrow pools. From the Ballantine Gateway northward, a distance of about half a mile, the park broadened out considerably and the woods ceased to be an important feature, much of the land being open fields or pasture with only scattering trees. They saved little of the poor tree growth and left a moderate number of the best trees, which have gradually formed broad-spreading meadow specimens, between which there are many pretty pastoral views. This formed a fine meadow landscape with simple, yet satisfactory beauty.[5]

The firm's approach to landscape design was summed up in the 1899 annual report of the Essex County Park Commission. They stated:

Regarding the relatively less population density around the northern part of the park than about the southern part, a condition which will probably always exist, we have designed to have a gradual diminution of artificiality and formality in the style of the improvements. We plan for the Northern Division, a general appearance of the plantings and the degree of neat lawns, from the garden-like treatment already adopted for the Southern Division to the stretch of simple natural meadow with scattering, broad-spreading trees and almost entire absence of shrubbery (except in the border plantings).

Branch Brook Park's Northern Division's open lawns are noted for its groves of trees and individual specimen trees. *April 18, 2009.*

In the same report, the Essex County Park Commissioners added their summary view of the of the work accomplished to date:

South of Fifth Avenue little construction work remains to be done, and the people have had the use and enjoyment of that section for several years. This past year, shelters of brick and stone have been erected in the Southern Division from designs furnished by Messrs. Carrère & Hastings, of New York. One is on the eminence overlooking the lake, known as Meeker's Mound, and another crowns the high ground at the corner of Parker Street and Fifth Avenue. The former cost $3,900 and the latter $3,660. The third is on the Clifton Avenue side of the park and is specially designed for the amusement of small children. It has a large court filled with fine white sand, where they can play, and a nearby shelter for the convenience of their mothers or attendants. Its cost was $6,020.[6]

In 1900, William C. Woolner made detailed plans of park benches. Notes on the plans indicate costs. "Cost of Lumber & Construction, 31 cts per running foot based on following schedule; 4" x 4" Posts $54.29, 2" x 4" beams $11.83, milling $20.00, totaling $86.12 per bench." This did not include any ironwork, so it is more than likely a design for wooden benches under the arbors. In February, Woolner created planting plan for the Middle Division and the following month, a planting plan for the portion between Clark's Pond and the Ballantine Gateway in the Northern Division. In July, Alling Stephen DeForest drew up a study for the general plan of the park and assisted another staff member the following month in preparing the overall general plan used for presentations. That October, Woolner and Emanuel T. Mische made planting plans for a portion between Clark's Pond and the Ballantine Gateway and for the vicinity of Clark's Pond in the Northern Division. In November, Edward A. Douglas revised the grading plans of several areas in the Northern Division. How appropriate that in December, Percy R. Jones made a study for a skating pavilion-boathouse for the Southern Division.

Postmarked in 1905, this postcard view of the sand court at Branch Brook Park shows how even a utilitarian structure could be designed with architectural style and built using sturdy materials making it a showpiece.

Work at the Olmsted Brothers firm progressed throughout 1901. In January, Percy R. Jones and Edward A. Douglas made a revised study and plan for the Elmwood Avenue entrance in the Northern Division. Plan #530 was an "as-built" plan of the Northern Division's pools and waterways indicating these had been constructed by this time. Alanson Phelps Wyman used the information to revise the planting plan for the Northern Division area adjusting to the lines of the pools and waterways as they had been built. In February, Henry V. Hubbard made a grading plan and cross sections for temporary walks in the Middle Division. In April and May, architectural draftsman Arthur H. Vinal made sketches for a women's shelter near the Ballantine entrance in the Northern Division, for a men's bathroom and shelter, and for a women's bathroom and shelter close to the sand court in the Southern Division. Emanuel Tillman Mische made a revised planting study for the Middle Division's springtime plantings. James F. Dawson and William C. Woolner designed the planting plan for Ballantine Gateway area.

Despite its unfinished state, the park was heavily used. On June 11, 1901, the **New York Times** reported that, on the previous day, the championship cricket match between the Newark Cricket Club and the Kings County Club of Brooklyn was held in Branch Brook Park. Newark won the low-scoring match.

In June 1901, a Newark architect, Charles Ackerman, designed the plans for a shelter and portable bandstands. Jones created a study for the arrangement of land to the west of the canal in the Southern Division. In September, Mische drew two cross sections of the canal banks south of Subway # 2 showing ultimate appearance of foliage (1) If hemlocks are planted and (2) If hemlocks were omitted. Jones made a study for the arrangement west of the canal in the Southern Division if the canal is abandoned. Wilbur David Cook, Jr., designed a preliminary plan for the portion of the park west of the canal between Sixth and Seventh Avenues in the Southern Division.

The shallow pools in Branch Brook Park's Northern Division reflect both sky and landscape. Here contestants participating in an annual bike race are mirrored in the water's surface as they speed toward the finish line. *April 18, 2009.*

By 1902, the demand for new plans from the Olmsted Brothers office was in decline. In January, James Frederick Dawson updated the planting plan for the Northern Division noting which trees had been planted and which were not yet planted. Percy R. Jones made a revised study for a mid-lake bridge at Fifth Avenue and a preliminary plan for the middle bridge in the Southern Division. Jones also worked on a compiled topographical map made in connection with studies for Sussex Avenue and the abandonment of the Morris Canal. He created a study for the most southern park drive crossing of the railroad, which at the time was the Delaware, Lackawanna & Western (DLW) and William C. Woolner made the preliminary sketch for the crossing while Jones made the preliminary plan for it with the assistance of Ralph Eldon Sawyer. Work on this railroad crossing continued into February as Jones drew the profile of the top of north retaining wall of DLW and sections of the Park Drive crossing it. No other plans were created in 1902.

Circa 1905. Taken by a talented amateur photographer, Arthur R. Grow, the exact location in Branch Brook Park seen in this photograph is not known. The trees, while no longer newly planted saplings, were still quite immature. *Courtesy of William A. Jordan.*

Another photograph in the series taken circa 1905 by Arthur R. Grow shows a typical day in Branch Brook Park as canoeists enjoy the lake. The classically inspired structural elements of the boat launch and Park Avenue Bridge are located in the park's Southern Division. The Park Avenue Bridge, designed by New York architects Carrère and Hastings, was restored in 2005 for a cost of $3,216,945. *Courtesy of William A. Jordan.*

In January 1903, Henry Vincent Hubbard made sketches for a fountain in the circular reservoir and in July, Percy R. Jones made revisions to the planting plan for the area around the mid-lake bridge. That August, Hans J. Koehler and Ralph Eldon Sawyer worked on plans and elevations for the area around the Bloomfield Avenue subway. Sawyer worked on revised preliminary grading plan for the mid-lake bridge. In December, Jones worked on a grading study and profile and several alternative plans for land west of the canal in the Southern Division. He then worked on a revised study for the Elmwood Avenue entrance in the Northern Division along with Wilbur David Cook, Jr., who made the revised plan. This work continued into 1904 as Edward Clarke Whiting made a grading study, cross sections, profiles, and a plan for the Elmwood Avenue entrance and Carl Rust Parker made a revised planting plan for the area around the entrance. That November, Sawyer and Jones created a preliminary study and plan for an entrance at Eighth Avenue. Jones also made a preliminary grading plan for the point of the park drive crossing the DLW Railroad in the Southern Division.

In November 1909, the Olmsted Brothers firm generated plan #675. This is the updated general planting plan for Branch Brook Park and three employees worked on it: Alling Stephen DeForest, Percival Gallagher, and John Charles Olmsted. It was 13"x 40"and the original 1901 plan was used as the base. In March 1910, Hans J. Koehler made a study for additional trees for the Southern Division. In March 1912, Herbert E. Millard made several studies for revised planting in the English Garden, Dutch Garden, Pine Tree Garden, Lotus Ponds, and perennial bank. By 1913, the park had 4.25 miles of roads and 11 miles of paths. No further work was asked of the Olmsted Brothers firm until 1920 when Herbert E. Millard made a sketch showing plan and elevation of the reservoir and Percy R. Jones made cross sections of the same area. In February 1921, Jones made rough grading studies of the old reservoir site.

This color postcard view postmarked 1908 shows the reservoir fountain in Branch Brook Park that was designed by Henry Vincent Hubbard. The buildings in the background are the original Barringer High School (on the left) and the Sacred Heart Cathedral with its towers still visibly under construction (on the right).

By 1907, this postcard view shows the vegetation on Clark's Island in the Northern Division of Branch Brook Park. No longer mere saplings, the maturing trees are reflected in the water of Clark's Pond.

Clark's Pond, just north of Bloomfield Avenue in Branch Brook Park has a fountain to keep its water circulating. *October 31, 2009.*

Although the Olmsted Brothers design philosophy was naturalistic rather than formal, they could incorporate formal planting schemes into their plans. As illustrated in the postcard postmarked in 1911, this garden arrangement fits into the overall scheme of Branch Brook Park.

Floral Display, Branch Brook Park, Newark, N.J.

63515

In the early 1920s, Harmon Hendricks presented the Park Commission a gift of 20 acres of land which extended the park northward into Belleville. Over the ensuing years, the Olmsted Brothers firm developed the plans for this, the most northern part of the park. During the year between June 1922 and July 1923, Percival Gallagher made a plan showing a portion of the property between Branch Brook and Belleville Parks. In January 1926, Walter F. Clarke drew topography of various sections for the Branch Brook Park Extension that ran from Heller Parkway in Newark to Mill Street in the neighboring town of Belleville and from the New York & Greenwood Lake Railroad to Quarry Street. In November 1926, James D. Graham and Lyle L. Blundell worked on a study of the Branch Brook Park Extension from Heller Parkway to Mill Street. Blundell also worked on a study for a greenhouse location for the concourse site at Sixth Avenue. In April 1927, he and Edward D. Rando created the preliminary plan for Branch Brook Park Extension. In September 1927, Walter F. Clarke created the planting plan for the Extension between Heller Parkway and Grafton Avenue.

In June 1928, Lyle L. Blundell and Henry McLaren revised the grading plan for a section between Greenwood Lake Branch of the Erie Railroad and Mount Prospect Avenue. In July 1928 and with revisions in 1931, J. Harry Scott created the general plan of the Extension to Mt. Prospect Avenue including Belleville Park and County Park Golf Course. In August 1928, Gordon Woodberry drew a planting plan showing the extent of the field collection of Japanese flowering cherry trees. In November 1928 and February 1929, Blundell and A. W. Phillips created a grading plan for a parkway along the Second River in the Extension. In January 1931, Clarke created planting plans for two sections of the Extension. One section was between South Orange and Greenwood Lake Branches of the Erie Railroad and the second section along Second River between Greenwood

One of the older cherry trees, perhaps planted in the late 1920s, in Branch Brook Park Extension, Newark, New Jersey. *April 18, 2009.*

Branch of the Erie Railroad and Mount Prospect Avenue. In January 1936, Clarke and Hans J. Koehler created a planting plan for part of the Extension section between Heller Parkway and Orange Branch Erie Railroad.

Beginning in 1899, when the area was first being transformed from swamp to park, the Essex County Park Commission has continually maintained the park and since the 1970s, assisted by the Branch Brook Park Conservancy group. Recent improvements to Branch Brook Park include: a new perimeter fence and entrance in the Southern Division in 2004; Middle Division relocated ballfields, grading, drainage, irrigation, sports lighting, scoreboard, new press box, parking improvements, pedestrian entrance improvements, amenities completed in 2006; fence and lights at pedestrian bridge completed in 2006; boathouse area landscape restoration in 2006; restoration of the historic Essex County Parks Administration Building completed in 2007; modernization and realignment of three baseball fields in the Extension completed in 2007; modernization of Cherry Blossom Welcome Center completed in 2008; pathway and lighting improvements, park entranceway enhancements, and cherry tree plantings completed in 2009; rehabilitation of Bloomfield Avenue Bridge at the cost of $3,028,890 completed in 2009; and the installation of, a new synthetic grass surface football and soccer field in the Middle Division named the Andre Tippett Field and completed in 2009.

Looking down from the former railroad bridge at the channeled course that the Second River takes through Branch Brook Park Extension. *April 18, 2009.*

Endnotes Chapter 5: Branch Brook Park

[1]History of Branch Brook Park from the Essex County Department of Parks, Recreation, and Cultural Affairs website: http://www.essex-countynj.org/p/index.php?section=af/system
[2]Frederick W. Kelsey. *The First County Park System; A Complete History of the Inception and Development of the Essex County Parks of New Jersey.* (New York, New York: J.S. Ogilvie Publishing Company, 1905): 112.
[3]History of Branch Brook Park, Essex County Department of Parks,

Recreation, and Cultural Affairs: http://www.essex-countynj.org/p/index.php?section=af/system.
[4]Essex County Park Commission. *Fourth Annual Report of the Board of Commissioners,1898-99.* (Newark, New Jersey: Grover Bros.,1900).
[5]Essex County Department of Parks. *Fourth Annual Report of the Board of Commissioners,1898-99.* (Newark, New Jersey: Grover Bros.,1900).
[6]Essex County Department of Parks. *Fourth Annual Report of the Board of Commissioners,1898-99.* (Newark, New Jersey: Grover Bros.,1900).

Chapter 6

Orange Park: Orange (1898)

Frederick W. Kelsey, a resident of Orange, was credited with the inception of the Essex County Park System. When he sat on the first Commission, he advocated for a park in his own town. The resulting Orange Park is a 47-acre, roughly triangular park bordered by Central Avenue, Olcott Avenue, Center Street, South Harrison Street, and Oakwood Avenue in the City of Orange. It is divided approximately in the center by a 1-1/2 acre lake. It is the County Park system's sixth largest park. Property for Orange Park was purchased in 1897 and such a large acquisition was thought wise at that time because it was the only available open space within the city's limits as these areas were rapidly being developed. Originally the land was low and marshy and served as a catch basin for surface water from the surrounding territory.[1] A music pavilion was located in the northern half of the park. On the evening of August 25, 1900, after three years of construction, the Olmsted Brothers designed park informally opened with a concert by Markwith's Brass Band.[2]

Orange Park has a unique history. The selection involved a continuous contending of differences between the commissioners themselves on the one side, and the almost unanimous sentiment of the public on the other side. Those favoring the project finally won, after two years of persistent effort. Apparently, when the roads were laid out forty years prior, this area was set aside with the idea it would eventually become a public park. Although the central area was a

low, swampy marshland, this was surrounded on each of the larger sides of the triangle with gentle slopes to higher ground the entire distance. The first commission agreed with the landscape experts that a park in this area would be desirable. However, the second Commission appointed in 1895 was no longer unanimous and had two different members than the first. The two, F. M. Shepard and Franklin Murphy, were vocal opponents of a park for Orange.

In 1895, Orange and East Orange officials sent letters and petitions to try to change the minds of the opponents. Their opposition was due to the high purchase price of one tract. About 16 acres of the proposed park was swampland, but the owner, seeking a higher profit and knowing that Orange desperately wanted to run a much-needed storm sewer through the property, refused to sell. Frederick Kelsey was given the authority by the Commission to deal directly with the reluctant landowner and authorized a maximum expenditure of $20,000. On December 7, 1896, Kelsey closed the deal on that parcel for $17,500. The Commission went ahead with the plans for Orange Park in December 1896. In 1898, the lines of the park were extended on the Central Avenue side about 700 feet and resulted in making the park, together with the finishing improvements inaugurated at the time, what has been frequently called, "the gem of the Essex County park system."[3]

This postcard printed in Germany circa 1905 shows the driveway of Orange Park in Orange, New Jersey. Due to the fact that there were many mature trees already on the land, John Charles Olmsted designed the roadways around them.

Amateur photographer and resident in Orange, K. B. Ward took this picture circa 1915 and kept it in his photo album. This photograph was labeled "Bandstand, Orange Park."

The 1899 Fourth Annual Report of the Essex County Park Commission included the following Olmsted Brothers entry regarding Orange Park.

Orange Park contains forty-seven acres and belongs to the class we have called "Local Parks." It is in the southern outskirts of the densely populated portion of the city of Orange, and it lies in a gentle valley with rich, moist meadows and beautiful trees. The low hills on each side of the park have suburban residences. The park is not a large one and all parts of it are fully visible from carriages passing it on the surrounding streets, so that we have preferred not to mar the beautiful meadows by running drives through them. This feature had already been determined upon, however, and it was thought best not to give it up. The under-drainage of the meadows had been planned and partly executed. In the case of the north meadow the water from the drains was intended to feed an artificial brook and the drains were kept higher for this purpose than they should have been. These sub-soil drains have not been changed but a few more have been added where needed. The plan adopted for taking care of underground water and storm-water in a pipe drain and of extraordinary stormwater in a shallow swale with gently sloping, grassy sides.

The existence of a little duck pond at about the middle of the park suggested the larger lake of over one acre. A lake of this sort is both attractive and appropriate in a low-lying park like this. The excavation had proceeded so far and the lake had one peculiarity that we felt obliged to object to. Much of the material excavated had been spread in the immediate vicinity of the pond, thus raising a dyke, with gently sloping sides about it. The adjoining natural ground was more or less covered by valuable trees, some of which had been heavily filled upon. The excavation continued until a uniform depth of eight feet was secured. Steep underwater slopes were substituted for long easy ones, except that there is a beach five feet wide under water needed for safety. It is proposed to draw the water down to a depth of three feet in winter so it will be shallow enough to be safe for skaters in case the ice breaks. The south end of the lake will be divided off by an inconspicuous fence and having been made very shallow and with sandy beaches can be used as a wading pool.

This photograph of Orange Park was taken circa 1905 by amateur photographer Arthur R. Grow. It shows the shallow swimming hole divided by a fence into separate sections, one for boys and the other for girls.
Courtesy of William A. Jordan.

In an opening of the grove occupying the middle portions of the park we have planted a formal concert grove. When the trees have grown up additional walks, and, if necessary, a drive encircling the grove may be added. It is to be hoped, however, that the present effect of breadth and continuity of the turf may not have to be broken by any more drives. In the grove south of the lake it is planned to have some seesaws, swings and other simple apparatus for children's amusements and a shelter with toilet accommodations. This structure, owing to the limited funds available, must, for the present, be of the cheapest sort. A more suitable cottage, with ample verandas and picturesque pergolas half-enclosing, and courts for infants, and affording shady seats for their mothers and attendants, is planned to take its place eventually. The same building will serve sufficiently well for the few hundred people who will be able to skate on the little lake.[4]

The Olmsted Brothers staff who worked on this park included John Charles Olmsted, Herbert J. Kellaway, Wilbur David Cook, Jr., Theodore Nicolesco, James Frederick Dawson, Edward Sturgis, Emanuel T. Mische, Edward A. Douglas, Alling Stephen De Forest, William C. Woolner, William H. Munroe, Herbert E. Millard, Lyle L. Blundell, H. A. Prime, Mr. Reed, and architectural draftsmen H. P. Richmond, and Arthur H. Vinal. The topographical maps generated by a local surveyor were received at the Olmsted Brothers' office in 1898. John Charles Olmsted drew park roads onto the topographical map. Herbert J. Kellaway created a grading plan with profiles and sections. A tree list was compiled in October 1898 and the positions were included on a grading plan in November. Edward Sturgis provided a sketch for a bandstand and H. P. Richmond created the preliminary

plan for the bandstand grove. John Charles Olmsted wrote a visit report in 1898. In 1899, Richmond made a sketch showing locations for trees to be moved near the southwest boundary. Throughout 1899, several plans for specific areas of the park were created but were not signed. These included grading plans and a planting plan for an area to be planted with bulbs—possibly the circular garden at the southern tip. In October 1899, Theodore Nicolesco produced the general plan for the park. In 1912, a planting plan (unsigned) for the south garden was rendered.

By 1899, the land was completely drained and converted from a marshy bog into a beautiful and usable playground. The lake was excavated near the center of the park. Little planting was necessary due to the fine character and abundance of trees already there. The rapid transition from the former swamp conditions to those of a completed park of unexcelled attractiveness gratified the public. The effective shrubbery borders and rising slopes on each side of the park, make an appropriate frame to one of the most attractive and restful landscape pictures that have resulted from modern park-making.[5]

The lake in Orange Park is no longer used for swimming but remains a popular spot for fishing and watching wildlife. *May 25, 2009.*

By 1913, Orange Park contained 47.63 acres, one mile of drives, and two miles of paths. The cost of the land totaled $149,418, and of the houses thereon, which were removed, $35,794. The improvements cost $134,854. The citizens living in the vicinity of this park contributed $17,275 in cash for its improvement. It now had tennis courts along with the wading pool, children's playground, and bandstand.[6]

The central part of Orange Park features groupings of mature hardwood trees that offer welcome shade on a hot spring day. *May 25, 2009.*

Carefully tended flower beds were located at the south end of Orange Park at the intersection of South Center and South Harrison Streets. During the 1950s and 1960s, tulips were the primary planting and the in the warmer months many wedding parties lined up there for group photographs. The children's playground, which was nestled in a grove of trees adjacent to the south shore of the lake, originally had swings, slides, merry-go-rounds, seesaws, an enormous sandbox, and a wading beach. The lake formed the geographic center of Orange Park and provided a focal point for many activities. Spring-fed and contained by a small dam, it was a notable ice skating venue in winter. On the south shore was a shallow wading beach for the children. A T-shaped fence originally divided the shallow into two sections, one for the boys and the other for the girls. This was removed by the 1920s. The north shore of the lake was identified by a little spit of land that protruded into the water and its weeping willow. As crime in the park increased during the 1960s, much of the surrounding vegetation was either cut back or removed to provide a safer environment for park-goers. The lily pond was a feature of the north end of the park near Central Avenue, and was unique due to its three-leaf clover design. Cast iron fountains used to be located throughout the park.[7]

In 1986, the north-south traverse roadway was closed to vehicular traffic, thus restoring the pastoral setting for recreational activities, as originally intended. Recent improvements, completed in 2004, include the installation of new equipment and rubberized safety surface in playground at a cost of $505,139. Renovation of the basketball court and construction of new restroom building was finished in 2006; and a renovation of park entrances, gardens, ball fields, pathways, and lighting and dedication

Orange Park was renamed Monte Irvin Orange Park in 2006 in honor of the Hall of Fame baseball player who grew up in Orange. *May 25, 2009.*

of Memorial to Orange Detective Kieran Shields for a cost of $1,272,507 was completed in 2007. A former lily pond in the north section of the park was revamped into a sitting area. The former pool has colored concrete with a parallel series of flowers and plants to reflect the original pool. In May 2006, Orange Park was renamed Monte Irvin Orange Park in honor of the hometown hero and baseball legend. A baseball pioneer, Monte Irvin (b. 1919) was among the first generation of black baseball players to break the color barrier of professional sports and play in the Major Leagues. He was a superb athlete and a mentor to younger players on and off the field. Even though his playing career ended over 50 years ago, he has left an admirable and lasting legacy and has been a role model and inspiration for generations.[8]

The circular flower garden remains an attractive feature at the southern end of Orange Park. *May 25, 2009.*

Endnotes Chapter 6: Orange Park

[1]History of Orange Park from the Essex County Department of Parks, Recreation, and Cultural Affairs: http://www.essex-countynj.org/p/index.php?section=af/system
[2]Don and Marietta Dorflinger. *Orange: A Postcard Guide to Its Past.* (Charleston, South Carolina: Arcadia Publishing, 1999).
[3]Frederick W. Kelsey. *The First County Park System; A Complete History of the Inception and Development of the Essex County Parks of New Jersey.* (New York, New York: J.S. Ogilvie Publishing Company, 1905).
[4]Essex County Department of Parks. *Fourth Annual Report of the Board of Commissioners, 1898-99.* (Newark, New Jersey: Grover Bros., 1900).
[5]Frederick W. Kelsey. *The First County Park System; A Complete History*

of the Inception and Development of the Essex County Parks of New Jersey.* (New York, New York: J.S. Ogilvie Publishing Company, 1905).
[6]Frank John Urquhart. *A History of the City of Newark, New Jersey Embracing Practically Two and A Half Centuries 1666-1913.* (New York, New York: Lewis Historical Publishing Company, 1915).
[7]Don and Marietta Dorflinger. *Orange: A Postcard Guide to Its Past.* (Charleston, South Carolina: Arcadia Publishing, 1999).
[8]Orange Park from Essex County Department of Parks, Recreation, and Cultural Affairs: http://www.essex-countynj.org/p/index.php?section=af/system.

Chapter 7
Eagle Rock Reservation: West Orange (1898)

In 1905, Essex County Park Commissioner Frederick W. Kelsey wrote:

> Whatever other property the Essex County Park Commission may acquire, there is no question that they have acted wisely in securing Eagle Rock and the land about it. This is the show place of Essex County. With the exception of opening roads through this reservation, some thinning of the natural growths and clearing in places the east brow of the cliff so as to open unobstructed views, little has been done in the way of improvement of this beautifully situated and densely wooded reservation. It remains largely in the primitive state as of years gone by. It is a place to delight an Emerson, a Thoreau, or a Ruskin, and to charm any lover of nature who revels in her rugged and unintruded haunts.[1]

Eagle Rock Reservation is a 408-acre park located in the central section of Essex County in the range of Watchung Mountains. The Reservation occupies the northeast corner of West Orange and a little strip of Montclair. The planned residential community of Llewellyn Park in West Orange, touches its southern extremity. The Township of Verona lies to the north. The reservation is bounded on the west by Prospect Avenue, on the south by Eagle Rock Avenue, on the east by Undercliff and Lloyd Roads, and on the north by a series of residential streets. By far the most striking topographical feature is the enormous trap dyke similar to the Palisades on the west bank of the Hudson River. Cliffs and precipitous slopes create the east slope of the mountain. The most comprehensive view is from Eagle Rock itself, a bold trap ledge with a cliff below it, forming part of the crest near the south end of the reservation. Lookout Point provides visitors with a spectacular view of suburban New Jersey east to the New York City skyline. A brook, which begins west of Eagle Rock, flows northward in a valley west of the crest to about the middle of the reservation, where it turns west to the foot of Stony Hill, and then southwest and west to the boundary. Before it leaves the reservation the brook receives several little branches, most of which, however, are dry in summer. Bridle paths and hiking trails criss-cross the reservation.

The first purchase of land took place in 1895, and the entire tract was finally consolidated in 1907. Frederick Law Olmsted, Sr., may have had a hand in the initial planning, but the majority of the park's design came from the Olmsted Brothers firm in the early 1900s. An historic building located on the crest is the old casino built in 1911. The term "casino" refers to an Italian style county dwelling. This was an open masonry shelter with a series of arches. It has since been transformed into the Highlawn Pavilion restaurant. This reuse saved the building, which had been slated for demolition.

In 1894, a trolley line began operating to the foot of Eagle Rock Avenue. This line was an extension of the Orange cross-town and ran via Washington Street. The idea behind its construction was to provide inexpensive transportation to Eagle Rock, which had become a mecca for Sunday picnickers because of its high elevation and magnificent view overlooking the cities. The promoters of the Eagle Rock line realized the impracticality of running a trolley to the top of the ridge because of the excessive grade. Instead, they counted upon their patrons climbing the last hundred feet up a zigzag path constructed along the side of the cliff. Automobile enthusiasts of that period held races up the cobblestone roadway of Eagle Rock Avenue that terminated in Eagle Rock Park.[2]

The Landscape Architect's report in the 1899 Essex County Park Commission Annual Report included a detailed description of the land and the planning for it. The Olmsteds found the area covered with a dense growth of trees resembling those commonly found in dry, rocky "wood lots." In the valleys where the trees grew in deeper soil and had more moisture, they were usually larger, but still crowded and slim. They surmised that visitors' general impressions would have been that the woods were dull and monotonous. The firm decided that this reservation, except for a few limited areas, should always be kept as a dense woodland, but managed as opposed to letting it grow untended. The landscape architects offered expert advice for managing such woodlands balanced with planning for an increasing number of visitors. The same advice was to also be applied to South Mountain Reservation. The existing trees in certain areas were to be thinned out, leaving only a few of the best to grow to imposing size and shape. On the rocky summits, views were to be kept open and near them create a suggestion of an alpine effect.[3]

Eagle Rock, Top of Orange Mountain.

Love from Vivian.
11/15/05.

Postmarked in 1905, this postcard of Eagle Rock Reservation shows the dramatic cliff face of Eagle Rock.

View of one of the hiking trails through the woods on the western part of Eagle Rock Reservation. The Olmsteds suggested that the majority of visitors would not venture far from the scenic views on the park's east side. *October 10, 2009.*

The magnificent views looking east to the New York City skyline from Crest Drive in Eagle Rock reservation. This is the heavily visited location of The Essex County September 11, 2001 Memorial. *October 10, 2009.*

The view westward from Crest Drive shows the pastoral land near the overlook that provides open space for casual strolls. The grassy area is dotted with specimen trees. The open space is bordered by the denser forest that covers the majority of Eagle Rock Reservation. *October 10, 2009.*

It may be assumed that most visitors will find by far the greatest interest along the eastern crest, with its inspiring bird's eye views, commanding elevation, picturesque cliffs and openness to the breezes. Some will drift back a short distance into the cool, deep shade of the western woods, but it will be a comparatively small number of visitors. Even in the wilder portions, it must be recognized that while woods are beautiful and inviting for their intricacy, mystery, and contrast with the ordinary haunts of man, they lose much of their beauty if frequented by large numbers of visitors. There are already patches of azaleas and other interesting bushes and many wild flowers in these open lands. There will be across these open tracts many agreeable local views and some views of distant hills which are worth while.

The drive and walk system will be designed not only for obvious, practical purposes, but also in such a way as to bring out the distinctive characteristics of different localities in the reservation. A crest line drive ought, if practicable, to continue to be obviously a crestline drive throughout its length. Where a terrace on the crest is needed for the convenient enjoyment of the view, it should be formed by building up a high retaining wall at the very outer edge of the cliff. In regard to the location of walks, they should be adapted to afford the visitor strong impressions as to the character of the scenery.

Also in a woodland, it is agreeable to occasionally get glimpses of the outer world and especially to see towering cliff-like margins of other masses of woods. Elsewhere the woods extend to the boundary and only need a little thinning out of tall-trunked trees. The addition of pines and hemlocks and shade enduring and evergreen shrubbery will be desirable generally along all the borders. In some other cases, where a wood is seen from a high view point, we should eliminate tall growing trees and substitute for them small growing sorts, such as flowering dogwood, hornbeam, hackberry, moosewood, gray birch, sassafras and the like. This will afford a more permanent open view and secure a more pronounced variation in the contour of the top surface of the woods.[4]

The employees listed as having worked on Eagle Rock Reservation included Frederick Law Olmsted, Jr., John Charles Olmsted, Frank A. Bourne, J. B. Herbst, Edward Sturgis, Percival Gallagher, William C. Woolner, Faris B. Smith, Emanuel Tillman Mische, Wilbur David Cook, Herbert J. Kellaway, Percy R. Jones, Edward A. Douglas, J. L. Doyle, William H. Munroe, C. R. Wait, Hans J. Koehler, A. John Halfenstein, Lyle L. Blundell, James D. Graham, John J. Sullivan, Edward D. Rando, Benjamin G. Donovan, John B. Moseley, Edward M. Prellwitz, and Walter F. Clarke.

In 1899, Frederick Law Olmsted, Jr., worked on a study for an entrance to the Reservation from Upper Mountain Avenue through the property of the Mutual Life Insurance Co. of New York. John Charles Olmsted, along with J. B. Herbst, Percival Gallagher, and Edward Sturgis, worked on the preliminary study showing the centerlines of the roads to be staked. In the summer of 1899, an inventory of trees on the Mutual Life Insurance Co. tract was created to accompany the plans. William C. Woolner drew the preliminary plan for the entrance through the property. In 1899, Faris B. Smith created a preliminary plan

for boundary at the northern end. Wilbur David Cook created a preliminary plan for portion of drive from the northwest line of Reservation to the middle North and South Roads.

In October 1899, Percival Gallagher created plans for planting pines and hemlocks, made an estimate of an area for the nursery, and created place names for the walks and groves. In January 1900, he

Ferns are just one of the many low-lying plants that thrive in dense woodlands of Eagle Rock Reservation. *October 10, 2009.*

created several large drawings, one was 44" by 162", showing the planting plan of the entire park. In 1900, Percy R. Jones created a study for Crest Drive and the location of a pond and John Charles Olmsted contributed his study for the main entrance from Eagle Rock Avenue. In 1901, Gallagher worked on a plan for the Eyrie entrance and Jones worked on grade study for the Administration yards and a profile of Stony Hill Road. He also created a smaller general plan of the entire reservation. Faris B. Smith worked on the plan for planting and woods improvement. In 1901, J. L. Doyle created the cross section of Eagle Rock across lake to boundary and William H. Munroe created a guide map of the reservation in a scale of 1"= 400'. The map is 41 inches tall by 82 inches wide. In 1902, Percival Gallagher made a sketch for arrangement of a Japanese garden. It is not known if this was ever created.

No other plans were generated until 1909, when architectural draftsman C. R. Wait developed rough plans for a shelter house, Casino, and refectory. The architects of the shelter were Bebb, Cook, & Welch Architects of New York. Hans J. Koehler created a plan for planting and woods improvement in the winter of 1909-1910 and in 1911, Jones made a study for connecting roads and walks with existing roads in the vicinity of the new Casino, which opened in 1912.[5] In 1919, A. John Halfenstein designed a community fireplace to be erected by the Camp Fire Girls.

Eagle Rock Reservation. These twisting, clinging vines rely on a maple tree for support. *October 10, 2009.*

In 1929, Gallagher and Lyle L. Blundell worked on a study for a new pavilion. Benjamin G. Donovan worked on a study for approaches to the Casino showing a new Essex County road. Edward D. Rando made a profile for proposed new entrance road from the realigned Eagle Rock Avenue. Emanuel T. Mische made a study for revision of a monument site. In 1932, Edward M. Prellwitz and Walter F. Clarke made studies of treatments for the northeast and north ends of the Reservation, which were alternatives to suggestions by the Montclair Planning Board.

Eagle Rock Reservation has bridle paths, hiking trails; a picnic area; softball diamond; and wildlife habitat to a wide range of flora and fauna. The acreage is predominantly comprised of a red oak forest, with a unique red maple wetland in the northern section of the tract. The Reservation also features the "Old Casino" located at the edge of the cliff, now converted into the Highlawn Pavilion restaurant. It is noted for its spectacular view and fine cuisine. A September 11th Memorial with sculpture and a plaza commemorates the location where hundreds viewed the 2001 tragedy. The vista toward New York has been one that has captivated visitors for over a century. Recent improvements include: the installation of a radio tower completed in 2005; construction of a gazebo, entrance upgrades, pathway improvements, landscaping and traffic safety enhancements, costing $982,000, was completed in 2009; and the expansion of the September 11th Memorial to include a monument dedicated to the Flight Crews, which was completed in 2009.[6]

AT THE TOP OF EAGLE ROCK AND THE PAVILION IN-THE-ORANGES, N. J. 014

Postmarked in 1944, this postcard shows the "Pavilion" also known as the Casino in Eagle Rock Reservation. This landmark building, which had been allowed to deteriorate, was saved from demolition by modernization. It reopened in 1986 as the Highlawn Pavilion.

Endnotes Chapter 7: Eagle Rock Reservation

[1] Frederick W. Kelsey. *The First County Park System; A Complete History of the Inception and Development of the Essex County Parks of New Jersey.* (New York, New York: J.S. Ogilvie Publishing Company, 1905).
[2] From History of Eagle Rock Reservation Essex County Department of Parks, Recreation, and Cultural Affairs:
http://www.essex-countynj.org/p/index.php?section=af/system.
[3] Essex County Department of Parks. *Fourth Annual Report of the Board of Commissioners, 1898-99.* (Newark, New Jersey: Grover Bros.,1900).
[4] Essex County Department of Parks. *Fourth Annual Report of the Board of Commissioners, 1898-99.* (Newark, New Jersey: Grover Bros.,1900).
[5] Joseph Fagan. *Eagle Rock Reservation.* (Charleston, South Carolina: Arcadia Publishing, 2002).
[6] Essex County Department of Parks, Recreation, and Cultural Affairs: http://www.essex-countynj.org/p/index.php?section=af/system.

Chapter 8
South Mountain Reservation:
Millburn, Maplewood, and West Orange (1898)

With such enchanting place names as Elf's Valley, Breezy Wood, and Mayapple Hill, South Mountain Reservation is the largest park in its most natural state in the Essex County system. The reservation encompasses over 2,000 heavily wooded acres in the south-central part of Essex County. South Mountain Reservation is situated between the first and second ridges of the northeast-southwest oriented Watchung Mountains, the English version of the Lenape name meaning "high hills." The West Branch of the Rahway River flows between the two ridges forming Elf's Ravine (shown on the Guide Map prepared by the Olmsted Brothers firm in 1902). A reservoir and watershed owned by the City of Orange lies in the northern tract. When first developed beginning in 1895, three municipalities shared this hilly terrain: Millburn to the southwest; South Orange Township on the east; and West Orange to the northwest. On November 7, 1922, South Orange Township was renamed Maplewood.

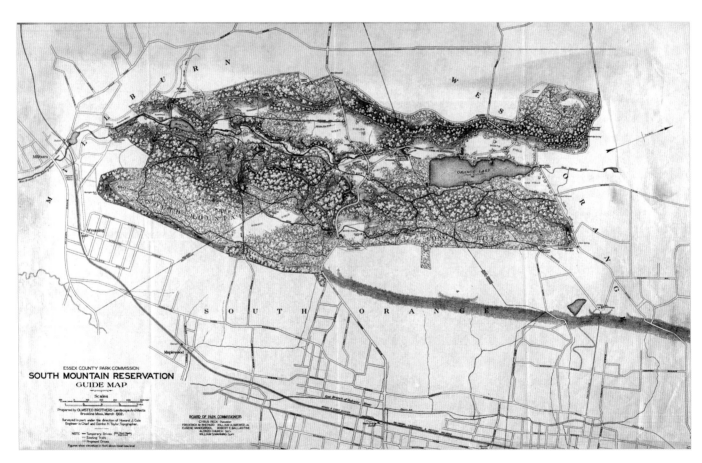

William H. Munroe and William G. Smith of the Olmsted Brothers drew this Guide Map of South Mountain Reservation in 1902. *Courtesy of Special Collections and University Archives, Rutgers University Libraries.*

South Mountain Reservation is comprised from numerous land purchases starting in 1895, shortly after the Essex County Park Commission was established. Due to deed ambiguities and landowner reluctance, by 1898 only half of the land needed had been purchased.[1] Nevertheless, the Commissioners secured the 2,000 acres, parcel by parcel, either by purchase or seizure over the next several years. In 1899, the Commission reported that approximately eight miles of service roads had been laid out through South Mountain Reservation. Getting to the Reservation itself initially proved difficult. The reservation was intended to be brought down to the Lackawanna Railroad station at Millburn, whence a walk only a trifle over half a mile would

At the very beginning, pleasure drivers utilized the roadways established in South Mountain Reservation. This postcard showing a chauffeur crossing a shallow Rahway River was mailed in 1908.

be needed to reach the southern end of the summit of South Mountain. The walk would be even shorter from Wyoming station, but the climb would be steeper. The access to the reservation by electric trolley was not very good. In 1899, the South Orange Avenue trolley stopped down in the valley, one and one-quarter miles from the reservation. The cable car road was better as it landed visitors at the top of the mountain. However, it was not in very active operation except in connection with entertainments at a summer amusement resort.[2]

The Landscape Architect's report for the Essex County Park Commission's 1899 Annual Report includes a wealth of information about the plans for the reservation:

> Geographically, South Mountain is a tremendous mass of trap rock, which has been thrust up through the beds of sandstone. The trap cliffs of South Mountain are remarkably continuous and regular in outline. The trap rock, while it is one of the hardest of stones, is filled with cracks, formed, no doubt, during the process of cooling. Moisture and frost act upon them quite readily causing the cliffs and crags and large masses to gradually crumble into smaller fragments, which roll down and form huge, steep, talus slopes. These precipitous slopes are now much bigger than the cliffs, though much less picturesque.

The trap rock has been carved by a shallow stream in South Mountain Reservation. This location is just above Hemlock Falls, which is five hundred feet further west. *November 8, 2009.*

The west branch of the Rahway River is a modest mountain stream, which runs nearly dry in summer. It is a roaring torrent after heavy rains owing to the steepness of the slopes, the valley's narrowness, and the thinness of the soil over the ledges. It is dammed in four or five places within the reservation. The uppermost dam is about half way from Northfield Avenue to South Orange Avenue. It forms the 57-acre Orange Reservoir, which is the main collecting and storage reservoir of the Orange Water Works. The valley continues to the northeast and drains into the Passaic River. There are very few houses in the reservation and but little open farming land, most of it being in the condition commonly called "wood lots."

The landscape of South Mountain Reservation is dependent upon its geology and topography much as the beauty of the human form is upon its skeleton and flesh. Without its clothing of vegetation, the reservation would be almost as ugly as the human form would be without skin and hair. It is as important to the full enjoyment of the reservation that its forest should be beautiful in its general effect as well as in detail. The forest is the one general characteristic and the drives and walks should also be laid so to lead visitors to commanding summits, to bold cliffs, picturesque ledges, steep declivities, and deep rocky ravines. These topographical features cannot be altered to any great degree, but they can be made more visible by removing interfering trees and more beautiful by adding suitable vegetation. New vista points should be established and those views that now exist should be kept open.

This photograph was taken c. 1905 by amateur photographer Arthur R. Grow. The picture shows a young man reading in the glen beneath Hemlock Falls in South Mountain Reservation. This location continues to be a popular destination for hikers. *Courtesy of William A. Jordan.*

The forestry of South Mountain Reservation demands much study, planning (in the broad sense), and actual work continued through a long period, in fact, never ceasing. Its former owners have held nearly all of the land as "wood lots." It is particularly noticeable that there are very few pine trees, hemlocks, ground hemlock, mountain laurel, holly, rhododendron, and other evergreen foliage, which does so much to beautify the wild woods of the mountainous regions of New Jersey. Monotony, deadly, dull monotony—that is the impression, which much of the woods will produce on visitors.

An intelligent management of the woods, with the aid of a few men and wagons can, in a few years, so alter and improve their appearance that a very different and much more agreeable impression will be produced, and afterwards the woods will always be growing in dignity and interest. The first thing is to prevent wood fires. With fires stopped, the undergrowth comes in and covers the ground, shading it where the trees do not do so effectively, thus preventing excessive evaporation of soil moisture and enabling the roots of the trees to continue to feed during droughts. The undergrowth also prevents the fallen leaves from blowing away. The dead leaves not only assist in shading the ground and producing leaf mould as fertilizer, but they prevent rainwater from flowing off rapidly, as it does on the smooth, hard soil of burned over woods.

A natural wood is both imposing, from the great size of some of its mature trees, and varied due to trees of all ages and types. Some trees, which have desirable appearances, can be given a better chance by thinning out about then even though they might not have survived the struggle naturally. Beech trees, for instance, are particularly liable to suffer from wood fires and are apt to be overshadowed by chestnuts and other rapid growing trees, yet the beech is perhaps the most beautiful of native forest trees. The differences that occur in nature, in the appearance of woods, owing mainly to conditions of soil and moisture, may desirably be simulated by design. The oaks are appropriate to the dryer, thinner soils; the beech, scarlet maple, tulip, and magnolia to deeper, moister soils or even in the case of the latter to positively swampy ground. It is reasonable to try to make this adaptation of tree growth to locality more obvious than it may happen to be. As a matter of design, it is more strikingly effective and interesting to come across parts of the woods where a particular tree is in marked predominance. Thus one may thin out to develop a beech grove or a white oak grove or a yellow birch grove. In other cases thinning may be done to open up about an uncommonly large individual tree, left over from a previous generation. We will leave a few of the best trees to stand singly on open ground or to plant thickly about them to restore the woods where it will be more appropriate to do

Laurels planted in the 1930s by the Civilian Conservation Corps in bloom at South Mountain Reservation. *April 25, 2009.*

so. Some places may be kept clear of trees permanently for the sake of the contrast to the dense woods and for providing views of the solid, bold cliff-like fronts. The occasional use of the scythe will usually suffice to keep bushes from getting too tall to be seen over.

If an area of grassland is large enough to warrant it, the best way to keep the grass short is by pasturing sheep upon it, but this can only be done if the expense of a shepherd with each flock can be afforded. Smaller areas can be kept sufficiently neat with the hay mowing machine or scythe. A combination of the bushy and grassy treatment produces pleasing effects where the good soil is interrupted by ledges or patches of thin soil. This is, in fact, what we designate the landscape of "bushy pasture," common in the northern states. It is both picturesque in general views and full of pretty details. Details in the abundance of flowers and in the variety of tints in the foliage and bark of the shrubbery, particularly in late summer, when the gorgeous golden

rods and asters are in bloom, and in autumn, when the last of these combine with the russet and purple foliage.

The forest is the predominant feature of this large reservation. Each year, fallen leaves enrich the soil. Prudent forest management has led to a healthy mixed forest in South Mountain Reservation. *November 8, 2009.*

The system of drives and walks for South Mountain Reservation should be so devised as to exhibit its strongly marked scenery effectively and so as to produce upon visitors a strong impression of each kind of scenery. There should be a real Brookside drive, true to its name, sticking to the brook from end to end of the reservation. There should be a drive on each of the two crest lines. There should be another drive along the top of the northwest slope of South Mountain from end to end of the reservation. There should be a wild, mountainside drive on the southeast slope of Second Mountain, sometimes at the foot of the crags, for cliffs and crags are most imposing when seen close at hand and from below. This will afford opportunities for impressive views of the valley and of the great extent of woods in it, stretching up over South Mountain in a continuous green carpet. There must be others for entrances and others to afford communication from the valley to the crest lines and to ravines, view points, picnic groves, and other points of interest. It would be extremely desirable to have a boundary road along the southeast boundary, following, approximately, the foot of the talus slope below the crest. The precipitous slope and cliffs above this road should be turned over to or secured by the Park Commission for a public reservation. This would be of great value, as it would preserve the most romantic and most conspicuous part of the mountain from destruction for the benefit of all those who live in the country below. It would also provide a local pleasure ground and a fine foreground for the large number of residences, which might be built above and below it in time.[3]

many sections and plans were made for each section. John Charles Olmsted worked on boundary studies at south end of the Reservation and drew a centerline through the "Pitcher Tract." Others show the property divisions and had notes by John Charles Olmsted, Edward Sturgis, and Percival R. Gallagher. They worked in suggestions from the County engineer in charge, H. J. Cole. In 1898, architectural draftsman Frank A. Bourne worked on plans of the pumping station, Wilbur David Cook, Jr., produced a sketch for suggested boundaries and approaches at south end of the Reservation, and Percival Gallagher made a preliminary study of the road system.

In June 1900, John Charles Olmsted presented a plan with planting notes, proposed roads, woodland improvements, and an Administration building on Taylor's topo maps. That August, William C. Woolner drew plans for the drive near Cherry Lane. Throughout 1901, John Charles Olmsted and Percival Gallagher created plans for all the sections. In 1902, William H. Munroe and William G. Smith drew the consolidated plan or guide map and Percy R. Jones drew a study for the administration building and grounds. Mr. Reed worked on preliminary plans for approaches at south end of Reservation and for proposed railroad station grounds. Carl Rust Parker wrote forestry notes on the planting plan in 1902. In 1905, John Charles Olmsted designed a plan of proposed distributing reservoir and 20-foot pumping main from Campbell's Pond pumping station to the distributing reservoir at the top of mountain near South Orange Avenue. In keeping with the forestry plan, hemlock and pine were planted, as were mountain laurel and wild azalea. Over 3,000 rhododendrons (at 43 cents each) were planted in 1910.[4]

The plans on file at Frederick Law Olmsted Historic Site shows that in 1898-1899 preliminary plans for South Mountain Reservation were drawn based on the topographic maps by Gorden H. Taylor. Because of the large acreage, the park was divided into

Stone bridges designed to fit into the forest scenery carry trails over the streams at South Mountain Reservation. *November 8, 2009.*

In 1913, the Commission purchased the Lighthope quarry tract at the southern end of South Mountain Reservation. On September 1, 1913, the stone crushing plant ceased operation. This came after many years of work in the course of which the beauty of the region was seriously marred and the section of the rock upon which Washington stood watching the retreat of one column of his army from Newark toward New Brunswick in November 1776, entirely carried away. The road from South Orange Avenue to Washington Rock—one of the historic spots of Essex County—is about one and three-fourths miles in length. While it winds through a beautiful stretch of woodland in which laurel, azalea, and rhododendron abounded, there are several beautiful vistas of the valley below before the visitor finally comes to the Rock itself with its commanding outlook.[5]

From 1909 to 1927, Hans J. Koehler supervised much of the planting and made extensive notes and revised plans covering various phases of the park's development. In 1920, Edwin M. Prellwitz prepared an outline plan of the property acquired east and west of Brookfield Drive including the New Jersey West Line Railroad and the Lighthope property. In 1924, Percy R. Jones designed the grading Plan for Eastridge Drive. In 1927, Milton F. Sherman designed the grading plans and details of the Bramhall Terrace in the vicinity of Washington Rock. In 1928, Raymond W. Aldrich and A. W. Phillips designed the plan for a parking area in the vicinity of Crest Drive and J. Harry Scott designed a planting plan for area around Bramhall Terrace. Lyle L. Blundell submitted grading and profile plans in 1929 to relocate Brookside Drive, which included an overpass across South Orange Avenue. In 1933, Joseph Bannon presented his planting plan for the proposed maypole field and J. Harry Scott and Carlton M. Archibald prepared plans for the vicinity of a proposed summit field.

During the 1930s, over 200 youths of the West Orange Company 1281, Camp SP-7, Civilian Conservation Corps worked for $1 a day each to create the trails, footbridges, and shelters. On January 8th, 1935, 125 of the young men went out on strike to protest the camp's mandatory 11 o'clock bedtime. The rebellion was short-lived, but even so, the fourteen ringleaders lost their jobs.[6]

According to the Essex County Park Commission web site (www.essex-county.org), South Mountain Reservation is now promoted for its ten picnic areas, nineteen miles of hiking and walking trails, twenty-seven miles of carriage roads for jogging, horseback riding, and cross-country skiing; an archery range; a Girl Scout camp; and the Washington Rock Lookout Historic Site. It continues to be the wildest of all the Olmsted parks in New Jersey.

Inscribed by an anonymous graffitist, South Mountain Reservation was designated "The Wild Park." *April 25, 2009.*

Endnotes Chapter 8: South Mountain Reservation:

[1]Frederick W. Kelsey. *The First County Park System; A Complete History of the Inception and Development of the Essex County Parks of New Jersey.* (New York, New York: J.S. Ogilvie Publishing Company, 1905): 40-41.
[2]Joseph Fagan. *Eagle Rock Reservation.* (Charleston, South Carolina: Arcadia Publishing, 2002).
[3] Essex County Department of Parks. *Fourth Annual Report of the Board of Commissioners,1898-99.* (Newark, New Jersey: Grover Bros.,1900).

[4] Frank John Urquhart. *A History of the City of Newark, New Jersey Embracing Practically Two and A Half Centuries 1666-1913.* Volume 2. (New York, New York: Lewis Historical Publishing Company, 1915).
[5]Essex County Department of Parks. *Twenty-fifth Annual Report of the Board of Commissioners, 1920.* (Newark, New Jersey: The W. H. Shurts Co., Printers, 1921).
[6]*New York Times.* January 9 and 10, 1935.

Chapter 9
Weequahic Park: Newark (1899)

Dominated by an 80-acre lake and bounded by Dayton Street, Meeker Avenue, Elizabeth Avenue, and the Weequahic Golf Course, Weequahic Park is located in the City of Newark in the eastern section of Essex County. It is the second largest developed park in the county system with 311 acres. U.S. Route 22 and the Lehigh Valley Railroad (Conrail) bisect the park. The name (pronounced Week-wake) stems from the Lenape term for "the head of the cove." Despite opposition to the acquisition in 1895, the first twelve parcels of land—approximately 265 acres of farmlands, fairgrounds, and swampland—were purchased between 1896 and 1899 at a cost of $220,000. Critics described it as merely a mosquito-laden bog. Nevertheless, the Essex County Park Commission took the step to reserve this land. The public quickly appreciated the advantages of the "reservation," as it was first defined, which prompted the Commission to change it into a park and offer a variety of recreational activities. In 2003, Weequahic Park was included as a Key resource in the Weequahic Park Historic Distinct listing in the New Jersey and National Registers of Historic Places. The Olmsted Brothers firm began working on the project in 1899.[1]

The Olmsted Brothers Landscape Architect's report in the 1899 Fourth Annual Report of Essex County Commission included the following summary of the firm's plans for Weequahic Park:

The landscape design will comprise the following features: First: The lake. Although the marsh is presently a beautiful feature of the landscape, being green with sedges and cat tail rushes, patches of golden rods, marsh mallows and other pretty wild flowers, it can scarcely be considered a desirable feature in the park. It is our plan to turn the marsh into a lake with wholesome gravelly shores and water of ample depth to prevent the undue growth of water plants, which would otherwise soon restore a shallow lake to its mosquito-breeding condition. We have adopted the plan to excavate the muck and sandy loam under parts of it, to the required depth. There will be over half a million yards of muck and earth to be excavated. This vast amount of material can be used to build up the shore where the trees are very thick, so as to provide room for the lake shore walk just outside of the trunks of the shore trees, but still under their spreading branches. Also, fill will be needed in several places to keep the lake circuit drive on good lines and within reasonable distance of the margin of the lake. The proposed islands, points, border between the circuit drive and the railroad, and the playfield areas will have to be filled upon to a good height to be well drained. A boathouse with broad, sheltering roof and verandas will be located at the north end of the lake nearest the city. This building will also afford accommodation for skaters in winter.

In the early 1900s, Newark photographer W.H. Broadwell printed his photograph of Weequahic Park on paper with a postcard backing. It captured a moment of two popular park pastimes: a family feeding the ducks and boaters on Weequahic Lake.

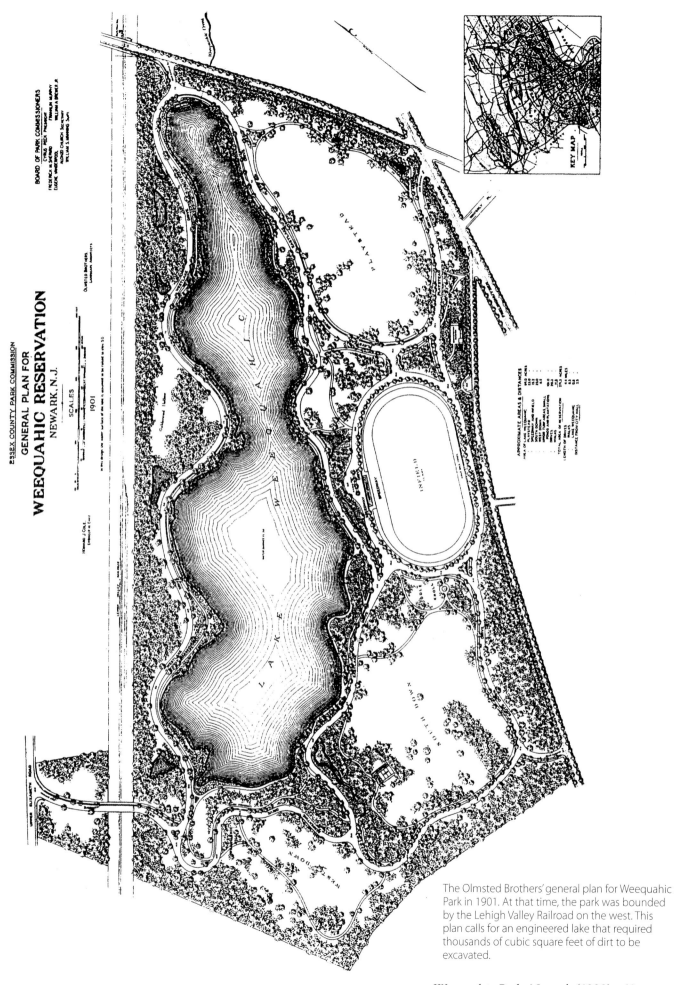

The Olmsted Brothers' general plan for Weequahic Park in 1901. At that time, the park was bounded by the Lehigh Valley Railroad on the west. This plan calls for an engineered lake that required thousands of cubic square feet of dirt to be excavated.

Weequahic Park: Newark (1899)   63

Second: The playstead. This open field containing twenty-three acres will allow hundreds of children to play upon and for their elders to roam. This playstead will be overlooked on two sides from a drive and will be surrounded by a walk in the shade of the border plantings and groves of trees. But little shrubbery is allowable except to conceal the boundary fence needed to protect the ground from short cutting. While the middle will be nearly level, the margins will have graceful undulations, lending variety of aspect to the frame of woods. A border mound along the low part of Waverly Avenue will be of great value in adding to the seclusion of the part of the lake circuit drive, which will be near it. A fieldhouse will be located at the east entrance near the streetcars. In the basement there may be dressing rooms and toilet accommodations. Above these there will be a shelter from rain or sun for a large crowd, and here light refreshments may be provided.

Third: The speedway. Southwest of the charming natural playstead area there is a racetrack, formerly used in connection with the county fair grounds. This man-made construction is completely hidden from the natural landscape portions of the park. This will be a track for speeding fast horses, surrounded by a wide walk for visitors on foot and a wide drive for visitors in vehicles or on horseback. Outside of this again there will be a walk on the hills at the ends. Within the speedway a kite-shaped bicycle track is planned to enclose a field for match and other games of baseball for men and older boys, who should not be allowed to play ball on the playstead.

Fourth: The pastoral district, south and southwest of the lake. This includes three hills and three valleys, mostly farm fields and pasture, but with a fine piece of wood, a few scattering trees and some good fence row trees. It is our plan to make this division of the park a comparatively wild and rough pastoral scene. We have planned for an outer circuit drive and a few walks will be needed. The lake circuit drive will afford views into this pleasing part of the park. A loop drive, branching from the drive surrounding the speedway and connecting with the lake circuit drive, will skirt the outer margin of the pasture land near the border plantings. It is proposed to keep the grass

Weequahic Lake is the dominant landscape feature of lower Weequahic Park. The trail around its edge is popular with walkers and joggers. It passes through woodlands following the designs of Andrew Auten and Wilber D. Cook, Jr. *April 12, 2009.*

short by pasturing sheep upon it. A shepherd and his dog will protect the sheep during the day from stray dogs, and keep the sheep out of the border plantations and thick woods where the undergrowth must be preserved to cover the ground, as it will be too shady for turf.[2]

Beginning in the spring of 1899, John Charles Olmsted, William C. Woolner, and Percy R. Jones created the preliminary plan of the park using topographical maps as the base. From 1899 to 1901, Percy R. Jones produced the majority of the grading plans including the design of the bicycle track. He selected the location for the boathouse that was to be built at the north end of the lake. William H. Munroe drew the preliminary plan creating the lake. In 1900, H. P. Richmond, a recent Harvard graduate with a degree in architecture, designed the field house located on Waverly Avenue. James Frederick Dawson, assisted by Faris B. Smith and Mr. Hemboldt, designed the preliminary planting plan for the entire park. In 1901, William C. Woolner revised the planting plan for the Waverly Avenue entrance and Emanuel Tillman Mische created a planting study for the section from the speedway to the south boundary on the east side of the park. That same year, Alanson Phelps Wyman designed a planting plan (revised study) for the temporary portion along Waverly Avenue. In 1902, Andrew Auten and Wilber D. Cook, Jr., designed planting plans for the area around the lake.

Weequahic Park's original western boundary was the Lehigh Valley Railroad, but in response to public demand, the Legislature authorized the acquisition of land that extended the park westward and up the hill to a new boundary along Elizabeth Avenue. By 1913, the cost of land purchases totaled $339,500, of the buildings thereon $38,050, and of the improvements to date $267,580.[3]

The open flat space of the playfield area of Weequahic Park were used for many types of sports and games. Here, the grass tennis courts are fully occupied on a summer's day. This color postcard, which lacks an exact postmark, dates to circa 1915.

TENNIS COURT IN WEEQUAHIC PARK, NEWARK, N. J.

Postmarked in 1907, this postcard shows a horse racing event that took place on the pre-existing Waverly Track that the Olmsted Brothers firm incorporated into the design of Weequahic Park.

On the Race Track, Weequahic Park, Newark, N. J.

Percival R. Jones continued to work on Weequahic Park and in 1910, he, Ralph Eldon Sawyer, and Edward L. Keeling prepared many plans for the new portion of the park west of the Lehigh Valley Railroad. In 1910, P.W. Dorr drew up the layout for the bridle path and worked on many plans including the westside ball fields through 1914. By 1914, Percival Gallagher created general planting plans and one for a formal garden near the tennis courts. Henry Pree and A. Chandler Manning designed plans for the area at Elizabeth and Meeker Avenues and the westside gardens.

Three buildings designed by New York architects Carrère and Hastings were constructed in the western section in 1916. They include the Divident Hill pavilion, the Tennis Building, and the Elizabeth Avenue Children's Pavilion. The Divident Hill pavilion was erected to celebrate the City of Newark's 250th Anniversary of its founding. It is located on the spot where on May 28, 1668, Commissioners of Newark and Elizabeth met to fix the boundary line (or divident) between the two municipalities. The Elizabeth Avenue Children's Pavilion serving the adjacent playground, is remembered for its formal classical design and rich architectural details. In 1918, Percival Gallagher drew up grading plans for Divident Hill, and Stanley Hart White created the planting plan. In 1922, John Halfenstein prepared a study for a rose garden and a month later Edward Clarke Whiting and Hans J. Koehler drew the plans for the garden. In 1924, Percy R. Jones developed the grading plan and Jacob H. Sloet developed the planting plan for the area around the statue of Governor Murphy that would be installed near Elizabeth and Meeker Avenues.

Percival Gallagher created the planting plan for the upper western section of Weequahic Park along Elizabeth Avenue. *October 31, 2009.*

The pavilion designed by New York architects Carrère and Hastings stands at the top of Divident Hill in Weequahic Park. It was built in 1916 to commemorate the City of Newark's 250th Anniversary of its founding. This is the location where officials from Newark and Elizabeth met to formally establish the boundary (or the divident) between the two municipalities. *May 23, 2009.*

The Elizabeth Avenue Children's Building in Weequahic Park was also designed by Carrère and Hastings. It has rich architectural details including an arcade, glazed terra cotta tile exterior, and arched ceilings clad with unglazed tiles. *May 23, 2009.*

Franklin Murphy (1846-1920) was born in Jersey City. He had been a soldier during the Civil War. After returning to Newark in 1865, he started a varnish business that would grow to become a national company. Murphy's aptitude for business translated into wealth and his political ambition took him from serving in the Newark Common Council in the 1880s into the office of New Jersey governor where he served from 1902 to 1905. Frederick Kelsey, also an early advocate for an Essex County Park System recounts inviting then state assemblyman Murphy to his dinner party in October 1894. Franklin Murphy was of the opinion "that what the public required and what he hoped would be accomplished was a system of parks and parkways which he, his family, and friends could enjoy now." He thought it best to bear in mind the future, but what was wanted were suitable parks immediately, and appropriate boulevards and parkways for reaching them.[4] In the 1890s, Murphy was an advocate for the legislation establishing the Essex County park system and upon its creation, was named one of the first Commissioners. Murphy's political focus included civic improvements. As governor, he supported labor standards, limits on child labor, tenement inspections, bank interest on state money, efforts to clean the Passaic River, and the state's first mandatory primary education law.[5]

The bronze sculpture was created by John Massey Rhind (1860-1936), a Scottish-born sculptor who had a studio in Alpine, New Jersey. The commemorative statue was commissioned by the Essex County Park Commission and was unveiled in November 1924. The inscription in brass letters affixed to the red granite base at one time read: "Franklin Murphy. 1846-1920. A friend of humanity endowed with rare civic zeal and executive foresight. An organizer and leader among men. Governor of this state 1902-1905."

Throughout the first half of the 20th century, the neighborhood around Weequahic Park developed into a middle-class residential neighborhood whose biggest asset was the park. It was inhabited primarily by a middle-class Jewish population and was home to a number of synagogues, yeshivas, and kosher restaurants. But the growth of outlying residential tracts in the 1950s and the development of interstate highways contributed to white migration to the suburbs all over the country. Weequahic's demographics already were changing before 1967, and the riots that ensued that summer provoked many of the remaining white residents to move outside Newark's boundaries.[6]

One such former resident is Cathy Bird Streeter who shared her remembrances.

When I was a small child living in Newark more than 65 years ago, some of my fondest memories are of Weequahic Park. How I remember the joy of the flower gardens, the beauty of the wonderful lake, the horse trails, the playgrounds with sand boxes, swings, and slides, the many statues and memorial structures, rolling down grassy hills, the walks through the wooded trails, and band concerts in summer. The park was the place I sneaked my first cigarette as a teenager. The park was pristine-clean. The benches were painted green every summer and the lawns were mowed and manicured. Park attendants made sure no one spoiled the park for anyone else. There were plenty of waste receptacles. The flower gardens always had a gardener on duty. Later, I married and lived in a nearby rented apartment. I would put my son in the carriage and walk to the park with him. In 1960 after my second child was born, we moved from Newark.[7]

Sculptor John Massey Rhind created this bronze statue of New Jersey Governor Franklin Murphy. The statue is located on a slight rise in Weequahic Park set back from and facing Meeker Avenue halfway between Elizabeth Avenue and the railroad tracks. *October 31, 2009.*

The Weequahic Park Association (WPA) was formed in 1992 to address the decline and neglect of Weequahic Park. The WPA is comprised of community residents who organized to stop the proposed demolition of the historic grandstand located in the park. It was the act of circulating a petition and collecting over 300 signatures that spurred the founding of the organization. The WPA is the first park conservancy group in Essex County to enter into a Partnership Agreement with the Essex County Administration for the expressed purpose of rehabilitating a park. The agreement allows the WPA to implement capital improvements in Weequahic Park and is patterned after the successful agreement between the City of New York that the Central Park Conservancy.

Recent projects include the Weequahic Lake Restoration Project, which was a comprehensive approach to environmental development completed in 2002. The $3 million project utilized community members and students, who participated in the research and study of the biological components of the lake. In 2003 and 2004, another student project, Rutgers University's Urban Forestry Weequahic Park Tree Inventory, examined the park's woods. Students conducted an inventory to gather specific information about each individual tree such as its species, height, trunk diameter, health, and environmental conditions within a prescribed area of the park. In 2004, the fieldhouse roof was repaired and tennis courts improved. In 2006, the playgrounds were modernized and the community building expanded. The installation of synthetic grass surfaced baseball field took place in 2007 and a six-station fitness course was installed in 2009.

Weequahic Park continues to be an important place of tranquil nature surrounded by a neighborhood of urban density. Joggers use the old half-mile racetrack where trotters ran decades ago. Gone is the historic grandstand, but not the conservancy group that first formed trying to save it. The fieldhouse services ballfields, basketball, and one of two playgrounds. The west section along Elizabeth Avenue is unique with its rolling hills and attractive monuments. This section also has tennis and paddleball courts, a playground, and a formal garden. The East Coast Greenway passes through the park and the scenic lake still attracts shoreline walkers. Summer concerts under the stars now often feature gospel and jazz musicians in what can be described the heart of Newark's vibrant Weequahic neighborhood.

The drive through the wooded area of the western section of Weequahic Park looks very similar to a winding country road. *October 31, 2009.*

Endnotes Chapter 9: Weequahic Park

[1] History of Weequahic Park from the Essex County Park Commission website.
[2] Essex County Department of Parks. *Fourth Annual Report of the Board of Commissioners, 1898-99.* (Newark, New Jersey: Grover Bros., 1900).
[3] Frank John Urquhart. *A History of the City of Newark, New Jersey Embracing Practically Two and A Half Centuries 1666-1913.* (New York, New York: Lewis Historical Publishing Company, 1915).
[4] Frederick W. Kelsey. *The First County Park System; A Complete History of the Inception and Development of the Essex County Parks of New Jersey.* (New York, New York: J.S. Ogilvie Publishing Company, 1905).
[5] Martin Paulsson. "Franklin Murphy." *Encyclopedia of New Jersey.* Eds. Maxine N. Lurie and Marc Mappen. (New Brunswick, New Jersey: Rutgers University Press, 2004): p. 550.
[6] Vinessa Ermino "Neighborhood Snapshot," *Star-Ledger.* November 22, 2007.
[7] Cathy Bird Streeter. Personal correspondence. March 16, 2009.

Chapter 10

Watsessing Park: East Orange and Bloomfield (1900)

Watsessing Park is located on 69 acres divided between the Townships of Bloomfield and East Orange, in the eastern section of Essex County. The two-section park is bounded by the Garden State Parkway, Dodd Street, and Bloomfield Avenue, and Glenwood Avenue and Cleveland Terrace. The meandering Second River (originally "Wigwam Brook") merges with Toney's Brook and flows through this long open park. It is the fourth largest park in the county system. The name is a modification of the Lenape words for hill (Watschu) and stone (Assan). The oldest section of the park comprises the first ten acres that were donated to the Essex County Park Commission by the City of East Orange in 1900. On October 23, 1900, the Commission appropriated $5,000 for immediate improvements, a sum sufficient, according to their landscape architect, to make it usable and attractive.[1]

The section in East Orange between Cleveland Terrace and Glenwood Avenue was the first to be designed. The archived plans in Brookline, Massachusetts, include a 1900 print of a topographical map overdrawn with planting notes by John Charles Olmsted and James Frederick Dawson. Herbert J. Kellaway designed a 5-lane running track. J. B. Herbst drew studies for grading plans and a study for sections to accompany the grading study. In 1901, William C. Woolner revised a planting survey that had been made in 1900. By February 1901, the planting plan included keyed planting locations and a plant list. An overview plan of the park was made in 1901 and it included the list of Essex County Park Commissioners and approximate areas of the different park sections. It includes a planting list.

The original section of the park in East Orange was extended south to Dodd Street in 1909 and Herbert J. Kellaway produced the planting plan for this extension. Warren H. Manning produced the planting study and Edward L. Keeling developed a planting plan around the area of Glenwood and Llewellyn Avenues.

By 1913, Frank John Urquhart stated in *A History of The City of Newark* that,

> The grounds have been laid out and planted and now constitute Watsessing Park. Additions have since been made within the town of Bloomfield in obedience to legislative enactments until the area of the park has grown to 70 acres. The cost of acquirement to date is $133,436. There is one half of a mile of paths. The improvement is not yet completed, but the available portion in East Orange contains a running track and athletic fields, and its use by the public is rapidly increasing.[2]

The brook through the East Orange section of Watsessing Park is channeled. Beech, sycamore, and maple are some of the variety of tree species in this section. *October 10, 2009.*

The older section of Watsessing Park in East Orange near Cleveland Terrace has a narrow section with mature trees. *May 9, 2009.*

This green spike fence encircles most of Watsessing Park. The Saturday morning cricket players were waiting for the rest of the team to arrive. They eventually went to the open playing field in the Bloomfield section south of the railroad tracks. *May 9, 2009.*

Even on rain-soaked weekend days, the playing fields are used for all sorts of activities at Watsessing Park. *May 9, 2009.*

The bandstand and concert grove near Bloomfield Avenue, originally donated to Watsessing Park by the Ladies of Bloomfield. It was renovated in 2004. *May 9, 2009.*

In 1908, the planning for the expanded park into Bloomfield began. This project was given a new project number (#2139). John Charles Olmsted made a preliminary study for paths and drives for the extended park on top of the topographic map provided by local surveyor A. Church. In December 1908, Percy R. Jones developed grading surveys. C. R. Wait made a sketch for a shelter house. Planting plans were drawn up in 1909 and Carl Rust Parker drew the final plan in 1910. In 1911, Frank W. Sherman and P. W. Dorr drew up the preliminary grading plans. Percival R. Gallagher drew the plan for the section east of the railroad and did not recommend putting a road in this section. In 1912, F. B. Martin and Marcus H. Dall drew up a planting plan for a section east of the railroad station.

In 1914, the Ladies of Bloomfield donated a concert grove and the Olmsted firm made various sketches for a proposed gateway. In 1928, the new field house was constructed. Russell N. Barnes drew up plans that had planting notes for the field house in addition to the terrace, sand table, teeter-totters, and cinder track. In the 1950s, a small section along the east side was taken when construction of the Garden State Parkway required it. Monies paid by the State of New Jersey for the right-of-way helped improve the Hendricks Field golf course in Belleville.[3]

Information included on the Essex County Park Commission website lists recent improvements. They include: pathway improvements and the installation of rubberized safety surface for playgrounds completed in 2003; revitalization of historic bandstand, basketball courts and park entrances and improvements to Lawn Bowling Green, finished in 2004; Renovation to the walking track, basketball courts, restrooms, lawn bowling building and park entrances, and the opening of an Off-Leash Dog Facility completed in 2005; and the modernization of Watsessing Park Field House for year-round use, finished in 2008.

Endnotes Chapter 10: Watsessing Park

[1]Frederick W. Kelsey. *The First County Park System; A Complete History of the Inception and Development of the Essex County Parks of New Jersey.* (New York, New York: J.S. Ogilvie Publishing Company, 1905): p. 285.
[2]Urquhart, Frank John. *A History of The City of Newark, New Jersey Embracing Practically Two and A Half Centuries 1666-1913.* Volume 2. (New York, New York: Lewis Historical Publishing Company, 1915).
[3]Essex County Department of Parks website: http://www.essex-countynj.org/p/index.php?section=af/system

Chapter 11

Anderson Park: Montclair (1903)

Postmarked in 1907, this real photo postcard shows Anderson Park from the Bellevue Avenue entrance only four years after it opened.

In 2010, this small, 15-acre, neighborhood park in Upper Montclair was listed in the New Jersey and National Register of Historic Places. It is bordered by North Mountain Avenue, Parkside Road, Belleville Avenue, and the railroad tracks of Conrail (formerly the New York & Greenwood Lake Division of the Erie Railroad). Originally called Montclair Park, the parkland was transferred to the Essex County Park Commission from the Town of Montclair in 1903. In 1909 the name was changed to honor its original donor, Charles W. Anderson (1848-1928). Fastened to a boulder near the northeast corner of Anderson Park, a bronze plaque has the following inscription. "The lands comprising this park were donated to the town of Montclair by Charles W. Anderson for the purposes of a public park and in June, 1903, it was taken into the Essex County Park System."

As early as 1896 C. W. Anderson became part of a town committee working to create a park that would have sprawled from Watchung Avenue all the way to Bellevue, bordered on the east by the railroad tracks and the west by North Mountain Avenue. Like much of county parkland, this land was originally low and swampy, and historic photographs show it as overgrown fields. But landowners wouldn't donate property, despite some of it being swampy and "considered by some a nuisance to the health and beauty of the town," as *The New York Times* put it. In the end, only Anderson donated land, and three buildings on what is now parkland were purchased and moved. With under-drainage and fill, the trapezoidal-shaped tract was transformed into a pastoral landscape of sprawling lawns with walkways bordered by groves of shade trees. In 1903, the 15-acre parcel was deeded to Essex County, and in 1905 the park formally opened.

Wintertime's frozen landscapes have a beauty most of us rarely see. The support structure of each tree is revealed without the fancy dressing of leaves. Anderson Park, Montclair. *January 24, 2009.*

The design for the pastoral park was completed on August 4, 1903, by the Olmsted Brothers firm. The employees who worked on the project were John Charles Olmsted, James Frederick Dawson, William Lyman Phillips, Percy R. Jones, William M. Humans, Wilbur David Cook, Jr., Ralph E. Sawyer, J. B. Herbst, Carl Rust Parker, Philip W. Foster, Edward Clarke Whiting, and T. C. Jeffers. By 1913, the *History of Newark* stated, "the county is indebted for this beautiful breathing space to the generosity of Mr. C. W. Anderson, It is treated in a simple informal landscape style and contains some fine trees. There are facilities for tennis and cricket."[1]

The Friends of Anderson Park, one of the most active of the conservancy groups in the state wrote on their website: "Much of the park's original shrubbery is gone now, and many of the trees planted have died or are showing their age, although a few trees are more than a century old. In the summer of 2006 the park enjoyed a $1 million makeover, acquiring more than 130 new trees and shrubs. Friends of Anderson Park is committed to furthering that rehabilitation in the spirit of the original Olmsted design."[2]

Several of the perimeter trees at Anderson Park are now 100 years old. *October 10, 2009.*

Anderson Park has no formal athletic facilities. The open fields support frisbee or soccer players and visitors just taking a stroll equally well. *October 10, 2009.*

Endnotes Chapter 11: ANDERSON PARK

[1] Urquhart, Frank John. *A History of The City of Newark, New Jersey Embracing Practically Two and A Half Centuries 1666-1913*. Volume 2. (New York, New York: Lewis Historical Publishing Company, 1915).
[2] Friends of Anderson Park, Inc. website, www.friendsofandersonpark.com, 2010

Chapter 12
Irvington Park: Irvington (1908)

Before 1890, Irvington was a small country village named Camptown with a population of 1,500 inhabitants, on the western border of the crowded city of Newark. With the construction of a trolley line in 1890, the land surrounding the village quickly transformed into a suburb. By 1905, there were 7,180 inhabitants and in only five years, the 1910 US census showed a population of 11,877. Population growth continued and, by 1930, the number stood at 56,733.[1] Irvington Park is a 24-acre, mid-sized, urban park bordered by Lyons Avenue, Grove, May, and Augusta streets in the Township of Irvington.

Irvington Park is the twelfth largest park within the Essex County system. In 1913, its location was near the center of Irvington's population. With the high land off Grove Street, with a fine view of the Orange Mountains, and the low and formerly swampy ground near Augusta Street, the park was developed along the lines of a playground. Its unique aspect is its three-tier grading design. On the lowest tier near, an artesian well feeds the 1.65-acre pond, which is deep enough for fishing and has often been the site of miniature sailboat races. The upper tiers have rows and groves of red oak, mulberry, dogwood, elm, and ash trees encircling spacious lawn areas.[2]

Irvington Park is an oasis of green in the summer months. *June 27, 2009.*

The fishing pond in Irvington Park is located in the lowest of three tiers. The fountain keeps the water circulating. *June 27, 2009.*

This Essex County park was established under authority of legislative acts passed in 1906 and 1910. The cost for acquirement was $65,000, and for improvements $30,703. Construction began almost immediately in order to transform the swamp into a pond for winter ice skating.[3] The Olmsted Brothers began to work on this park in 1908 and the following staff members took part in the park's development: John Charles Olmsted; Percy R. Jones; A. Comerford; Henry Hill Blossom; P.W. Dorr; Walter J. Clarke; Carl Rust Parker; Edward L. Keeling; Hans J. Koehler; and Lyle L. Blundell.

The Olmsted Brothers received the topographic maps in 1908 and, in the summer, Percy R. Jones made a preliminary sketch and grading plan for the park. Walter J. Clarke drew profiles and cross sections to accompany the grading plan. In 1909, F. B. Martin created the planting plan. In 1910, Edward

L. Keeling made a planting plan for the southern addition to the park. In 1912, P. W. Dorr created the general plan of the park. No additional plans were drawn until 1930, when the firm produced a grading plan for the area around a bandstand.

Irvington Park officially opened in the summer of 1913. In 1914, an addition was approved that included ballfields, tennis courts, and broad lawns sloping to the west from Grove Street to Augusta Street. Work on this portion, including a new fieldhouse, was completed the following year. A well was driven to supply water to the wading pool, which has been closed due to pollution and a fountain was installed for aesthetic and practical purposes. The appearance of the park has changed little over the years.

According to the Essex County Department of Parks, recent improvements include: Lighting upgrades and the installation of rubberized safety surface in the playground were projects completed in 2003; the renovation of basketball courts, tennis courts, walking track, and park entrances completed in 2004; and the construction of a two-story addition to the community building completed in 2006.

The basketball courts in Irvington Park were recently upgraded by the Essex County Park Commission. *June 27, 2009.*

Irvington Park has a unique three-tier design and the fields on all levels are encircled by groves of mature hardwood trees. *June 27, 2009.*

Endnotes Chapter 12: Irvington Park

[1] Alan A. Siegel. *Irvington*. (Charleston, South Carolina: Arcadia Publishing, Inc., 1997); p. 78.
[2] Essex County Department of Parks website: http://www.essex-countynj.org/p/index.php?section=af/system
[3] Frank John Urquhart. *A History of The City of Newark, New Jersey Embracing Practically Two and A Half Centuries 1666-1913*. Volume 2. (New York, New York: Lewis Historical Publishing Company, 1915).

Chapter 13

Riverbank Park: Newark (1908)

Riverbank Park is located in the east side section of Newark bounded by Raymond Boulevard, and Market, Van Buren, and Somme Streets. A portion of the park across Raymond Boulevard has 1000 feet of waterfront access on the Passaic River, and includes land that once held the Morris Canal. At 10.77 acres, it is the smallest park in the Essex County park system and yet, the demands on it are great. It has been intensely developed for recreation. The remaining natural areas are along the riverbank.[1]

In the early 1900s, the drive to establish Riverbank Park was led by Franklin Murphy. The Murphy Varnish Company was in the Ironbound section of Newark, and Murphy wanted people like his workers to have a patch of green and a place to swim in their own neighborhood. Murphy loved Weequahic and Branch Brook Parks, but he realized that they were remote from the densely populated, working class portions of Newark.[2] This park was created in response to the demand from the citizens and following an act of the Legislature passed in 1906. It started as a smaller park of 5.75 acres and by 1913, its development was not yet entirely completed. The planning was similar to that of Eastside Park, accentuating the playground feature. The land cost $155,342 and the improvements $26,810.[3]

The first acreage for this park was acquired in 1907 and the Olmsted Brothers firm first designed the plans for what can be considered the middle section. The topographical maps were delivered to Brookline in March 1908. John Charles Olmsted and Percy R. Jones drew a preliminary plan of the park. In June 1908, architectural draftsman C. R. Wait drew a sketch for park building and P. W. Dorr drew details of steps and curbs. D. B. McAllister worked on the grading plan that included the Passaic River, Morris Canal, Passaic Avenue buildings, tank, wading pool, outdoor gym, and playfield. In 1910, F. B. Martin and Ralph Eldon Sawyer worked on the planting plan for the park

The mature trees along the park's walkways in Riverbank Park remain as part of the original Olmsted Brothers planting plans. *October 11, 2009.*

including a playfield, lawn, wading pool, outdoor gym, women's outdoor gym, Administration building, dressing rooms, men's and women's shelter (bathrooms), Morris Canal, and Passaic River. In 1912, P. W. Dorr and T.C. Jeffers created the plan of the park used for presentations.

The modern light fixtures mimic early 20th century design forms. This is in keeping with the historic time period of Riverbank Park's establishment. *October 11, 2009.*

Initially, the park was half the size it is today. Until the 1920s, the second largest metal processing enterprise in the United States, Balbach and Sons Refining and Smelting Company, was located where the baseball field is today.[4] After that land was purchased, the Olmsted Brothers were asked to design the new section. In 1927, Lyle L. Blundell and Edward D. Rando drew up the preliminary plan that had the three sections of park including a baseball field, football field, game ground, shelter, field house, tennis courts, promenade, and outlook over the Passaic River. Both Rando and Blundell along with Carroll A. Towne worked on the grading plans for the location of a pool over the Morris Canal, the grading study around the new grandstand, and the planting plans for the baseball field, grandstand, football field and track, field house and tennis courts. Arthur Dillon, a New York City architect, designed the grandstand.

In the 1990s, the park was threatened with a proposal to develop it into a minor league baseball stadium. Due to the efforts of a determined Ironbound community and organizations like SPARK (Save the Park At RiverbanK), the planned baseball stadium was defeated. It was built on Broad Street. As part of the planning, contaminants were found in the park's soil and it was closed for an environmental cleanup.

Riverbank Park has become the locale for the popular sport of soccer. Three Ironbound soccer leagues hold contentious negotiations over rights to the soccer fields here, in Independence Park, and in Weequahic Park. Raymond Boulevard, a major road, separates the heavily used main section of the park from the open and natural section along the riverbank. The riverbank has been left undisturbed, and it provides a rare stretch of open waterfront in a largely industrial area.

Riverbank Park was listed in both the New Jersey and the National Registers of Historic Places in 1998. Recent improvements include: the installation of a synthetic soccer field, scoreboard, fencing, and landscape improvements completed in 2003, and general improvements completed in 2006.[5]

The baseball stadium grandstand at Riverbank Park was designed by New York architect Arthur Dillon and built in 1930. *October 11, 2009.*

The soccer field at Riverbank Park is located inside an oval, five-lane running track. *October 11, 2009.*

Endnotes Chapter 13: Riverbank Park

[1] Essex County Department of Parks website:
http://www.essex-countynj.org/p/index.php?section=af/system
[2] J. Bennett, from website of Friends of Riverbank Park at http://www.newarkhistory.com/riverbank.html, December 2005.
[3] Frank John Urquhart. *A History of The City of Newark, New Jersey Embracing Practically Two and A Half Centuries 1666-1913*. Volume 2. (New York, New York: Lewis Historical Publishing Company, 1915).
[4] J. Bennett, from website of Friends of Riverbank Park at http://www.newarkhistory.com/riverbank.html, December 2005.
[5] Essex County Department of Parks website:
http://www.essex-countynj.org/p/index.php?section=af/system

Chapter 14

Glenfield Park: Montclair (1910)

Glenfield Park is a 20-acre park located in Montclair, with a small corner extending into Glen Ridge. It is in the central section of Essex County and is the thirteenth in size in the county park system. Bordered by Maple, Woodland, and Bloomfield Avenues, and the former Delaware, Lackawanna & Western Railroad, Glenfield Park serves as a community park. Most of its visitors walk to it from the surrounding neighborhoods. The Town of Montclair gave the original acreage to the Essex County Park Commission in 1910.

In 1905, Montclair park advocate William B. Dickson wrote the following letter to the Montclair Town Clerk:

> The tract now known as Glenfield Park on Maple Avenue, originally a beautiful ravine in which many trees still survived, was for the most part now an unsightly dumping ground for town rubbish, part of the level ground being occupied by the Poor House. Being adjacent to the Lackawanna Railroad, the first impression of Montclair received by newcomers was decidedly unfavorable. In fact, on our first visit to the

town in 1901, it having been recommended to us by a Pittsburgh friend who had relatives here, we "viewed the landscape o'er" after the train pulled out of Glen Ridge and were disgusted with the outlook. Our estimate of the character of the town was not improved when the train bumped over the grade crossing at Bloomfield Avenue and landed us at the old Lackawanna station, so we remained at the station and took the next train back to New York. Only the plea of our friends that we had not seen the real Montclair led us to make another visit, which resulted in our settling here.

> The tract was held by several owners, one of which had recently subdivided his part into 20-foot lots on which a number of shacks had been erected. An attempt to acquire the entire property required courage, persistence, and money, but fortunately our Committee under the able Chairmanship of Mr. Sawyer, was able to command all of these and with the hearty co-operation of the town officials, the property was acquired.[1]

This postcard of the wading pool at Glenfield Park was never mailed. It shows the former wading pool and field house that once stood near the corner of Bloomfield and Maple avenues.

The 1909 Crane map of Montclair show this land with the name, "Maple Avenue Park." This park preserved a rare bit of wildlife habitat in the midst of a bustling metropolis. While the largest section of the acreage was transformed into a pastoral park with recreational activities, in the southeastern corner of the park, the ravine at Toney's Brook was allowed to remain a picturesque glen with natural streamside vegetation. This creates a habitat favorable to a variety of wildlife, including several species of songbirds. The glen has been an educational resource in environmental education programs. The thick vegetation along Toney's Brook also aids in buffering the traffic noise from Bloomfield Avenue.[2]

The Olmsted Brothers employees who worked on this design include: John Charles Olmsted; Percy R. Jones; F. A. Hammond; P. W. Dorr; Herbert E. Millard; Ralph Eldon Sawyer; John J. Sullivan; T. C. Jeffers; Lyle L. Blundell; and Edward L. Keeling. The topographical maps showing the public school, summer school, and poor house were received in 1910. The study plan by John Charles Olmsted was revised and finished in March 1910. F. A. Hammond and Percy R. Jones drew the preliminary plan for the park. Herbert E. Millard made a tree list on the topographical maps. There was an effort to conserve the trees already on this site. The grading plans drawn by P. W. Dorr include notes about adjusting grade to save trees. Herbert E. Millard drew a study for the planting plan in 1910 and created the final plan in 1912 after trees had been removed. In 1912, Ralph Eldon Sawyer drew up the general plan of the park.

The 1913 *History of Newark* had an entry about this park paying homage to the neighboring town of Montclair.

This park contains 21.75 acres. It was presented to the county by the town of Montclair, with the exception of a tract containing 1.91 acres which was purchased in order to straighten the boundary lines and bring the park out to Bloomfield Avenue. The cost of this property was $20,860. The cost of the improvements to the park was $26,310. The fund for the improvement of this tract, including the purchase of the additional land, amounts to $100,000 and was authorized by the Legislature of 1909. The estimated cost of the improvements is $60,000. The plans provide for one main entrance at the corner of Bloomfield and Maple avenues and the other at the corner of Maple and Woodland avenues.[3]

The wooded section of Glenfield Park left natural includes a ravine that follows the course of Toney's Brook. *May 9, 2009.*

The Olmsted Brothers firm performed no further planning work until 1931. John J. Sullivan drew a map of the corners of the park in the vicinity of Maple Avenue. Lyle L. Blundell made revision of the walks on Maple Street side of the Park included additional planting in this area, showed the existing planting line near a proposed school building. An unsigned plan from this time also shows a proposed new administration building, large playground apparatus, and a game ground.

During the 1960s and 1970s, an increased demand arose for recreational sites from the neighborhood residents. A community center, home of the Montclair Grass Roots, was established in the park's field house in 1974. Along with the community center are field hockey and football fields, softball fields, tennis courts, lighted basketball courts, a large playground, and a fitness court. Recent improvement projects include: Playground resurfacing completed in 2003; general improvements included the installation of an 8-station exercise course, reconstruction of the basketball and tennis courts, and renovation to community building for over $1 million, completed in 2006.

This is the Glenfield Park House, home of the Montclair Grass Roots summer camp program. *May 9, 2009.*

Architecture often incorporates stylized forms from nature. The columns at Glenfield Park's field house look like a tree truck and the false timber trim curves like tree branches. *May 9, 2009.*

Endnotes Chapter 14: Glenfield Park

[1]William B. Dickson. Letter to Montclair Town Clerk in June 1905. On file at the Montclair Public Library, Montclair, New Jersey.
[2]Essex County Department of Parks website: http://www.essex-countynj.org/p/index.php?section=af/system

[3]Frank John Urquhart. *A History of The City of Newark, New Jersey Embracing Practically Two and A Half Centuries 1666-1913*. Volume 2. (New York, New York: Lewis Historical Publishing Company, 1915).

Chapter 15

Yantacaw Park: Nutley (1912)

Yantacaw and Yanticaw are used interchangeably as the name of this park, which is in the Township of Nutley in the eastern section of Essex County. It is a mid-sized park and the eleventh in size in the county park system. It encompasses 29 acres on both sides of the curving Third River roughly bordered by Chestnut Street on the north; Passaic Avenue on the east; Centre Street on the south; and Vincent Place and Warren Street on the west. Park Drive on the east border separates the picturesque river valley from the upper flatland where the ballfields are located. Two township parks border the Essex County park: Booth Park to the south and Memorial Park to the north.

The park's name is of native American derivation. The name Yanticaw, widely used throughout the town of Nutley, had its origins from an early local Indian ceremonial dance of thanksgiving called Yantacaw. It stems from the Lenape words meaning "place of the wood boundary." Tradition informs that the native inhabitants made an annual trek to the seashore to catch fish and to gather shells used for cooking and eating utensils. On their way they gathered at a spot where the present Third River flows into the Passaic River in Nutley. This site was recorded as "Yountakah" on a 1666 deed made between Captain Robert Treat and the Indians. In 1895, John R. Clark and Dr. Thomas E. Satterthwaite began campaigning for creation of a county park along this riverbank.

The Third River winds through Nutley and was channeled as it passes through the pastoral Yantacaw Park. *June 27, 2009.*

In 1908, the Town Commission decided under pressure to send a representative to a hearing in Newark. It was John R. Clark who pushed through a plan for a Nutley Park in the Essex County Park Appropriations bill on May 5, 1909. A year later Clark appeared before the Town Commission to report that a map had been prepared to preserve the natural beauty of the Third River "Along Yanticaw and Bear Creeks" from Harrison Street to Passaic Avenue. Through the efforts of Charles B. Vroom of Nutley and the Nutley Improvement Association the claim was made to the county that Nutley had been paying its share of a county tax for 17 years, had seen beautiful parks rise everywhere else, but had none of its own. Vroom haunted the Commission meetings and finally won $40,000 to buy land and $200,000 for its development into a park. In 1911, the land was finally acquired.[1] The 1913 *History of Newark* included an entry on Yantacaw Park. "This park was located in obedience to an act of the Legislature passed in 1911, providing park facilities for Nutley. Its boundaries have not yet been fully determined and no improvement has been attempted. So far as acquirement is concerned the commission has secured nineteen acres at a cost of $39,242."[2]

The steep stairway connects the two levels of Yantacaw Park. The cast concrete balustrade has regularly spaced holes, a trait that appears elsewhere in the Olmsted Brothers designed park. *June 27, 2009.*

The bridge carrying a wide footpath over the Third River also has the same cast concrete balusters seen in the staircases. This bridge marks the location of a dam that formed a pond when Yantacaw Park first opened in the 1910s. *June 27, 2009.*

The topographical maps were sent to the Olmsted Brothers office in July 1912. The following employees worked on this park design: Percy R. Jones; Edward L. Keeling; P. W. Dorr; John J. Clune; Mr. Jeffers; C. R. Wait; Mr. Martin; Percival Gallagher; and John A. Bigelow. Percy R. Jones created a preliminary profile on centerline of road and Edward L. Keeling worked on the preliminary grading plan. In 1913, P. W. Dorr and John J. Clune worked on sections and profiles of the road from Chestnut Street to Centre Street and of the shore walks east and west of the small lake (that has since been removed). Dorr made revised grading studies for the north boundary road and the north section of the park. In August 1913, Mr. Martin created the planting study. John A. Bigelow drew a sketch and studies for a shelter and comfort station.

By 1914, Yantacaw Park had become a reality.[3] The swampy lowlands had been drained and the Third River was channeled. The spillway, bridge, and paths had been laid out following the Olmsted Brothers designs. The picturesque steep slopes were left covered with woods and grand staircases were installed to allow access to the park's lower level.

Today, the park's distinguishing features include a fieldhouse, football and baseball fields, a playground and support building, unique terrain sloping down to the river, two foot bridges, shuffleboard, bocce, lighted basketball court, and a mall of linden trees. Recent improvements include: the installation of new equipment and rubberized safety surface in the playground completed in 2003; path paving completed in 2006; and reconstruction of Park Way to address flooding and enhance aesthetics, which were completed in 2008.

The Olmsted Brothers always grouped trees in such a way to provide diversity and contrasting colors and shapes. Here two in a row create a framed view to one of the lawn areas in Yantacaw Park. *June 27, 2009.*

The allée of linden trees is located in the eastern section of Yantacaw Park along a pathway that connects the service building to Passaic Avenue. *June 27, 2009.*

Endnotes Chapter 15: Yantacaw Park

[1] Essex County Department of Parks, Recreation, and Cultural Affairs: http://www.essex-countynj.org/p/index.php?section=af/system
[2] Frank John Urquhart. *A History of the City of Newark, New Jersey Embracing Practically Two and A Half Centuries 1666-1913*. Volume 2.

(New York, New York: Lewis Historical Publishing Company, 1915).
[3] John Demmer. *Nutley.* (Charleston, South Carolina: Arcadia Publishing, 1997 reprinted 2002).

Chapter 16
Grover Cleveland Park: Caldwell and Essex Fells (1915)

Grover Cleveland Park is the seventh largest park in the Essex County park system. It consists of 41 acres located in the western section of Essex County along the border between Caldwell and Essex Fells. It is bounded by Brookside Avenue on the north, Runnymede Road on the west, the abandoned Erie Railroad on the south, and Westville Avenue on the east. This park has a combination of pastoral landscape and natural woodlands. There are manicured lawns, tree lined walks, and three acres of waterways, which includes Pine Brook and a small lake at the southwest corner of the park.

In the 1910s, the Essex County Park Commission questioned the need for a park in this locality as it was a suburban area with open green spaces, unlike the crowded urban areas, such as Newark, which had a greater need for parks. However, the Commission determined that the lands to the west of the Second Mountain were developing so rapidly that if postponed, the good land for parks might no longer be available and would be more expensive later. Grover Cleveland Park was the only new park established by the Park Commission in 1913.[1] The parkland was acquired between 1913 and 1916 and was named after President Grover Cleveland who was born in Caldwell. He was the 22nd and 24th President of the United States. The Olmsted Brothers were asked to develop a park plan designed to make a large portion of the area usable for recreation purposes.[2]

The pond and visitors center are the main focal points of the southwest section of Grover Cleveland Park. *October 22, 2009.*

The following Olmsted Brothers staff members worked on this park: Arthur E. Spooner; Edward L. Keeling; P. W. Dorr; Percival Gallagher; Robert Fuller Jackson; C. R. Wait; and Chandler A. Manning. The topographical maps were delivered to the offices in Brookline in April 1914. A preliminary plan and grading study was drawn up in January 1915. This plan included a sketch of a shelter and field house, four tennis courts, and some paths. The paper plan was 37 inches high and 85 inches long. Percival Gallagher made notes on it in April 1915. Walks were created through a hemlock grove near Runnymede Road, which was said to be the finest group of these stately trees in Essex County.

Robert F. Jackson worked on the plan and elevation of a shelter near the wading pool. He also created a perspective, elevations, plans, and detail for a shelter and loggia as well as a detail of a pool curve and end of arbor along with architectural draftsman C. R. Wait. Percival Gallagher and P. W. Dorr worked on a cross section of ball field and elevation of the backstop wall. A general planting study was completed in June 1915. In September 1915, Edward L. Keeling drew a plan showing the proposed land taking east of the present park. A planting study was finished in December 1915 and revised one year later. In the summer of 1915, work on the actual park had begun. The laborers created the tennis courts, baseball fields, a playground, sand court, and wading pool, and they constructed a shelter house to service all the facilities. The park improvements were completed in 1916.

In January 1917, the Olmsted Brothers office produced a new topological map showing the location of the paths, lake, and brook. In February 1917, they produced a planting plan that included the stream, tennis courts, shelter, wading pool, sandboxes, ball field, and pond. It also included a planting list. P. W. Dorr made a revision in the location of the walk south of the children's playground shelter to eliminate the steps. In August 1917, a preliminary plan and grading study showed the positions of groves of trees.

Grover Cleveland Park was under construction during World War One. In an effort to carry out its policy of aiding the conduct of the war in every possible way, instead of seeding the lawns, the Essex County Park Commission decided to turn them into farming plots. Corn was planted in 1916 and harvested becoming feed for the animals that were kept at the other county parks.[3]

This postcard of Grover Cleveland Park was postmarked in 1940. The view shows the outlet of the pond as it flows into Pine Brook Creek.

Many of the trees in Grover Cleveland Park are labeled as part of the nature center educational mission. This mature willow oak provides shade on a sunny June day.

On July 24, 1927, *The New York Times* reported that the park's footbridge had been washed away after a tremendous storm, which caused flooding throughout the region. The bridge was rebuilt. Also in 1927, proposals called for a shelter for the children and a comfort station for the park. New York based architect Arthur Dillon was selected to design a building, which was constructed in 1928.[4] Storms in July of 1945 eroded the banks of Pine Brook and approximately 250 feet of old stone wall was destroyed. The wall was rebuilt, as was the west abutment of the footbridge that crosses the stream opposite Gould Place. Picnic tables and fireplaces were reconditioned in the hemlock grove on the knoll east of the lake.[5]

Recent improvements include: The installation of new equipment and rubberized safety surface in playground completed in 2003; the replacement of Runnymede Road Bridge completed in 2003; park beautification, path paving, and the renovation of Children's House and tennis courts completed in 2004; and the modernization of the skate house and baseball field in 2006.

This view is looking toward the Children's House from the fenced playground. New York architect Arthur Dillon designed the elegant Tudor Revival style community building that was built in 1928 in Grover Cleveland Park. *June 20, 2009.*

A cobblestone carriageway in the woods of Grover Cleveland Park has not yet been completely covered. *June 20, 2009.*

Endnotes Chapter 16: Grover Cleveland Park

[1]Essex County Department of Parks, Recreation, and Cultural Affairs: http://www.essex-countynj.org/p/index.php?section=af/system
[2]History from the Grover Cleveland Park Conservancy, http://www.groverclevelandpark.org/Thepark/history.html
[3]History from the Grover Cleveland Park Conservancy, http://www.groverclevelandpark.org/Thepark/history.html
[4]Thirty-third Annual Report of the Essex County Park Commission, 1928.
[5]Forty-seventh Annual Report of the Essex County Park Commission, 1945.

Chapter 17

Belleville Park: Belleville (1915)

Belleville Park is a mid-sized 32-acre park in the Essex County system. It is located on the border of Belleville and Branch Brook Park in Newark. Belleville Park is bounded by Belleville Avenue to the north; Parkside Drive to the east; Mill Street to the south; and Hendricks Field to the west. Branch Brook's famous "Cherry Blossom Land" is contiguous with this park and together, they create a continuous green strip over 2-1/2 miles long. The land was acquired in 1915 and designs were drawn in the following years. Some grading had been done in the summer of 1916, but the main development did not begin until the spring of 1921. The park opened to the public in 1922. The delay between design and major construction was due to the difficulty of obtaining labor during World War One.[1] The park was designed by the Olmsted Brothers firm and, even today, retains most of the original pastoral landscaping seen in its winding paths and sweeping lawns ringed with trees.

The topographical maps were received in May 1915 at the Olmsted Brothers offices in Brookline. The following staff members worked on this park: Percy R. Jones, P. W. Dorr, Percival Gallagher, T. C. Jeffers, Jacob Sloet, and Arthur E. Spooner. Only two of the plans were signed. In June 1915, Percival Gallagher wrote field notes and included the elevation of a spring, the profile of John Street with sketch of the spring, locations of trees, and sketch of a spillway. By February 1916, the staff had created the preliminary plan for the park. A grading plan was completed by March 1916 showing tennis courts, boy's ball field, little folks field, and the treatment of the old quarry, which was to be determined on the ground. A preliminary plan showing the locations of planting beds and tree pits was created in August 1916. In December 1916, Percival Gallagher produced a sketch and elevation of a wall. The unsigned planting plan for the park was produced in February 1917 showing the tennis courts, hillside, boy's baseball field, little folks' field, and little children's playground. In February 1917 the firm produced plans for typical steps and ramps with the specifications that they were to be of rough stone laid in cement, and the stones for steps to be not less than one and a half foot long. In October 1917, a sketch showed the revisions to paths in the vicinity of the old quarry.

This walkway to Belleville Park is lined with cherry trees. This creates a visual continuation of the neighboring Branch Brook Park, which erupts each spring with an abundance of blossoms. Belleville Park was designed beginning in 1915 and constructed in the early 1920s. *April 18, 2009.*

Evergreen trees divide the park into sections and the characteristic border mounds and plantings isolate the park from the city streets. Its semi-formal character is composed of native, rare, and ornamental trees and shrubs. In 1917, to aid in the war effort, these fields were planted with corn. The park represents an early example of urban rehabilitation, as there is a former industrial site within its boundaries. A depression on the south side of the park represents all that is left of an old rock quarry.[2]

The stucco field house costing $15,577 was constructed by 1921 to accommodate those using the nearby tennis courts and baseball field. A building of similar design, costing $11,782, was located near the children's playground, wading pool, and sand courts.[3] This building still exists.

According to the Essex County Department of Parks, recent improvements include: playground and bathroom building construction completed in 2005 and improvements to the Seniors Building completed in 2006. Belleville Park's distinguishing features include a new senior citizens center, playground, bocce courts, four softball fields, two soccer fields, quarter-mile jogging path, and connections to Hendricks Field Golf Course and Branch Brook Park.

Many of the original plantings from the 1920s, such as these oak trees, remain standing in Belleville Park. They create a dense canopy of shade over the walkways each spring and summer. *August 11, 2009.*

Endnotes Chapter 17: Belleville Park

[1] Essex County Parks Commission. *Twenty-sixth Annual Report of the Board of Commissioners, 1921*. (Newark, N. J.: Baker printing Co., 1922); p. 10.
[2] Essex County Department of Parks, Recreation, and Cultural Affairs: http://www.essex-countynj.org/p/index.php?section=af/system.
[3] Essex County Park Commission. *Twenty-sixth Annual Report of the Board of Commissioners, 1921*. (Newark, N. J.: Baker printing Co., 1922); p. 10.

Chapter 18
Vailsburg Park: Newark (1917)

Vailsburg Park is located in the Vailsburg area of Newark on 30 acres of land surrounded by tight-knit urban neighborhoods. The park is bounded by South Orange Avenue on the north, Oraton Parkway on the east, Vailsburg Terrace on the south, and South Munn Avenue on the west. This is a mid-sized park heavily used primarily by neighborhood residents. It is the tenth largest park within the county park system and is in the eastern section of Essex County. In 1915, the county legislature enacted into law the issuance of $500,000 in bonds specifically for the creation of a park in Newark's Vailsburg Section. The bill provided for a referendum and on November 2, 1915, Essex County voters approved the project. The bonds were issued by the Board of Chosen Freeholders and the proceeds turned over to the Essex County Park Commission in September 1917.

The Essex County Park Commission included the following information about Vailsburg Park in their 1920 Annual Report:

Vailsburg Park was planned to meet the needs of a rapidly growing population in the northwest section of the City of Newark. It also had the advantage of removing a dilapidated amusement park, "Electric Park," which many residents had found objectionable. The general plan for Vailsburg Park included a band stand with concert grove in the fine group of trees near the northeast corner of South Orange Avenue and Devine Street, with a garden to the west near South Orange Avenue. A field house was to be provided at about the center of the park, east and west, and approximately opposite Fifteenth Avenue. The greater part of the area between the field house and the concert grove and garden was to be taken up with lawns to be used for baseball and football, and were to be so constructed that they could be flooded for skating in winter. The park was to total about nine acres. The girls' playground and a wading pool opposite were to be located south of the field house. The plan called for the wading pool to also have sand courts and a shelter. A mall with flowerbeds was planned to separate the girls' playground and the wading pool. The south end of the park was reserved for tennis courts.[1]

Vailsburg Park is an oasis of green in the midst of a heavily developed residential section of Newark. Visitors come here to rest, feast their eyes on the beautiful greenery, and experience nature. *May 25, 2009.*

The majority of the Olmsted Brothers plans were not signed; however, the following members of staff are known to have worked on this park: Henry Pree, Percy R. Jones, Walter Clarke, P. W. Dorr, Thomas E. Carpenter, Paul Wood, J. Louis Doyle, Joseph F. Bannon, Edward Clarke Whiting, Charles W. Eliot, and Benjamin G. Donovan.

Several of the historic streets no longer exist as a result of the construction of the Garden State Parkway in the 1950s. The Olmsted Brothers received the topographical maps in March 1917. In May 1918, studies were made for connections of the park off Myrtle Avenue and an entrance from the Oraton Parkway. Studies for foliage to accompany the preliminary plan were made. In June 1918, the park boundary near Myrtle Avenue and 16th Avenue was under consideration by the Park Commissioners in order to take less land. The issue was resolved and by October 1919, the topographical map of the smaller park was delivered. A planting plan showing the location of trees in "Elm Canyon" was generated in February 1920. In December 1920, a profile plan for the walkways was produced.

Percival Gallagher approved the first grading plan and cross sections in January 1921. The same month, sketches for a park shelter were drawn and Thomas E. Carpenter made revisions to the southern boundary to provide for street adjacent to the park. A study for the grading of the South Devine Street mall was made in December 1920 and revised in September 1921 as was the location and alignment of the park drive. In October 1921, Edward Clarke Whiting made a study for a drive along South Devine Street. A revised grading plan was produced in November 1921 and Thomas E. Carpenter created a planting plan.

The interior field in Vailsburg Park is larger than those found in other Essex County parks. Four baseball fields share a common outfield forming this large central open space. *May 25, 2009.*

The eight-foot high border mounds around the perimeter of Vailsburg Park absorb the city noises. In this photograph, the high border mound is on the left. *May 25, 2009.*

In July 1922, a grading site plan was drawn for the site of a war memorial. The staff produced a park extension along 16th Avenue and in April 1923 they made a study for an entrance on line with Linden Avenue. A study was made for a group of buildings in 1920 and in September 1923, the firm of John H. and Wilson C. Ely, Architects of Newark designed the children's shelter, field house, and comfort station. These were considered to be of the English cottage type of buildings with walls of weathered trap rock and roofs of variegated Vermont slate. They had spacious covered loggias. They were half-timbered in a weathered finish to give the appearance of growing out of the ground.[2] The field house, children's shelter, and comfort station were built in 1923.

Although park construction was begun in 1917, two-thirds of the grading and planting was finally complete by 1922. The Olmsted Brothers designed broad lawns to give a feeling of spaciousness, while large trees abound on the perimeter of the park, surrounding the ball fields, playgrounds, and bandstand. The perimeter mounds are some of the most effective in the parks that I visited. The peacefulness in the center of the open space of this park was quite striking considering the busyness of the surrounding urban neighborhood. In 1922, the Parks Commission wrote in the annual report; "The sloping mounds of plantings, green play areas, winding paths, the children's wading pool and playground are marked contrast to the unsightly heaps of debris and the water-filled depressions of a year ago."

During both World Wars, the U.S. Army erected tents in Vailsburg Park and used the park for training, embarking, and recruiting. A maintenance building was built in 1940. In 1952, two softball diamonds were eliminated by the U.S. Army, which leased a small portion of the park for an anti-aircraft gun site. The Army vacated the site in 1960.[3]

Recent improvements include: the installation of rubberized safety surface in the playground completed in 2003; and Phase 1 and 2 General Renovations, with the installation of new synthetic grass baseball field, modernization to five natural turf baseball fields, and improvements to the playground and park entrances completed in 2007. This park's distinguishing features include five softball and hardball baseball fields; two soccer fields; updated playground and shelter; a field house; a Senior Citizens Center with bocce courts; lighted basketball courts; and a half-mile jogging path.

The wading pool, sand court, and shelter at Vailsburg Park are closed and shuttered. This building was designed by the firm of John H. and Wilson C. Ely, Architects of Newark and built in 1928. *May 25, 2009.*

Endnotes Chapter 18: Vailsburg Park

[1] Essex County Park Commission. *Twenty-fifth Annual Report of the Board of Commissioners, 1920.* (Newark, N. J.: The W. H. Shurts Co., Printers, 1921): 8.
[2] Essex County Park Commission. *Twenty-seventh Annual Report of the Board of Commissioners, 1922.* (Newark, N. J.: Colyer Printing Co. 1923): 5-6.
[3] Essex County Department of Parks, Recreation, and Cultural Affairs: http://www.essex-countynj.org/p/index.php?section=af/system

Chapter 19
Verona Park: Verona (1921)

Verona Park is a 54-acre park with a small lake in the southern part of the Township of Verona. This is the fifth largest park within the Essex County Park system. It is bordered by Bloomfield Avenue on the north, Porcello Lane and Park Avenue on the east, the Montclair Golf Course on the south, and Lakeside Avenue on the west. Once an old swamp, the lake was first formed in 1814 when Doctor Gone dammed the Peckman River to provide waterpower for a gristmill. In the 19th century, the Verona Lake Park Association owned much of the property including the lake. Weeping willow trees dotted the edge of the lake and winding paths offered places to stroll.

Even before it became a county park in the 1920s, the public had been going there to bathe, picnic, and enjoy the amusements, which included a merry-go-round and boat rentals. Essex County first began acquiring land for the park in 1920. Demand for this acquisition had been increasing for some time, but action was delayed due to economic conditions caused by World War One. To acquire part of this land owned by the Erie Railroad Company, an agreement was made allowing Erie to retain a right-of-way across the park by means of a bridge. Sketches showed a bridge with a series of high arches that spanned the lake and roadway. Fortunately, this bridge was never constructed. The landscape plans prepared by the Olmsted Brothers were approved the same year Verona Park was acquired. Actual development did not start until several years later due to court proceedings concerning condemnation of some of the land. There was no inconvenience to the public during the delay because the park was already being used for boating, bathing, skating, picnics, and band concerts.[1]

The majority of the Olmsted Brothers' plans in the archives at Brookline are not signed. The following staff members are known to have worked on the park: Frederick Law Olmsted, Jr., Percy R. Jones, Percival Gallagher, Henry Pree, Charles W. Eliot, J. Harry Scott, James L. Greenleaf, Thomas E. Carpenter, Henry C. Nye, Edward D. Rando, Lyle L. Blundell, Dana W. Clark, Hans J. Koehler, Joseph Bannon, and John J. Sullivan.

The topographical maps were sent to the Olmsted Brothers in September 1919. Percy R. Jones presented a preliminary study in July 1921 that included the locations of the paths, boathouse, and picnic grove. In February 1922, the office received a topographical map showing the locations of the pre-existing boathouse, canoe house, tool houses, boiler house, carousel, five dwellings, and two barns. Henry Pree worked on a grading plan and Charles Eliot worked on a study for a footbridge, a grading study for the concert ground, and a study for a bathhouse in July 1922. Percy R. Jones worked on a plan showing the profiles on axis of walks. The preliminary plan for the park created by Percival Gallagher and Henry Pree in 1922 included the little folks lawn, hillside for sledding, bathhouse, beach, sunken garden, boat house, concert grove, overlook, picnic grove, and play field.

This picture postcard from 1906 shows Verona Lake Park when the lake was the center of attraction at the privately owned park.

AMONG THE LILIES. VERONA LAKE, N. J.

The 13-acre Verona Lake continues to be the focal point of this park for both humans and wildlife. *October 22, 2009.*

In July 1925, Percy R. Jones developed a study for a possible railroad crossing of the park. As mentioned above, the right of way for the Montclair Branch of the Erie Railroad went through the park. In December 1926, Thomas E. Carpenter and J. Harry Scott worked on a planting plan for the area near Bloomfield Avenue. In 1927, a boathouse, two comfort stations, and the bandstand had been built and, in October, Edward D. Rando made a planting plan for the areas around them. The dam was reconstructed in 1928 and Lyle L. Blundell made a grading plan with revisions for the area. The final plans for the 36-foot footbridge over the narrow part of the lake were received in January 1929. They were signed by Robert S. Sinclair Pres.; A. M. Reynolds, Chief Engineer; J. H. Phillips, Deputy; and A. Burton Cohen, Construction Engineer. The same company also created a plan for a reinforced concrete bridge near Lakeview Place. After the footbridge was constructed, Edward D. Rando made a planting plan for that area.

The 36-foot span carries a path over the lake in Verona Park at the point where it narrows. *May 9, 2009.*

The paths around the lake at Verona Park are popular with walkers and joggers. *October 22, 2009.*

In 1929, the Olmsted Brothers received a map showing property adjacent to Verona Park. Lyle Blundell worked on a preliminary study for an area around the Administration shelter. In 1931, the firm received a map of the western portion of Verona Park, showing fill along Lakeside Avenue and existing paths, and Dana W. Clark made a plan showing the proposed paths. In August 1931, Hans J. Koehler created the planting study and Joseph F. Bannon developed the planting plan for the area along Lakeside Avenue. Koehler also rendered the study for Japanese cherry tree locations along Lakeside Avenue in December 1931 and John J. Sullivan drew up the plans in January 1932.

In the 1930s, a Work Projects Administration project involved lakeshore protection and maintenance. The 1941 Annual Report of the Essex County Park Commission stated, "The inlet channel was cleaned, banks were graded, and large boulders were placed to prevent scouring action of the stream." The east boundary of the park was graded and prepared for planting. Excess material from the excavations was used to fill in the low areas at the south end of the park.[2]

Verona Park's distinguishing characteristics include: the 13-acre lake with its photogenic ornamental bridge, a modernized and expanded boathouse, a new children's garden and playground, tennis courts, 1.2-mile fitness course, a softball field, bocce courts, and a bandstand. Recent improvements include: playground resurfacing completed in 2003; the lake shoreline stabilization project and the development of Children's Garden, tennis courts, entrance enhancements and restroom building completed in 2005; and the renovation of Verona Lake Dam and the development of five-station exercise course and improvements to landscaping and pathways completed in 2008.

The section of the park north of the Verona Lake displays the planting scheme developed by Thomas E. Carpenter and J. Harry Scott in 1926. *October 22, 2009.*

Endnotes Chapter 19: Verona Park:

[1] Essex County Department of Parks, Recreation, and Cultural Affairs: http://www.essex-countynj.org/p/index.php?section=af/system
[2] Essex County Park Commission. *Forty-third Annual Report of the Park Commission of Essex County, 1941.* (Newark, N. J.: 1942).

Chapter 20

Memorial Park: Maplewood (1922)

Memorial Park is in the Township of Maplewood in Essex County. It is not part of the Essex County system, but a municipally owned park. It is bounded by Baker Street on the southwest, Dunnell Road on the northwest, Oakland Road on the north, and Valley Street on the southeast. It was designed by the Olmsted Brothers and they began work in 1922. The park is located on both sides of the East Branch of the Rahway River, which flows through the town. During the nineteenth and early twentieth centuries, the Township of Maplewood had many changes in name and boundaries. Originally part of South Orange, Maplewood retained its rural quality through the early 1900s as there were many farms and woodlands with only a few main streets. But change was beginning to occur as a few entrepreneurs realized the town's potential as an attractive suburb along the train line. By the mid-1920s, Maplewood was experiencing dramatic, community-wide growth. In her 1948 book ***Maplewood Past and Present: A Miscellany***, Helen B. Bates wrote that when she was a young woman, "a large part of Memorial Park between the railroad station and Valley Street was meadowland where cows grazed. There was long ago a boardwalk from Valley Street running through. At one point there was a stile, which had to be climbed over and from there the boardwalk continued."[1]

Shortly after the incorporation of the Township of Maplewood in 1922, the Olmsted Brothers firm was hired to create a plan for a park in the center of town.[2]

Memorial Park is located on both sides of the East Branch of the Rahway River, which flows through Maplewood Township. *May 23, 2009.*

Although most of the plans were not signed, the following employees were recorded as having worked on this park: G. A. Lewis, Joseph Bannon, Percy R. Jones, Henry Pree, Thomas E. Carpenter, and J. Harry Scott. The original plan called for a lake, wading pond, a promenade, playground, open fields, groves, a hill for coasting in the winter, flower gardens, and a ball field. The entire park was to be crossed with paths and walkways, which were to be lined by hundreds of trees for shade and seclusion from the street.[3] By August 1922, the outline plan showing the park boundaries had been prepared. The Olmsted Brothers also prepared grading studies with profiles and cross sections. The unsigned preliminary plan was created in December 1922. Grading plans of the various sections of the park were produced in March 1923. A planting study for portion of park bordering Dunnell Road was created in April 1923 and Thomas E. Carpenter created the planting plan that same month.

At first named Maplewood Park, the town changed the name to Memorial Park in 1928 to honor those Maplewood veterans who died in action in World War One. A bronze plaque is affixed to a large boulder off Baker Street. It reads: "This park is dedicated as a Memorial to the men and women of the Township of Maplewood who served their country in the World War 1914-1918."

In the intervening years, the park has been cared for by the Maplewood Parks and Shade Tree Department. Members have kept the trees in good health, tended the English yew, planted hundreds of bulbs throughout the park in addition to planting the flower beds with begonias, salvia, canna lilies, and other flowering perennials.[4]

The large pond in Memorial Park sustains lily pads and is a favorite location to see the resident mallard ducks. *May 23, 2009.*

The variety of mature trees in Memorial Park create a visual feast of overlapping natural shapes, colors, and textures. *May 23, 2009.*

Endnotes Chapter 20: Maplewood Park

[1]Bates, Helen B. *Maplewood Past and Present: A Miscellany*. (Princeton, New Jersey: Princeton University Press, 1948); pp. 163, 174.
[2]Township of Maplewood Master plan 2004.
[3]Arline Zatz. *New Jersey's Great Gardens: A Four-Season Guide To 125*

Public Gardens, Parks, and Arboretums. (Woodstock, Vermont: The Countryman Press, 1999); p. 111.
[4]*Ibid.*

Chapter 21
High Point State Park:
Montague and Wantage Townships (1923)

Of all the parks in New Jersey that the Olmsted Brothers played a role in designing, High Point State Park is both the most northern and by far the largest. The Olmsted Brothers' philosophy toward this expansive acreage is contained in their detailed November 7, 1923 report that was written shortly after the park was opened.

High Point Park, a gift to the State of New Jersey by Colonel Anthony R. Kuser and his wife Mrs. Susie Dryden Kuser, is a reservation of natural scenery comprising some 10,000 acres. It is situated along the ridge of the Kittatinny Mountain in the extreme northwestern part of the state and comprises the well-known High Point (elevation 1823 feet), the highest land in New Jersey. This fact gives the reservation its special character, one that may be called unique among the growing number of state parks in the country. But what is perhaps more important, considered as a public park, is the singular quality of the views by reason of the somewhat isolated position of the mountain with reference to the general trend of the Appalachians. Thus the views westward across the valley of the Delaware are particularly effective in the afternoon light and comprise the best local scenery of the park. From the High Point southward the Kittatinny range takes a pronounced southwesterly curve. And to the east, one looks down upon the cultivated farmlands that occupy the rolling valley lands between the Kittatinny Mountain range and the range comprising Sparta, Hamburg, and Pochunk Mountains.

The view looking southwest from the High Point monument shows Lake Marcia and the Kittatinny Mountains at the horizon. *May 27, 2009.*

The Olmsted Brothers report included information about how the traveling public could enter the park. They concluded that the best approach to the summit was on the road to Port Jervis from Sussex by way of Coleville (now Route 23). They discussed the composition of the forestlands in the region, which in 1923, included Stokes Forest and Swartswood Lake Forest. The forest on Kittatinny Mountain was comprised of hardwood trees of which several varieties of oak were in abundance. Dead chestnut trees were also abundant at the time, due to a severe blight. Pines and hemlocks, white cedars and rhododendrons were largely in the neighborhoods of streams and swamplands. "On the extreme summits and ridges, the vegetation is sparse and stunted. This is especially true of High Point itself, which presents a generally bare, rocky aspect. Its conelike form is distinctly mountainous in character rising above the general level of the forest cover."

The sun broke through the clouds for a moment illuminating the mixed hardwood forest found at High Point State Park. *October 1, 2009.*

The report continues: "A singularly fortunate feature of this elevated region is the existence of several lakes, two of which, Lake Marcia (20+ acres) and Lake Rutherford (60+ acres) are within the limits of the park. Lake Rutherford being the source of water supply for the town of Sussex, is excluded from consideration as a usable feature of the park except as an object to look upon and enjoy as such."

As his private country retreat, Colonel Kuser developed just the area around Lake Marcia. He erected a high fence to form a range for game animals. He built a gate-lodge and a large mansion house on the site of a one-time hotel. A road connected the gate lodge and house with a few turning and parking spaces befitting a private drive.

The Commission was established to convert the private estate into a public park to be used for general park purposes and specifically by campers, camping parties, and vacation outings of non-profit societies. The plan called for this park to be preserved as a nature reservation. Power was given the Commission to lay out, construct, and maintain roads or pathways and to connect them with other public roads outside and adjacent to the park. The Olmsted Brothers' role was to create a balance between the public demand for outdoor recreational opportunities versus the ability of this particular area to provide them. The Commission was mindful of the potential for high demand indicated by both the national movements of establishing state parks and the growth of the summer camp and scouting movements. The attraction of High Point as a pre-existing tourist destination with its summit and former hotel coupled with the advent of the good roads movement combined to make High Point an attractive place to develop.

The Olmsted Brothers organized their planning efforts around the pre-existing conditions, and provided a general suggestive scheme for development. The draftsmen were Benjamin G. Donovan, Faris B. Smith, and Percival Gallagher. They recommended purchasing as much of the surrounding property as possible in order to control the vistas. The gate-lodge on the Port Jervis road became the convenient point around which the system of roads was drawn to access the various sections of the park. The Olmsted firm proposed creating a main road with a 13-mile circuit and a system of smaller secondary roads including the road that arrives close to but not at the peak itself. The firm intentionally avoided ending the road at the exact summit leaving it free for people to climb the last section. The area around the summit was planned to be used by casual day visitors, thus the campgrounds were located elsewhere.

The firm recommended that the Kuser mansion be used as the Park's administrative headquarters and possibly also as housing for the state offices of the Fish and Game Commission and Forestry Department. They recommended that the driveway to the mansion be changed to keep

Lake Marcia has a swimming beach on its south shore and the north shore remains in a more natural state. High Point State Park. *May 27, 2009.*

pedestrians and automobiles as far apart from each other as possible. They also recommended that the paddock for the game animals be reduced in size and made less obtrusive while remaining at the edge of Lake Marcia, the source of the animals' drinking water. The firm suggested that the camps be located in the vicinity of Mashipacong Pond and they also provided their thoughts of the best location for a golf course. The firm stressed the importance of good design to establish architectural character of the buildings and other structural elements. Signs, fences, and the like "should be simple and dignified in character without filigree and affectation. Thoroughness and substantiality should distinguish all work in public parks." The firm also made the wise recommendation to limit additional plantings to those pre-existing species of flora.

It is the general observation concerning the adaptation of parkland to public uses, that it is always difficult to forecast what the maximum demands are likely to be. In the case of almost everything that becomes popular with the public, the capacity is quickly overreached, and in seeking to expand, oftentimes the very thing that makes the place attractive is destroyed or so far injured as to result in disappointment. In parks of natural scenery that is particularly true, for the very nature of the elements of landscape cannot withstand the presence of large numbers of people without damage, if not complete destruction.[1]

High Point Park was officially opened by Governor Silzer with ceremonies held at noon on Wednesday May 23, 1923. The Sussex Concert Band played at the porch of the Kuser mansion. A grand luncheon was served to the assembled national and state dignitaries. The park was open to the public on Memorial Day, May 30, 1923. In the ensuing years, many of the Olmsted recommendations were implemented such as the road improvements, acquisition of more land, creation of park architecture with character, elimination of the elk park, and the establishment of the campgrounds. Other suggestions, such as the construction of a golf course and the grand 13-mile circuit drive were never implemented.[2]

The Olmsted Brothers received the topographical maps in September 1923. In October 1923, Benjamin G. Donovan and Faris B. Smith created the plan of the park to accompany the company's November 7, 1923 report. Percival Gallagher created his study plan in August 1923. The proposed State Forest Park was drawn in a 16" x 42" plan in September 1924. The Olmsted Brothers involvement ended after they provided their report. Most of the park's facilities and structures were designed following the Olmsteds' suggestions by park staff and constructed by laborers of the Civilian Conservation Corps. This was a federal program during the Great Depression of the 1930s that provided jobs for young men and women in the forests, parks, and historic sites nationwide. The 220-foot High Point Monument was designed by New York architects M. S. Wyeth and F. R. King was constructed by the Hoffman Construction Company between 1929 and 1930. Also paid for by Colonel Kuser, the completed structure was dedicated to the veterans of America's wars who were from New Jersey.[3] It remains the most visited attraction in Sussex County.

This undated photo postcard from the 1920s shows the Kuser mansion. This was once the estate house of Charles St. John, which Kuser purchased in 1910 and remodeled. Unfortunately, the building was allowed to deteriorate and was demolished in 1995. High Point State Park.

The clouds cleared just for a moment letting the setting sunlight illuminate the High Point State Park monument. A plaque affixed to the monument states; "The base of the monument is erected on the highest point in the State of New Jersey." *October 1, 2009.*

Endnotes Chapter 21: High Point Park

[1]All of the text above is condensed from the planning report produced by the Olmsted Brothers, Landscape Architects in 1923. *High Point Park, New Jersey; A Report Concerning Its Development*. (Brookline, Massachusetts; Olmsted Brothers, 1923).
[2]Ronald J. Dupont, Jr., and Kevin Wright. *High Point of the Blue Mountains*. (Newton, New Jersey: Sussex County Historical Society, 1990).
[3]Peter Osborne. *High Point State Park and the Civilian Conservation Corps*. (Charleston, South Carolina: Arcadia publishing, 2002).

Chapter 22
Library Square: Plainfield (1924)

The City of Plainfield's Library Square is composed of one city block of level ground. It is dotted with mature trees and it has diagonal walkways that begin at the four corners and wind to a crossing in the center where there is a small central plaza with benches and a fountain. The square is located between West 8th Street; College Place; West 9th Street; and Arlington Avenue. It is included within the boundary of the Van Wyck Brooks Historic District, which is listed in the New Jersey and National Register of Historic Places. It was developed as a park on the block adjacent to the Plainfield Public Library long before the Olmsted Brothers were asked to submit their designs. Their input is a modification to a pre-existing park. The Library was originally located on the adjacent block in a Second Empire-style building completed in 1886 that faced Park Avenue. In 1912, an addition funded in part by Andrew Carnegie was constructed facing Library Square and fronting on College Place. In 1968, a modern library building replaced this complex of two older buildings.[1]

The records at the Frederick Law Olmsted National Historic Site indicate that the Olmsted Brothers draftsmen for the modifications to Library Square were Edwin Prellwitz and Percival Gallagher. This small project, begun in 1924, only generated five plans, which included a plan for improving Library Square, a design for the center of the square, and a suggested treatment for the center of the square. April M. Stefel, Landscape Architect with the Plainfield Planning Department recently stated that she considers it to be an Olmsted park.

> The basic design is and continues to be two intersecting diagonals with a feature at the intersection. I have seen a tree and now a fountain as the focal point. In the late 1980s the City of Plainfield received green acre funding to upgrade the park. I was on the historic preservation commission at the time and made sure the new design was sensitive to the former. The dead tree that was the focal point was removed and replaced with the fountain. The entrances to the park at the diagonals were widened. No trees were removed. Since that renovation two additional trees, native species, were planted in the park to replace those that were damaged by a severe storm.[2]

Because of its small size, typical Olmsted design elements such as the open pastoral grounds and groves of trees were not permissible for this green space. Nevertheless, it remains an important indicator that this important company of landscape architects attended to even small projects during the decade when it was at its most busy.

Library Square in Plainfield is a small city park with crossing walkways and a central plaza. The Olmsted Brothers produced modifications to a pre-existing park in the 1920s. *October 14, 2009.*

Endnotes Chapter 22: Library Square

[1] History of the Plainfield Public Library on the Library website at: www.plainfieldlibrary.info/AboutUs/History.html
[2] April M. Stefel, Landscape Architect. Personal e-mail communication, December 17, 2010.

Chapter 23
Union County Park System

"Dedicated to public use forever, a Park System will preserve present beautiful features of our County and will make new beauty spots for succeeding generations. To carry the project through is a duty we owe to our selves, our children and our children's children." On his 1943 pictorial map of the Watchung Reservation, Jack Manley Rosé included the above motto of the Union County Park System. The decisions that were made with great foresight in the 1920s have lived up to the promise as the grandchildren of the founding generation, are now enjoying the public parks in Union County.

John Cunningham wrote a history of the Union County Park Commission in 1971. He stated that Union County enjoys more than 6,000 acres of parkland in every section of the county due to an inspired sheriff who hoped to save "his" stream and who elicited enough support from his fellow residents. The catalyst for conservation was Union County Sheriff James E. Warner who knew every foot of the Rahway River, from its source in the Watchung Mountains to its mouth at the Arthur Kill. He wanted to see the river returned to the pristine condition he had remembered from his youth. Warner wrote to the *Cranford Citizen* during the winter of 1919, pleading for the salvation of the Rahway River as a fitting memorial to the young men who had died in World War One, just then concluded. Cranford Township Committeeman Collins took up the cause and dedicated himself to making it more than just a poetic wish. Editorials in the *Rahway Record*, the *Westfield Leader* and the *Cranford Citizen and Chronicle* supported the proposal. The major editorial boost came on May 5, 1919, when the *Elizabeth Daily Journal* declared that Warner's idea was "a duty rather than an opportunity."

Warinanco Park is a Union County park in Roselle. It is known for its gardens and the groves of magnolia trees, which bloom in an explosion of pastel colors and fragrance each spring. *April 26, 2009.*

The county park movement caught many other people in its grip. Henry Kreh, Jr., of the Elizabeth Chamber of Commerce organized a Union County Park Association and more than 400 men and women responded, many from Cranford. The group was soon stymied when the 1920 U.S. Census indicated Union County was short 100 people. New Jersey law required that a county must have 200,000 residents before a Park Commission could be established. The group canvassed every Cranford home and secured enough signed affidavits to increase the Union County population past the 200,000 mark. Soon after, the official United States Census reaffirmed that Union County's population was indeed 200,157.

One other action needed to be taken. Supreme Court Justice James J. Bergen, sitting in Elizabeth, had to be petitioned to appoint a temporary commission to study the population's sentiment regarding a county park system. Henry Kreh, Jr., took the petition to the courtroom without an appointment and was denied a hearing. However, the kindly judge asked for a special meeting and then readily agreed to appoint a commission. He suggested that Henry S. Chatfield, a prominent Elizabeth banker, might make a good commissioner. Chatfield responded enthusiastically as he was an advocate of county parks having often used the nearby Essex County parks. On April 30, 1920, Judge Bergen appointed the temporary commission of Henry Chatfield, Arthur Rindge Wendell of Rahway, Charles Hansel of Cranford, Caxton Brown of Summit, and Percy H. Stewart of Plainfield.

The temporary commission was given two years and a small budget of $10,000 to study the park needs and desires of Union County however, the group reported back in less than five months and returned most of the unused funds. A report written by the Olmsted Brothers and submitted on the July 5, 1921, outlined the comprehensive county park system. Their recommendations urged Union County officials to act quickly before still-open lands became crowded with buildings and divided by highways. The Freeholders placed the issue on the November 8, 1921 ballot, asking voters to decide whether a permanent Park Commission should be appointed. The approval would carry a hefty price tag: $2.5 million to be spent however the Commissioners chose, without political interference or favor. Determined resistance sprang up in Elizabeth and Plainfield, where more than 60 percent of all county residents lived. Elizabeth's mayor favored parks but felt that other needs were more urgent. Voters who streamed to the polls on November 8 included many women, who had recently won the right to vote. The park supporters won handily. Judge Bergen appointed the first Union County Park Commissioners on November 19, 1921. He named Chatfield, Wendell, Hansel, and Brown, as expected, and then surprised park boosters by appointing as the fifth commissioner Charles A. Reed, a Plainfield attorney who had bitterly fought the idea of establishing an all-powerful county parks commission.

The first Union County Park commissioners were men on a mission. They first met on December 20, 1921, elected Henry S. Chatfield as president, and continued by convening two or three times each week, on weekends and spare afternoons to scope out potential parkland. The commissioners quickly established an office at 286 North Broad Street, Elizabeth, and by February 1922, had made the two most important professional moves. First, they hired the Olmsted Brothers firm, as the commissioners all were very familiar with the Essex County parks and were impressed with the comprehensive planning report written the year before. Percival Gallagher was the chief landscape architect who consulted with the Union County Park Commission and who was a master in his own right. Secondly, the commissioners persuaded Princeton graduate and thirty-five year old W. Richmond Tracy, to leave his job as chief bridge builder for the Bronx River Parkway Commission and become the first paid engineer and secretary of the Union County Park Commission. He would remain employed until his retirement in 1957. The high caliber of the Union County Parks is due to the quality of Tracy's oversight.[1]

The Olmsted Brothers comprehensive plan envisioned a link between the two county park systems, with the Watchung Reservation in Union County connecting to the South Mountain Reservation in Essex County. The plan for a park system emphasized the importance of creating a series of interconnected parkways along the Rahway River, the Elizabeth River, and a cross-county parkway traversing east to west linking the Watchung Reservation and Elizabeth River. One large central park, Warinanco Park, and a series of smaller neighborhood parks, such as Wheeler Park were planned. The parks were designed in the same tradition as the Essex county parks using the naturalistic pastoral landscape style. The plan envisioned a series of boulevards connecting the county together, of which Westfield Avenue is example.[2]

At the outset the Commission planned a system of seven tracts, comprising 3,100 acres. Land was bought at a fair price or condemned and appraised when the asking price was excessive. Out of 150 parcels, there were only eleven instances of acquisition by condemnation. A few public-spirited owners donated several tracts. Union County had several departments working along with the Park Commission. As soon as enough planning and land acquisition had taken place, the Union County Construction and Maintenance Department started their work. That Department hired a large work force in 1923. At the time, nearly everything was done by hand and teams and wagons were hired to haul materials. Power equipment such as shovels, tractors, and trucks came into general use by the end of the 1920s.[3]

The shorelines along the small lake in Rahway River Park in Rahway feature irises that bloom in the late spring. *May 31, 2009.*

By 1925, the largest unit under development was Watchung Reservation. It had already been used for camping, swimming, and boating. Next in attractiveness was Echo Lake Park of 123 acres. Warinanco Park in Roselle, at the border with Elizabeth, had a running track, ballfields, and playgrounds, with a concrete stadium that seated 3,500 people. The banks of the Rahway and Elizabeth Rivers were being turned into parks from Rahway to Millburn. Altogether, a sum of $1.9 million had been spent in less than three years and the acquisition of land was undertaken in the nick of time to forestall an embarrassing rise in prices.[4]

The Commission had acquired its first land through a generous donation, when, on January 18, 1922, the Wheatena Company gave the Park Commission four acres of already developed parkland along 2,300 feet of the Rahway River front near the Wheatena plant in Rahway. The Commission continued making rapid progress. In November 1925, the *New York Times* had an article summarizing the Union County Park Commission's first four years:

> It is in this country of copses and dense timber of second and third growth, with streams winding through it, and with here and there a lake, that the Union County Park Commission is doing a great work of reclamation, landscape architecture, and the making of recreation fields. To President Henry S. Chatfield and his fellow Commissioners is due credit for bold conceptions and energy in carrying them out. Some of the material with which they had to deal was forbidding—mere swamp, saw grass, and dwarfed trees. Out of it they have made beauty spots and havens of rest. Echo Lake Park with its wild little tarn, now boasts of a dam and waterwheel. Cedar Brook Park, crossing the Randolph Road, in

Plainfield, was an unsightly spot when the landscape architects began to prepare a paradise.

On November 21, 1926, the *New York Times* contained a follow-up article by Raymond H. Torrey, in which he noted that the Union County Park Commission had benefited greatly through the growing national trend of giving gifts of land for public beneficence. He cited several Union County donations that had rounded out various parks including gifts from Mr. and Mrs. Otis Wright of Westfield, Judge A. J. David, Judge A. A. Stein, and Karl Schaeffer of Elizabeth, who gave a lake and river frontage on the Rahway River.[5]

In 1928, a $1 million bond was approved by the voters, to cover a two-year period of land acquisition and development of county park projects. A few of the projects under contemplation were the development of the Elizabeth River parkway and the acquiring of land for two community parks, one to serve Roselle Park and one to be a center for Garwood, Westfield, and Cranford.[6] The onset of the Great Depression stopped many park development plans; however, the Commission kept building through the use of the Civilian Conservation Corps and Works Progress Administration laborers. In 1938, the Park Commission received a federal matching grant of $67,500 through the Works Progress Administration for park improvements.[7] Work continued on the park system into the 1960s with the Echo Lake-Nomahegan Connection being the last of the Olmsted guided projects. In 1978, the Park Commission was eliminated through referendum and the care and maintenance of the parks fell to the Union County Department of Parks.

The concept for the comprehensive Elizabeth River Parkway was first drafted in the Olmsted Brothers 1921 report. In 1926, the Park Commission requested that the Olmsted Brothers submit plans for a few sections, which the archived records indicate the company produced. The later Park Commission reports indicate that the Elizabeth River Parkway project did not get underway until after World War Two. By this time, the staff of the County Engineering Department would have produced the plans. The 1946 report indicated land had been acquired and that the Elizabeth River Parkway plans called for flood detention basins which would greatly alleviate flood conditions for several miles along its course. The 1957 report indicated that several sections had received playing fields and picnic areas. Only the "Pruden Section" from South to South Broad Streets in Elizabeth had been landscaped. Although the Olmsted Brothers firm initiated the idea for this meandering parkway, the actual parks along its banks, with the exception of Mattano Park, were not designed by them.

The Olmsted Brothers firm not only designed a comprehensive overall plan for Union County, but created many individual parks with great natural qualities. There were major parks in the cities, smaller parks for other communities, and a nature preserve, the Watchung, all which were linked by river corridor parkways and transportation parkway. Olmsted scholar, Charles E. Beveridge, has called Union County's park system "a jewel" because it is one of the most fully realized surviving park systems designed by the Olmsted Brothers.[8] Each Olmsted designed park in the Union County park system is highlighted individually in the following chapters.

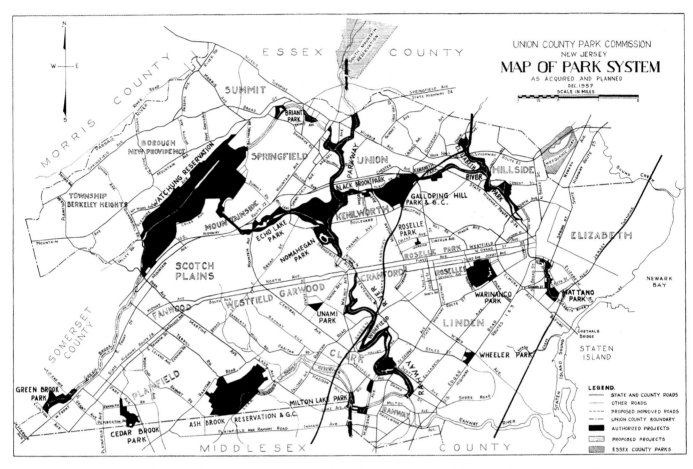

The 1957 report of the Union County Park Commission was illustrated with this overview map of the Union County park system. The Olmsted Brothers' system of connected parks is one of the most comprehensive in the country.

Endnotes Chapter 23: Union County Park System

[1]John T. Cunningham, "To Benefit the Whole Population…" published by the Union County Park Commission, Elizabeth, New Jersey, 1971.
[2]April M. Stefel. "A Short History of the Union County Park System."
[3]Union County Park Commission. *Twenty-five Year Report of the Union County Park Commission 1921-1946*; pp. 36-37.
[4]*The New York Times*. November 8, 1925.
[5]Raymond H. Torrey, "Jersey County Parks Extend Their Bounds; Union Follows Essex in Developing a System of Open Tracts That are Readily Accessible to Its Large centers of Population," *The New York Times*, November 21, 1926.
[6]*The New York Times* article November 12, 1928
[7]*The New York Times* article "521 PWA Projects Added to Program," October 30, 1938.
[8]From The Union County 150th Anniversary Magazine, 2007; p. 26.

Chapter 24

Green Brook Park:
Plainfield and North Plainfield (1922)

Green Brook Park is located at the border of two counties in the City of Plainfield in Union County and North Plainfield in Somerset County. The namesake brook, which flows from west to east, is the dividing line of the two municipalities. The park is roughly bounded by Parkview Avenue and Myrtle Avenue on the north; Gerund Avenue on the east; West Front Street and Park Drive on the south; and Clinton Avenue on the west. The park was listed in both the New Jersey and National Register of Historic Places in 2004.

In the Annual report for the City of Plainfield in 1913, out-going Mayor Percy H. Stewart wrote about the consolidation of the two communities that bordered the Green Brook, Plainfield and North Plainfield. In an indication of "City Efficient" thinking, he stated,

> The question of the consolidation of the City of Plainfield with the Borough of North Plainfield has been mooted from time to time. We are experiencing now the inconvenience of having two municipal governments interested in problems, which affect us as a single community, such as the water supply, sewage, fire protection, police, schools, parks, lighting and hospitals. A united city could lay out broad connecting avenues and a park system along the line of Tier's pond and the brook. The land should be acquired now, before there is too great an increase in its value and such a park system would be desirable, not only from the point of view of health and the beautifying of the city as a whole, but also because of the great increase in value, which would accrue to adjacent property. After the acquisition of the land, a certain amount could be spent from year to year in improvements, so that the burden upon the taxpayer would not be too great at any one time.[1]

Wise words; however, the two municipalities remained separate. In 1921, the City of Plainfield bought the land along Green Brook, which would be semi-developed into a park. In January 1926, the City donated the parklands to the Union County Park Commission.

The following Olmsted Brothers employees worked on Green Brook Park: Percival Gallagher, Joseph Bannon,

The Green Brook runs through the park for which it is named. Here the winter color scheme is a mix of beige and gray. *February 22, 2009.*

The same view of the brook in Green Brook Park shows the bursting springtime greenery. *May 17, 2009.*

Prentiss French, G. A. Lewis, William Bell Marquis, Charles W. Eliot, Arthur B. Clarke, Paul E. Wood, Leon H. Zach, J. Harry Scott, Walter Popham, Henry Pree, Benjamin G. Donovan, Hans J. Koehler, Edward A. Douglas, Percy R. Jones, Thomas E. Carpenter, James A. Britton, and Kenneth Newton.

The Olmsted Brothers began designing Green Brook Park based on topographical maps drawn in 1919. By January 1922, Percival Gallagher drew up a plan for a report to the Union County Park Commission. The maps showed the watersheds of Story Brook and Green Brook. In March 1922, Prentiss French developed a map showing a proposed expansion. The outline map of the park showing adjacent properties was created in July 1922. That summer, Percival Gallagher and Joseph Bannon worked on a grading study that indicated Green Brook, a ditch, a sidewalk, and a bridge and Gallagher and Charles W. Eliot prepared a grading study for the east portion of the park. In August 1922, the Olmsted Brothers received the plans for a bridge over the Green Brook designed by H. C. Van Enburgh and J. C. Bauer, Union County Engineer. William Bell Marquis and Charles W. Eliot created the 43 x 108-inch study layout of the park. Smaller plans showing individual areas were also produced during 1922. These included profiles of the drives and a general plan for development between Clinton Avenue and Sycamore Avenue.

Percival Gallagher prepared the large planting plan of the park in September 1922. That month, Mr. Eliot and Arthur B. Clarke worked on a general grading plan for the park between Myrtle Avenue and West End Avenue. In autumn 1922, William Bell Marquis worked on grading plans and a detail for a concrete wall at the West End Avenue Bridge. Clarke and Marquis collaborated on the plan showing the location of the fence and posts at Compton Avenue. In November 1922, Marquis and Paul E. Wood collaborated on a sketch for a service building. Leon H. Zach and Marquis prepared a grading plan for a boulder slope, an entrance at Compton Street, and a wading pool. Hans J. Koehler prepared a plan for proposed fall planting.

In January 1923, the firm made a plan showing details of typical steps and walls. J. Harry Scott and William Bell Marquis worked on a general plan study for layout of drives and walks. Also in January, Koehler and Benjamin G. Donovan created two planting plans, one for the western portion from Clinton Avenue to Compton Avenue and the other for the eastern section from Compton Avenue to West End Avenue. Marquis created a study for the method of procedure in building new line of the brook and a related study for the work in building the new brook channel. Walter D. Popham and Hans J. Koehler prepared three preliminary planting studies in December. In the summer of 1923, Edward A. Douglas produced a study for a swimming pool and Paul E. Wood sketched a design for a pavilion. In January 1924, Paul E. Wood worked on sketches for the Clinton Avenue, West End Avenue, Compton Avenue and Albert Street entrances.

Percival Gallagher developed the planting plan for Green Brook Park in 1922. *May 17, 2009.*

In March 1924, the park's land was extended between Sycamore and Gerund Avenues and Percy R. Jones worked on the grading plans for this section. Jones, and Austin Scott worked on this new section devising the grading plans in May 1924. The two also created a preliminary plan for an athletic field north of the brook. In the same month, Jones and Percival Gallagher produced a foliage study indicating lawns, trees, and plantings. In July 1926, James A. Britton produced a sketch for a bandstand. Planning for an extension of the park in neighboring North Plainfield, from Stein Avenue to West End Avenue, began in December 1926 when the topographical maps were delivered to the Olmsted Brothers. Thomas E. Carpenter worked on a planting plan for the extension.

The Report Of The Union County Park Commission 1947-1957 indicated that some erosion control work was accomplished along the brook with the construction of 1,529 linear feet of concrete retaining walls. Flooding often besets the Green Brook. In 1950, a masonry field house was constructed to provide bathrooms and storage space for the nearby playground. A concrete footbridge replaced two, old wooden bridges.[2]

The overall effect of the Olmsted Brothers work was that Green Brook Park in Plainfield became a good example of a former swamp and dump transformed into a delightful pastoral park with a meandering brook as its centerpiece.

The changing autumn colors are reflected in the duck pond in Green Brook Park. *October 14, 2009.*

Endnotes Chapter 24: Green Brook Park

[1] Annual Report of the City of Plainfield, New Jersey 1912.
[2] *Report of the Union County Park Commission 1947-1957*; p. 19.

Chapter 25

Echo Lake Park: Mountainside and Westfield (1923)

Echo Lake Park is a 147-acre Union County park nestled along the foot of the Second Mountain. It is near the geographical center of Union County and it straddles two municipalities, Mountainside and Westfield. The original site of this park was an old farm with a dammed millpond known as Echo Lake. At the time of acquisition, this was the only lake fed by Normahiggin Brook. An ideal area for a second lake existed in the west section and this was flooded to form two lakes connected by the brook. Much of the surrounding woodland remains untouched and forms a wildlife sanctuary. The main drive through the park passes the lakes, a gazebo and waterwheel, a pavilion, picnic areas, a playground, and the boathouse on the upper lake. The most picturesque structure in the park is the gazebo near the waterwheel at the edge of the lower lake. Photographers and artists find this an ideal subject. Across the park drive from the gazebo is a pavilion with a refreshment stand, fireplace, and bathrooms. A boathouse and refreshment stand in a larger building are located at the upper lake.[1]

The Olmsted Brothers received the locally produced topographical maps in August 1923. The preliminary plan for the entire park, which is 55" x 104" was drawn up that same month. The following employees were known to have worked on this park: Percy R. Jones; Percival Gallagher; Leon H. Zach; George Bradley; Lyle L. Blundell; Thomas E. Carpenter; Benjamin F. Glover; J. Harry Scott; Carl Rust Parker; Edwin M. Prellwitz; Thomas E. Carpenter; Carlton M. Archibold; Johan Selmer Larsen; Frank H. Malley; Henry C. Nye; James D. Graham; Gordon Woodbury; Milton F. Sherman; A. G. Scholtes; and Joseph Bannon.

The first day of spring in Echo Lake Park shows a sunny reflection of the natural woodlands that surround the lower lake. *March 21, 2009.*

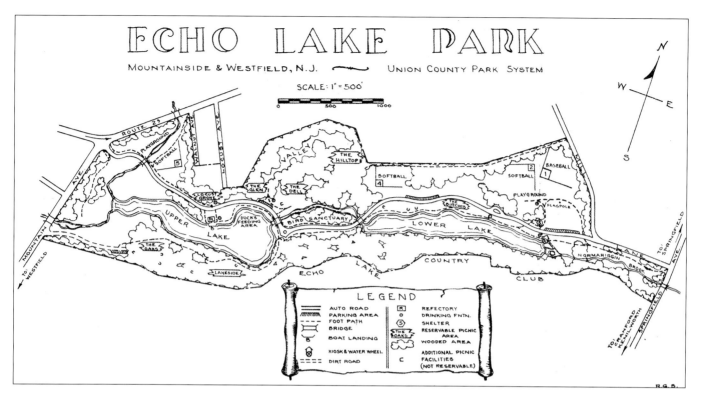

ECHO LAKE PARK

MOUNTAINSIDE & WESTFIELD, N.J.   UNION COUNTY PARK SYSTEM

SCALE: 1" = 500'

LEGEND

═══	AUTO ROAD	R	REFECTORY
▓▓▓	PARKING AREA	o	DRINKING FNTN.
- - -	FOOT PATH	S	SHELTER
	BRIDGE	THE OAKS	RESERVABLE PICNIC AREA
	BOAT LANDING		WOODED AREA
	KIOSK & WATER WHEEL	C	ADDITIONAL PICNIC FACILITIES (NOT RESERVABLE)
----	DIRT ROAD		

This map of Echo Lake Park was drawn circa 1950 and printed in a brochure produced by the Union County Park Commission.

In March 1924, preparatory drawings for a comfort station, a water wheel, and a summerhouse at the lower lake were prepared. Thomas E. Carpenter drew the planting plan in August 1924. Lyle L. Blundell worked on the grading plan for the vicinity of the pavilion and shelter in September 1924. In October 1924, the grading plan for the eastern section was created. Blundell made a study plan for the vicinity of the dam. In November 1924, Percy R. Jones designed the grading plan for the north side of the lake westward to the future bridge at the west end of the lake.

In September 1924, the architectural plans for the water wheel and attendant gazebo from local architects Hollingsworth and Bragdon of Cranford, New Jersey were completed. The firm, made up of Frank Hollingsworth and William B. Bragdon, had been established in 1915. Hollingswood was a 1902 graduate from the University of Pennsylvania, with a B. A. in architecture, who lived in Cranford as did Bragdon, who was a 1901 graduate of Harvard College. The 1925 Report from the Commission shows the newly constructed pavilion noting that G. A. Newman was the General Contractor.

In March 1925, Lyle L. Blundell revised the grading plan for the western section showing the location of the pines

The gazebo at the edge of Echo Lake has been in many photographers' images. It was designed in 1924 by Hollingsworth & Bragdon, Cranford architects. *October 14, 2009.*

copse atop a hill and Thomas Carpenter designed the planting plan for the vicinity of the pavilion and shelter. In May 1925, Edwin M. Prellwitz designed the plan for the walls and grading around the gazebo and Percy R. Jones drew the profile plan of the centerline of the park drive. In June 1925, J. Harry Scott worked on the general grading plan and in July a grading plan for the northwest section showed a temporary dam for the proposed upper lake. This plan was revised in November 1925.

Echo Lake Park: Mountainside and Westfield (1923)   113

Work was carried out as funding permitted. By 1925, the Park Commission report stated that;

> The easterly side of the park is practically completed including extensive improvements to the old dam, the construction of an old-fashioned water wheel and shelter house, a boat landing, an attractive pavilion, several miles of paths, 24 acres of turf, two baseball fields, and several planting areas. The westerly end of the tract has been graded and will be planted in the fall of 1925. Paths have been cut through the woods making the area available for picnic parties, horseback riders, and lovers of nature. A nursery has been started in this tract to provide for the future plantings of the Commission.[2]

The grove of pine trees stands at the top of a small hill in Echo Lake Park and offers a hilltop view of the upper lake. *March 21, 2009.*

In November of 1926, Raymond H. Torrey wrote in *The New York Times* that "Echo Lake Park in Westfield has always been known as a natural beauty spot, and is now being improved for larger use without marring any of the original features. The original lake, an old mill pond, will be supplemented by another by damming Normahiggin Brook higher up, more than doubling the present water surface for boating and skating."[3] From 1947 to 1957 there was a program of silt removal and nearly 10,000 cubic yards of silt from Upper Echo Lake was removed. The dredging allowed the State Fish and Game Commission to initiate a program designed to improve fishing conditions in Upper Echo Lake. Additional picnic fireplaces and tables were also constructed in an attempt to keep pace with increasing demands.[4]

This view is looking east from the west end of the upper lake in Echo Lake Park. In 2009, new plants were installed around the entire perimeter in an attempt to discourage Canadian geese from taking up permanent residency. *October 14, 2009.*

Endnotes Chapter 25: Echo Lake Park

[1]Union County Park Commission. "Echo Lake Park; Mountainside and Westfield," brochure circa 1950.
[2]Union County Park Commission. *Report of The Union County Park Commission 1923-1924-1925*; p. 34.
[3]Raymond H. Torrey, "Jersey County Parks Extend Their Bounds; Union Follows Essex in Developing a System of Open Tracts That are Readily Accessible to Its Large Centers of Population," *New York Times*, November 21, 1926.
[4]Union County Park Commission. *Report of the Union County Park Commission, New Jersey 1947-1957.* (Union County Park Commission, 1957): 17.

Chapter 26
Warinanco Park: Roselle (1923)

Warinanco Park is located in the borough of Roselle on the border with its neighbor to the north, the City of Elizabeth. The park is bounded by East 3rd Avenue to the north, Acme Street and Watson Avenue on the east, St. George Avenue (Route 27) on the south, and Thompson Avenue to the west. It is the largest park in Roselle and part of the Union County park system. The name Warinanco comes from one of the three Lenape chiefs who conveyed this part of New Jersey to European settlers in the 17th century. The park, built on former farmland, features a small lake, a promenade, several groves, and gardens. The first president of the Union County Park Commission, Henry Summers Chatfield (1864-1933), is memorialized with a tulip garden, thus its official name, Henry S. Chatfield Memorial Garden. An azalea garden is dedicated to the memory of Caxton Brown of Summit (1879-1952) who was an effective leader in creating the Union County Park Commission. He was a member of the original commission, its president for eleven years, and served continuously from 1921 to 1952. The oak trees in the George Washington Memorial Grove were planted in 1932.

A postcard from the 1930s captures the beauty of the Henry S. Chatfield Memorial Garden in Warinanco Park in the springtime. When called on to do so, the Olmsted Brothers designed small and simple formal elements as part of their designs.

The Olmsted Brothers firm began working on the plans in 1922 based on topographical maps submitted by the local civil engineers Luster & Luster. The following Olmsted Brothers employees worked on this extensive park: J. Harry Scott; Percival Gallagher; Faris B. Smith; Paul Wood; Benjamin G. Donovan; A. John Halfenstein; Percy R. Jones; Gordon J. Culham; Thomas E. Carpenter; Carl Rust Parker; Benjamin F. Glover; Carlton M. Archibald; Gordon Woodberry; Henry C. Nye; Russell N. Barnes; Jack E. Pulver; Walter Clarke; A. G. Scholtes; and Henry Vincent Hubbard.

In March 1923, the firm created a study of the preexisting vegetation. After Percival Gallagher and Carl Rust Parker visited, the grading plan was produced in May 1923. The plan included playfields, a children's playground, tennis and athletic fields, a meadow, a woodland, a lake drive, a bridle path, and walkways. A. John Halfenstein drew preliminary study plans for an arbor, wading pool, and restroom building. That month, the firm also created a grading plan and a planting plan for the vicinity of an athletic field, a study for a grandstand at the fields, a study for the administration buildings, a grading plan for a mall and concert grove, and a general grading plan. Percy R. Jones created the profile on centerline of roads and, in June 1923, he rendered a general grading plan.

A driveway with an accompanying bridle path makes the circuit of the park. These are so arranged as to bring those using them to the best points of view, to enjoy the landscape scenes and to reach the several special features of the park such as the "Spinning Woods," an existing growth of old trees on the westerly side of the park.[1]

The Olmsted Brothers' preliminary plan for Warinanco Park is dated March 20, 1923. *Courtesy of the Union County Division of Park Planning & Maintenance.*

In August 1923, the centerline profiles for Linden Avenue and Center Street were drawn up and the firm produced a detail of the walls, steps, balustrades, and concourse. Percy R. Jones made cross sections to accompany the road profiles. In September 1923, the firm created a study for a bridge and a grading study for the Rahway Avenue entrance. In October 1923, staff members produced grading plans for the southwest and northwest sections of the park. They also produced sketch plans for the fountain court, boat landing, bandstand, and the terminal treatment for the mall. The lake was laid out in November 1923. In December 1923, the firm worked on the grading plan for the east and southeast sections of the park. By February 1924, the preliminary planting plan was created and Percy R. Jones drew a study plan for an open channel outlet for the proposed lake. In March 1924, the firm produced a sketch for an entrance to the park mall, a plan for Cascade Brook, and grading plans for the southwestern section of the park and the athletic field. In April 1924, the firm produced a grading plan for the northeast section of the park.

The tulips are in radiant full bloom at the Henry S. Chatfield Memorial Garden in Warinanco Park. *April 26, 2009.*

This rain swept day in early spring allowed this view of what the Olmsted Brothers labeled *The Mall* on their preliminary plan. Four parallel rows of trees create aisles, the center one of which has been paved. *April 4, 2009.*

In May 1924, Carl Rust Parker drew the plan showing areas of proposed cuts and fills and Elizabeth, New Jersey, architect, C. Godfrey Poggi designed plans for the administration building. In June 1924, the planting plan was created for the east and southeast sections of the park. A plan showing the limit of the autumn planting and a general grading plan were produced in July 1924. In September 1924, Thomas E. Carpenter produced the planting plans for the north, northwest, east, northeast, and southeast sections of the park. In October 1924, the firm produced details for the athletic field fence and curb for the concourse. In January 1925, Carl Rust Parker created a progress map showing the various fields, a flower garden, boathouse, and bandstand. That same month, the firm created planting plans for the area around the Administration building and the vicinity of the athletic fields. In February they produced a general grading plan and a grading plan for the Rahway Avenue entrance. In March 1925, the staff produced grading plans for the northwest section, mall, and concert grove and created a study for trellised seats near the children's playground. In September 1925, the firm recorded the planting that was done up to this point. December 1925, the firm created a plan for the location of pine trees. The Park Commission report written in 1926 shows that the pergola, comfort station, and wading pool at the Little Children's Playground had been completed.

In January 1926, the planting plan for the northeast section of the park was revised. During the summer of 1926, Runyon & Carey engineers designed electric lighting for the park.

In 1929, the Olmsted Brothers created planting plans for the vicinity of the Administration building, along the boundary next to an apartment building, and along the north and northeast boundaries of the park. Work in 1931

With their smooth bark, beech trees are typically the recipients of harmful carvings. Nevertheless, the trees will most likely outlast most of these relationships. *April 4, 2009.*

included creating the plan for flowering cherry trees around the lake and creating the as-built drawing of the lake itself. The landscape plan for a small slab bridge and the treatment of the banks were created in March 1939. In January and March of 1945, Carl Rust Parker designed the azalea garden, which was later expanded in 1955.

In the 1940s and 1950s, parking areas were introduced into the park and wooden curbing was replaced by pre-cast concrete.[2] Now the park features a bicycle path; boating and boat rentals; a skating center (built in 1964), which is home to Westfield High School's ice hockey team; tennis courts and running track; winding walkways; football, soccer and baseball fields; a playground; and a water spray for children in the summer.

The azalea garden is dedicated to Caxton Brown of Summit, New Jersey. In the 1920s, he was an advocate for the establishment of the Union County Park Commission. *April 26, 2009.*

Endnotes Chapter 26: Warinanco Park

[1]Union County Park Commission. *Report of the Union County Park Commission 1923-1924-1925*; p. 22.
[2]"History of the Union County Park System; Special Feature, Warinanco Park." Warinanco Park Tour Committee: Elizabeth, New Jersey, 2010.

Chapter 27

Rahway River Park: Rahway (1923)

Rahway River Park is a 133-acre park located in the City of Rahway. It has highly irregular boundaries as it follows the meandering path of the river through the municipality. The park is bounded by suburban developments. Parkway Drive encircles the major section of the park that is not along the banks of the Rahway River. There are two main entrances, one off St. George's Avenue (Route 27) and the other off Valley Road. Constructed from land formerly comprised of swamps, garbage dumps, and overgrown fields, the park, since 1923, combines natural areas along the river and open pastoral fields used for recreational purposes.

In 1926, Raymond H. Torrey wrote an article for *The New York Times* that summarized the first four years of work of the Union County Park Commission. He wrote,

> The preservation of the Rahway River, the largest stream in the county, was a most fortunate and appropriate feature of the park development. This riverway is growing in beauty and in public use as the acquisition of practically its entire length, by gift and purchase, proceeds. Several lakes, for boating in summer and skating in winter, have been built, extending the available water area and adding to recreational utility as well as creating new beauties. The Union County Park Commission has benefited largely through the growing tendency to public beneficence in gifts to park systems, which has been displayed throughout the country. Among donations which have been highly useful in establishing and rounding out the various units were the Rahway Poor Farm of forty acres, added by that city to the Rahway River Park.[1]

The Olmsted Brothers began work on this park in 1923. The following employees contributed to the design. Percy R. Jones, Percival Gallagher, J. Harry Scott; Benjamin G. Donovan, Carlton M. Archibold; George Bradley; Edwin M. Prellwitz; Joseph Bannon; Edward Clarke Whiting; Thomas E. Carpenter; Edward D. Rando; L. Palmer Lavallee; A. W. Phillips; William Lyman Phillips; Thomas D. Price; Jack E. Pulver; Henry C. Nye; Walter Clarke; Gordon Woodberry; Lyle L. Blundell; James D. Graham; Russell N. Barnes; and Frederick G. Todd.

The local topographical maps were generated in 1922 and in June 1923, Percival Gallagher made a sketch of

Rahway River Park. The numerous properties along the river were mapped in April and June 1923. By December 1923, the plan showing taking lines was created. It was revised in February 1924 and Percy R. Jones added notes to it in December 1924. In June 1924, Percy R. Jones produced the plan for the section from St. George Avenue to Valley Road in Rahway. In December 1924, Percival Gallagher created a general plan for the Poor Farm section. In February 1925, Percy R. Jones and Percival Gallagher created a study plan for a 120-foot boulevard crossing the park to connect with Wiltsie's corner. In March 1925, Percy R. Jones created

Rahway River Park features this large lily pond next to the Rahway River. Wildlife abounds including fish, turtles, cormorants, and Canadian geese. *May 31, 2009.*

study plans showing the playgrounds, tennis courts, and a football field. The preliminary plan for the section between Valley Road and St. George Avenue, including the Poor Farm tract, was made. A grading plan for the former Wheatena property was also made In September 1925. The firm produced a profile to accompany plan #94 and Percy R. Jones revised the study plan for the eastern portion of the park. The firm produced the grading plan for the eastern portion of the Poor Farm section to Valley Road and St. George Avenue.

In December 1925, Jones created profiles to accompany the plans for the eastern portion. In March 1926, the firm created a study plan showing proposed boundary on the east side of the Poor Farm section. In May 1926, Percy R. Jones produced a plan of cuts and fills. In May 1927, A. W. Phillips designed a plan for a spillway from the lake to the Rahway River. In June 1927, the firm produced a detail plan for a bridge over the spillway. Lyle L. Blundell produced a grading plan for the Rahway River Waterworks in July, which was revised that November. In August 1927, Jack E. Pulver provided details of the spillway. Additional planting plans were generated in September 1927 and September 1929. In March 1929, the firm produced a sketch plan for a swimming pool for the Poor Farm section and in June 1929, they made the study plan. Prellwitz was overseer of this project. In August 1929, Russell N. Barnes produced the planting plan for the area around the swimming pool. This planting plan was revised in October 1929. In June 1930, the firm created a revised grading plan for the Poor Farm section showing a swimming pool with swimming beach, bathhouse, football field, and a wading pool in the section off of St. George Avenue.

By 1930, the Commission's Report stated the following were complete: the swimming pool and bathhouse at the Lincoln Highway (Route 27) section, a bowling green and sports fields, several playgrounds at Rahway and Springfield, and the preliminary development of various sections of the parkway drive through Rahway, Clark, Linden, Cranford, and Union.[2]

Top right:
A turtle takes advantage of the sunny day to dry out its shell on the bank of the lily pond. *May 31, 2009.*

Right:
The northern section of the Rahway River Park consists of the natural banks of the Rahway River. Native sweet gum trees have star shaped leaves that each autumn turn bright shades of yellow, red, and purple. *November 7, 2009.*

In the fall of 1946 and spring of 1947, the Rahway Chapter of the American War Dads dedicated 41 newly planted pin oaks and 17 dogwood trees to commemorate those Rahway residents who perished in military service. A masonry field house was built in 1950 to supply bathrooms, a shelter, and refreshments to visitors using the nearby picnic areas, athletic facilities, and children's playground. Four tennis courts were resurfaced to improve playing conditions, and metal nets installed, and additional picnic areas with fireplaces were established.[3]

In April 1948, Gordon Woodberry created the grading plans, cross sections, and road profiles for a new park drive, which was south of the state highway between Walnut Avenue and South Park Drive. In December 1952, the firm produced a plan for the location of a memorial flagpole and in October 1955, they made a sketch plan for the Wendell Memorial. This memorial stands near the swimming pool and the bronze plaque has the following text; "In Memory of Arthur Rindge Wendell of Rahway and Summit, 1876-1952. An ardent leader in the establishment of the Union County Park Commission. Served 1921-1952." Rahway River Park is one link in the chain of the magnificent greenway that courses along the Rahway River through Union County.

Constructed in 1950, the masonry field house at Rahway River Park is located near a playground and picnic area shaded by mature oaks and beech trees. *November 7, 2009.*

Endnotes Chapter 27: Rahway River Park:

[1]Raymond H. Torrey, "Jersey County Parks Extend Their Bounds; Union Follows Essex in Developing a System of Open Tracts That are Readily Accessible to Its Large Centers of Population," *New York Times*, November 21, 1926.

[2]Union County Park Commission. *Report of the Union County Park Commission, New Jersey 1929-1930;* p. 17.
[3]Union County Park Commission. *Report of the Union County Park Commission, New Jersey 1947-1957;* p. 21.

Chapter 28

Cedar Brook Park: Plainfield and South Plainfield (1923)

Cedar Brook Park is located in the southern section of the City of Plainfield and a small part is located in the adjoining municipality of South Plainfield. It is roughly bordered on the north by Randolph Road; on the west by Kenyon Avenue; on the south by the Middlesex County line; and on the east by Park Avenue and Rose Street. Cedar Brook is very narrow and shallow brook coursing through the park into a small lake in the southern section. Its unique attraction is a Shakespeare Garden, one of only a few in the country. This pastoral park was listed in both the New Jersey and National Register of Historic Places in 2007.

In 1925, the Union County Park Commission stated;

Of the finished areas in the park system, none presents a more striking contrast to the original state than Cedar Brook Park with its 78 acres of swampland, including the city refuse dump, now transformed into green turf with curving drives and paths and surrounded by border planting. The first step was to excavate a new and larger brook channel, in graceful alignment and with banks properly protected from erosion. This channel was excavated by steam shovel, paved with stone, and the banks higher up lined with sod. The excavation of 33,000 cubic yards of material in the southerly part of the tract served the double purpose of creating a picturesque lake of four acres and providing fill for elevating the lowlands.[1]

The Olmsted Brothers employees who worked on this park include: Percy R. Jones; Carlton M. Archibald; George Bradley; Faris B. Smith; Robert F. Jackson; Percival Gallagher; Lyle L. Blundell; J. Harry Scott; Jacob Sloet; Carl Rust Parker; Thomas E. Carpenter; Joseph Bannon; Edwin M. Prellwitz; Edward D. Rando; Henry C. Nye; Milton F. Sherman; James D. Graham; Walter Clarke; L. Palmer LaVallee; and A. G. Scholtes.

In December 1922, a preliminary plan of the park was submitted for the Union County Commission to review. The park plan was laid out on the topographical maps in May 1923. In June 1923, topographical maps were used to show the placement of the roads. In January 1924, Percy R. Jones created the grading plans, which would be revised several times in 1924. In March, Jones drew the plan for the proposed location of the fire station, bridle path, and brook channel. Specific drawings showing the cross section of the brook with its gravel bottom, boulders laid in place, and sloped walls were also created at this time. The preliminary plan of the entire park that Jones drew was dated February 11, 1924. The Board of Park Commissioners and Percival Gallagher approved the plan for issue. The plans showed the meadow, children's lawn, a baseball diamond, wading pool, and lake. In April 1924, a planting study was created for the area around Randolph Road and Kenyon Avenue. In May and June of 1924, Robert F. Jackson drew preliminary plans and later created more detailed drawings for two bridges. The later drawing showed a concrete bridge

In 1926, Raymond Torrey wrote about the newly established Union County park system, stating that the City of Plainfield had given Cedar Brook Park to Union County and it was one of the donations that was highly useful in establishing and rounding out the various park units. "It is one of the best examples of the work of the landscape architect and engineer. Seventy-eight acres of stump and swampland were made into a preserve with great beauty, in which fine trees were saved and their attraction supplemented by natural planting of shrubs and herbaceous plants indigenous to the vicinity."[2]

Cedar Brook Park, Plainfield, New Jersey   2

This linen-era picture postcard shows the small lake in Cedar Brook Park, a popular spot for fishing and bird watching.

The lake at Cedar Brook Park reflects the newly-renovated pavilion. *November 7, 2009.*

faced with stone. In July, Jackson also designed a spillway off the lake. Percy R. Jones designed the plans for a wading pool and a sand court in July 1924.

In August 1924, Thomas E. Carpenter developed two planting plans; one for the area around the vicinity of the lake and the other for the northwest portion of the park. In November 1924, a revised grading plan of a ford to take the place of the bridge over the creek was drawn up. In March 1925, Jacob Sloet created a planting plan for the area between the two bridges. In July 1925, a revised grading plan for the lake was produced and Jackson designed a footbridge of I-beams and wood. The planting plan for the eastern section of the park was designed in August 1925. In December 1925, Percival Gallagher drew up a study plan for the Randolph Road-Stelle Avenue (Kenyon Gardens) area. In March 1926, Edwin M. Prellwitz created a grading plan for a paved brook channel at Randolph Road and Stelle Avenue. A new electric light scheme designed by Runyon and Carey Consulting Engineers was created in January 1926. In September 1927, a planting plan was generated for the Park Avenue entrance. In March 1932, Percival Gallagher generated a sketch and a study plan for a proposed iris garden. A memorial shelter was designed at the request of Senator Reed in March 1943.

In the 1940s and 1950s, the Iris Garden was touted as one of the best in the country, but that is no longer extant. The Shakespeare garden remains intact, due to eighty years of continuous care from members of the Plainfield Garden Club.

The small Cedar Brook runs along the western edge of the park perpendicular to Randolph Road. Thomas E. Carpenter designed the planting plan for this section in 1924. *June 13, 2009.*

Percival Gallagher drew the preliminary sketch plan for the Shakespeare Garden in March 1927 and in May 1927, Lyle L. Blundell produced the planting plan for it. It is one of only one hundred such gardens worldwide, one of only seven or eight in this country. The Shakespeare Garden, initiated by Mr. Howard C. Fleming of the Plainfield Shakespeare Society in 1927, was originally meant to be but a small garden in a corner of Cedar Brook Park. However, the Park Commission was more ambitious and hired the Olmsted Brothers to design it. Gallagher's plan included two long beds, each one hundred feet long, and seventeen smaller flowerbeds. The beds were planted under the expert guidance of Mrs. Annie Burnham Carter, who remained Plainfield Garden Club chairwoman for at least eighteen years. Only about forty-four different plants and shrubs are mentioned in Shakespeare's writings, so other 16th and 17th century herbs and perennials supplemented the forty-four. The beds, all laid out geometrically, were edged with brick, according to the custom of the times. To give the garden literary interest, the botanical and folk names, and quotations about the flowers were put on stake labels.[3] In 2007, the Shakespeare Garden was 80 years old and the Plainfield Garden Club celebrated with a boutique and plant sale accompanied by music by the Plainfield Symphony.

The elements of the Shakespeare Garden include many of the plants mentioned in William Shakespeare's writings. *June 13, 2009.*

Endnotes Chapter 28: Cedar Brook Park

[1] Union County Park Commission. *Report of the Union County Park Commission 1923-1924-1925;* p. 28
[2] Raymond H. Torrey, "Jersey County Parks Extend Their Bounds; Union Follows Essex in Developing a System of Open Tracts That are Readily Accessible to Its Large centers of Population," *New York Times*, November 21, 1926.
[3] Victoria Furman. "The Plainfield Garden Club, 1915-1965."

The bare bones of the Shakespeare Garden in Cedar Brook Park can best be seen in wintertime. Percival Gallagher developed the plan in 1927. *March 21, 2009.*

Chapter 29

Watchung Reservation: New Providence, Mountainside, and Scotch Plains (1925)

Watchung Reservation is a 2,002-acre county-owned woodland located in the Boroughs of New Providence and Mountainside and the Township of Scotch Plains. It is part of the Union County Park system. The Reservation is roughly bounded by Glenside Avenue and Interstate Route 78 on the north, Summit Road on the east, suburban developments on the south, and New Providence Road on the west.

On November 21, 1926, Raymond H. Torrey of *The New York Times* wrote about the Union County Park Commission's activities. He stated;

> The Watchung Reservation, four miles long and reaching 575 feet above sea level at Peckman's Tower, with wide views over the lowland to New York harbor, has the same position in the Union County system, which the Eagle Rock and South Mountain Reservation have in the Essex County park system. Like them, the Watchung Reservation will be kept largely in its present natural state. Deer run wild and smaller game and birds are numerous. The lake is used for bathing and boating and a Boy Scout camp has been established on its shore. Facilities for athletic sports, motor parking, a riding stable and bridle paths and many miles of trails for walkers have been provided. Lake Surprise is stocked with perch and bass and Blue Brook is a trout stream. Among donations to the Union County Park Commission, which have been highly useful in establishing and rounding out the various units, was a donation of fifty-three acres in the Summit section of the Watchung Reservation by Carroll P. Bassett.[1]

The following Olmsted Brothers employees worked on the designs for this woodland preserve: George Bradley; Percy R. Jones; Carlton M. Archibald; M. Corse; Percival Gallagher; Benjamin G. Donovan; Clarence DeForest Platt; Thomas E. Carpenter; Edward A. Douglas; Thomas D. Price; Lyle L. Blundell; and Russell N. Barnes.

Lake Surprise is one of the attractive features at Watchung Reservation. *November 7, 2009.*

The topographical maps were locally drawn and delivered to the Olmsted Brothers office in 1922. In September 1923, the lands within the proposed reservation were shown on a 42" by 120" topographical map drawn by Frank J. Hubbard, C. E. of Plainfield and John J. Kentz of Summit. Plan #4, dated February 1924, has tentative plan and redesign for Ackerman Avenue by Percy R. Jones. Plan #8, of June 3, 1924, has preliminary plan for portion of the west boundary road. This was revised in January 1926. In May 1925, Mr. Corse drew a sketch plan for the stables, office, and garage. In June 1925, the administration site on the south side of Silver Lake was designed in study plans and included the bathing beach and boat dock. A study showing the placement of roadways was created in July 1925.

The ease with which people can reach remote places by the automobile has brought about the coming together of many people, in one place. This brings about an extinction of wild or natural vegetation, which is the special attraction of the woodland reservation. The problem therefore, is to devise ways which will provide adequate accommodations for the public without losing the very elements that make the place what it is.[2]

The grading plan for the stables and approaches to them was created in October 1925. This area included the west ride, east ride, training track, stable, and auto parking lot. In December 1925, a grading plan for a proposed road from Glenside Avenue to Oakridge Avenue was produced. In February 1926, Thomas E. Carpenter designed the planting plan for the same area that included an English hurdle fence in the exercise ring.

In March 1927, Edward A. Douglas designed the plan for the area through the Beattie property north of Glenside Avenue and in July, an "as-built" drawing of the reservation was produced. In August, the staff created a plan with the profile and cross sections of the road from Surprise Lake to Glenside Avenue and the grading plan for an addition to the stable. Two years later, in January 1929, the firm produced a study for the administration building, which included additional parking, a terrace, men and women's bathrooms, and vistas to the lake. In March 1929, the staff designed a planting plan for the campsites along the loop road and a study for the arrangement of the cottage, boathouse, field house, parking around the playing field in the area of Silver Lake and New Providence Road.

Watchung Reservation is a heavily wooded park and the guiding philosophy of its treatment is to keep it as natural as possible. Trails through the woods have trail blazes but that is about it. *October 4, 2009.*

The 1947-1957 Union County Park Commission report included this passage:

The fast growth in interest and attendance at the Trailside Nature Museum necessitated the building of an addition in 1951 to the building that first opened ten years earlier. This provided more room for displaying exhibits, better sanitary facilities, and a larger lecture room. Constant improvement is being made to facilities at the Watchung Riding Stable to keep pace with the intensive use of this area. The original riding stable was destroyed by fire on April 15, 1957. A new fire-resistant stable 212 feet long, had been built at the original site, also a separate barn for storing hay and straw, and a new office, assembly room, and caretaker's apartment are now under construction. Concrete posts and wooden rails have replaced the decaying wooden hurdle fence; sand has been used to replace cinders in the track for better drainage and footing; and a living fence of multiflora rose bushes has replaced an old wooden fence. Better floodlighting to improve late afternoon and evening riding conditions and a small vending service for the public has been added. A 78 by 24-foot masonry shelter including a refreshment stand and sanitary facilities, was constructed in the fall of 1957 in the loop section near Lake Surprise. Throughout the Watchung Reservation, more than 7,000 linear feet of pre-cast concrete posts and rails have replaced wooden guard rails dating back to the CCC days. The new rails are made to simulate logs for a pleasing effect and have eliminated costly maintenance.[3]

Watchung Reservation remains primarily a large woodland and is an oasis for nature surrounded by suburban development of ever increasing density.

This young beech tree in Watchung Reservation appears to be trying to avoid receiving more carvings as it leans southward and away from the trail. *November 7, 2009.*

Endnotes Chapter 29: Watchung Reservation

[1]Raymond H. Torrey, "Jersey County Parks Extend Their Bounds; Union Follows Essex in Developing a System of Open Tracts That are Readily Accessible to Its Large centers of Population," *New York Times*, November 21, 1926.

[2]Union County Park Commission. *The Report of The Union County Park Commission 1923-1924-1925.* p. 16.

[3]Union County Park Commission. *Report of the Union County Park Commission, New Jersey 1947-1957.* (Union County Park Commission, 1957): 22.

Chapter 30
Wheeler Park: Linden (1925)

Located along one of the busiest sections of US Highway 1 in the City of Linden, John Russell Wheeler Park is a twenty-acre oasis of calm. Morses Creek bisects the small pastoral park, which is bounded on the north by South Wood Avenue, on the east by Route 1 (known as Edgar Road), on the south by South Stiles Street, and on the west by Kennedy Drive and West Simpson Avenue. In 1923, Linden began advocating for a community park and, to that end, an ordinance that proposed the purchase of the Colomon Danninger and John Fedor tract was passed. A year later on December 1, 1924, the newly designated parkland was turned over to the Union County Park Commission for its care, custody, and control as a park. By 1926, the park's name had been selected to commemorate John Russell Wheeler, a marine and the first soldier from Linden to die in World War One.[1]

The Olmsted Brothers employees who designed this park include: Percival Gallagher; Edwin M. Prellwitz; Thomas E. Carpenter; Joseph Bannon; Percy R. Jones; Gordon J. Culham; Carlton M. Archibold; James A. Britton; Henry C. Nye; Lyle L. Blundell; Russell N. Barnes; Walter F. Clarke; Raymond W. Aldrich; and Wolcott E. Andrews.

Postmarked in 1937, this picture postcard showing Wheeler Park in wintertime was sent with a summertime message about playing baseball. Morses Creek was dammed at one point, but now flows freely through the park. The bridge has also been replaced with a more modern structure.

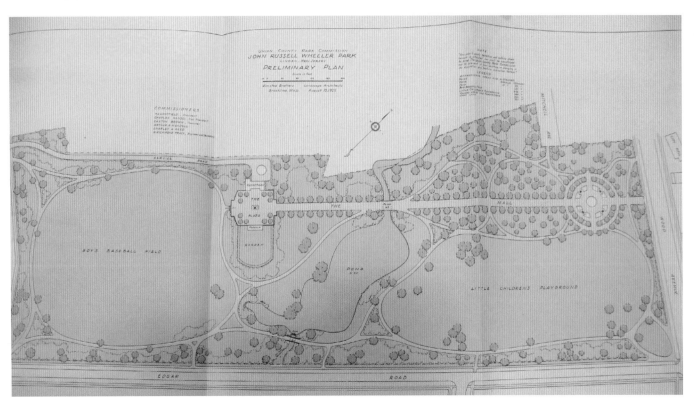

The Olmsted Brothers preliminary plan for John Russell Wheeler Park dated August 10, 1925 was included in the Union County Park Commission Report. *Courtesy of the Union County Division of Park Planning & Maintenance.*

In April 1925, Percival Gallagher produced the study plan for the proposed park. In June 1925, Edwin M. Prellwitz created the preliminary grading and layout plans as well as corresponding profiles. Developmental work began in the summer of 1925 with the removal of debris and dead and superfluous trees. In August, the firm created the preliminary plan with a baseball field, plaza, garden, pond, and playground. Additional plantings along Wood Avenue and Edgar Road were designed in August 1925. A sketch was made for the area of the triangle around the Linden City Hall, which included a war memorial. One plan was produced in December 1925 showing the location of linden trees near Wood Avenue and Edgar Road. In February and March 1926, Thomas E. Carpenter produced the planting plans for the park. In May 1926, Joseph Bannon created detailed studies for the central mall, a dam, and a footbridge with a balustrade. In August 1928, the general property key map was produced. Walter F. Clarke created a planting plan for the area along Edgar Road (now Route 1) in March 1929. In March 1931, the firm designed sketches for the area for the pool and bathhouse and a grading study plan for the extension of the park to Stimson Avenue. Lyle L. Blundell developed the grading plan for the extension.

The mall leading from Wood Avenue invites visitors to promenade through the park. The original bathhouse built in 1931, was destroyed by fire in 1945. By 1947, a fireproof masonry model was constructed in its place.[2] Aerial photographs of Linden taken in 1940 and 1947 show that the pond was eliminated and the creek returned to a more natural channel during these years. The Union County Park Commission included a short summary of the development of this park in their 1947-1957 Annual Report. It stated that an additional two acres along Stimson Avenue had been developed into a lawn area. The paved parking area adjoining the swimming pool was doubled in size to accommodate 80 cars.[3]

Wheeler Park in Linden is more popular in the summer when the pool opens. On this rainy February day, the park had only a few visitors. *February 22, 2009.*

It's hard to believe that there is a six-lane roadway approximately fifty feet to the east of this field in Linden's Wheeler Park. The border mound along US Route 1 reduces most of the traffic noise. This northeast section of the park was designed in 1925. *August 1, 2009.*

Endnotes Chapter 30: Wheeler Park

[1] Lauren Pancurak Yeats. *Linden, New Jersey*. (Charleston, SC: Arcadia Publishing, 2002); p. 42.
[2] Union County Park Commission. *Twenty-five Year Report Of The Union County Park Commission, 1921-1946*; p. 27.
[3] Union County Park Commission, 1947-1957 report.

Chapter 31
Mattano Park: Elizabeth (1926)

Mattano Park is a small urban park located in the City of Elizabeth. It is bounded by South Fifth Street on the north; Fifth Avenue on the east; and nestled in an elbow of the Elizabeth River on the south and west. The Olmsted Brothers' report of 1921 stated that a park in this heavily populated section of Elizabeth would be crucial for providing opportunities for public recreation.[1] The former salt meadow and bleak, low-lying land that existed along this section of the Elizabeth River was transformed over time into a managed park with a border mound, groves of trees, a rose garden, managed open fields, and recreational facilities. The park consists largely of a large open field used for recreation and sports with small groves of mature trees along both streets. There is a ten-foot grass-covered berm along the riverbank. The park is named for the most important chief of the Lenapes and one of the signers of the original deed when white settlers purchased this tract.[2] The park was originally designed with the names of Elizabethport Park or Elizabeth River Park. By 1930, the name Mattano had been selected. The 1928 Park Commission Report stated:

This photograph taken by Mr. Fieldman on April 3, 1926 shows the wasteland that the Olmsted Brothers firm would transform into Mattano Park. *Courtesy of Union County.*

> This tract of 47 acres has been acquired and is being developed as rapidly as circumstances and funds permit. Over 125,000 cubic yards of filling material have been used to bring this area up to the necessary grade. It is planned to make this unit a typical neighborhood park providing facilities for band concerts, boating, bathing, playgrounds, picnic and various forms of athletics. One of the main features will be a rose garden, the gift of a prominent citizen of Elizabeth. Although boating along the river never became a popular attraction, the pastoral fields and play areas within the groves of trees would entice many residents to the park.[3]

The following Olmsted Brothers staff worked on the design of Mattano Park: Percival Gallagher, Percy R. Jones, Edwin M. Prellwitz, Walter F. Clarke, Thomas E. Carpenter, Oliver F. Hooper, James T. Greenleaf, Robert Sterling Yard, Jo Ray, Henry C. Nye, Gordon Woodberry, Russell N. Barnes, Edward D. Rando, Carroll A. Towne, Wolcott E. Andrews, J. Roland Smyth, and Sen Yu.

The topographical maps of the area were sent to the Olmsted Brothers office in February 1926. Percy R. Jones produced preliminary studies and an outline plan showing the suggested grades on the border streets in March 1926. Several studies to detail alternative treatments of the Elizabeth River were produced on the topographical maps. Percival Gallagher produced the preliminary plan of the park in April 1926 and Percy Jones produced the grading plans that month. Edwin M. Prellwitz made some revisions in July and the two collaborated to produce the final grading plan in February 1927. Walter Clark worked on cross sections to accompany the plans and Samuel M. Green made the planting plans of the north and east borders and, in March 1927, of the children's playground and vicinity. The planting plan produced autumn of 1927 by Thomas E. Carpenter and Walter Clark was later revised in 1929, 1930, and 1931. In 1928, Robert Sterling Yard and Percival R. Gallagher produced plans of a location for a swimming pool. In January 1929, Gordon Woodberry and Edwin M. Prellwitz, rendered the planting plan for the children's playground and created a plan for the wading pool that March. Prellwitz also created a sketch for a field house.

In March 1929, Russell N. Barnes produced a planting plan for the park and in June, created the preliminary plans for a rose garden (for the northeast corner of the park). In July, Walter F. Clark and Edward D. Rando produced the details for the rose garden's construction and gardening. In May 1929, C. Godfrey Pozzi and William B. Beagdon, Architects of Elizabeth, New

Jersey, submitted their plans of the field house to the Olmsted Brothers to use for creating their planting plan. Barnes produced the planting plan in January 1930. In March 1931, Barnes also revised the rose garden and J. Roland Smyth drew a sketch for a rose arbor.

The 1930 Report of the Park Commission stated that the children's playground with a wading pool was complete, the field house constructed, and the grading and filling operations were taking place in several locations including the rose garden.[4] By 1931, the rose garden was complete and by 1947, the playing fields for baseball, softball, and soccer were in operation. The New Jersey Turnpike Authority realigned Trenton Avenue in the 1950s and the park was reduced in size by several acres. In 1953, soil stabilization efforts were instituted, which continued into the 1960s.

As the needs of the community changed, construction projects took place to create sports fields and to install a skateboard park. The field house was replaced by a new recreational building in the southeastern part of the park. It was during this time that the rose garden disappeared. Union County has plans to reinstall it following the original design of Olmsted Brother employee Russell N. Barnes.

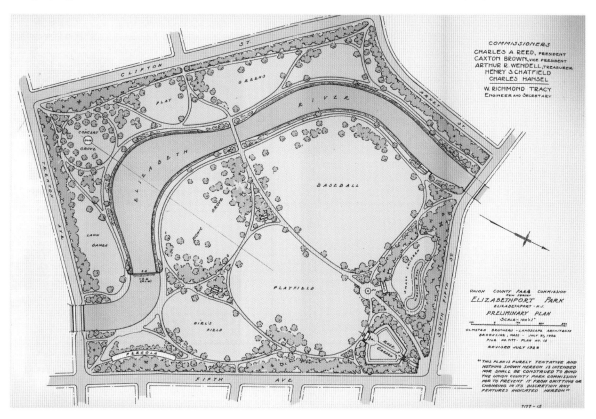

The Olmsted Brothers' preliminary plan for Elizabethport Park is shown revised and dated July 1928. The park was renamed Mattano Park in 1930. *Courtesy of the Union County Division of Park Planning & Maintenance.*

The three sections of Mattano Park include a grove of trees closest to South Fifth Street, a large open space (seen on the right), and a natural area along the bank of the Elizabeth River (in the foreground). *August 1, 2009.*

Endnotes Chapter 31: Mattano Park

[1]Olmsted Brothers, Landscape Architects. "Report to the Union County Park Commission." Brookline, Massachusetts, July 5, 1921; p. 10.
[2]The Union County Park Commission. *Twenty-Five Year Report Of The Union County Park Commission 1921-1946;* p. 19.

[3]Union County Park Commission. *Report of the Union County Park Commission 1926-1927-1928*; pp. 27-28.
[4]Union County Park Commission. *Report of the Union County Park Commission 1928-1929-1930*; p. 15.

Chapter 32

Nomahegan Park: Cranford (1925)

Nomahegan Park, in Cranford, comprises 95 acres of woodland bounded by Kenilworth Avenue to the north; Riverside Drive to the east; Park Drive to the south; and Springfield Avenue to the west. The name comes from "Noluns Mohegan" a name the New Jersey Lenape were called in the Treaty of 1758. This is translated as "women Mohegans" or "she-wolves" and was applied to Lenape men in scorn by Iroquois warriors.[1] This park developed as part of the much larger Rahway River Parkway project and there were a dozen plans specific to Nomahegan, as noted in the title blocks. This heavily wooded park represents another successful land use conversion from swampland used as a dump to attractive recreational center in the suburbs.

In April 1925, the Olmsted Brothers firm produced a sketch showing the proposed revision and lake in the section near Springfield Avenue in Cranford. These plans were part of the Rahway River Parkway project. In May 1925, Joseph Bannon created the general plan for the Sperry Farm subdivision. In July 1925, the firm created a study plan for the lake near Springfield Avenue in Cranford and a grading plan for the section along Springfield Avenue to which Percival Gallagher added field notes in August 1925.

In June and July 1926, Percival Gallagher developed the grading plan for this park. The plan, which is on file at the Union County Division of Park Planning and Maintenance, shows the acreage between Springfield Avenue to the west

Nomahegan Park's main attraction is a small lake with curving contours. The surrounding lawns are bordered with a variety of trees creating a pastoral setting for park visitors. *October 14, 2009.*

and Kenilworth Avenue to the north. It called for an outer ring roadway, a much larger lake with a centered island, and four bridges. The plan showed locations for a boathouse, six tennis courts, and a stream connecting the lake to the Rahway River. In August 1926, the firm changed the border mound. A plan from October 1926 contained additional data on a culvert at the northwest corner of the park. In February 1927, the firm developed a planting plan for the park and a more detailed planting plan for the border mound along Springfield Avenue. In November 1927, the Olmsted Brothers produced a revised grading plan for this park.

By 1929, the Park Commission had obtained additional lands to the west of the river and in their 1930 report, indicated development work was underway. The regulation baseball field was complete and work was progressing on the lake and adjoining areas including the construction of a concrete culvert and the sub-grading of the southerly section of the park drive.[2]

By 1947, a smaller lake (following the lower half of the contours seen on the plan) was completed along with picnic grounds. A large parking area was built along Springfield Avenue in 1959. In December 1964, the firm developed the planting plan for the park entrance road off Springfield Avenue. The Cranford Centennial Committee donated 100 Japanese cherry trees to the park in 1971, to commemorate the township's centennial. These were planted along the lake's edge near Springfield Avenue. The fitness trail through the wooded section was constructed in 1985.

This heavily wooded park has limited sections of development that include the pond, athletic fields, a bicycle path, a fitness trail, picnic areas, and a playground. Trails connect it to Lenape Park to the north. Dr. Patrick L. Cooney of the New York, New Jersey Botany Club noted the abundance of vegetation in the less developed section along the pond and the connecting Rahway River. The trees included box elder maples; red maples; sweetgums; American sycamores; and three types of oak trees; white, pin, and red. Shrubs included: privet; multiflora rose; and blackhaw viburnum. Vines included Asiatic bittersweet; greenbrier; and poison ivy.[3] The new East Coast Greenway trail passes through the park.

A young Great Blue Heron searches for a fish dinner in the shallows of the lake in Nomahegan Park. *October 14, 2009.*

The woodland that existed prior to the creation of Nomahegan Park was allowed to revert to its natural swampy state. *May 17, 2009.*

The stone bridge built over the Rahway River in Nomahegan Park. Sweet Gum trees' star-shaped leaves display a wonderful variety of colors each autumn. *October 14, 2009.*

Endnotes Chapter 32: Nomahegan Park

[1]Federal Writers' Project. *New Jersey, a Guide to Its Present and Past.* (New York: The Viking Press, 1939); p. 547.
[2]Union County Park Commission. *Report of the Union County Park Commission 1928-1929-1930*; p. 17.

[3]New York, New Jersey, Connecticut Botany Online www.nynjctbotany. org/njnbtofc/nomahegn.html

Chapter 33
Briant Park: Summit and Springfield (1930)

Briant Park is a 30-acre Union County park located within the City of Summit and the Township of Springfield. It is often also called Briant Pond Park. The land was originally part of the homestead of Oliver J. Hayes (1802-1861), a 270-acre estate that was located roughly between Morris Avenue and Springfield Avenue, and Hobart Avenue and the defunct Rahway Valley Railroad. When Mr. Hayes died, his will stated that the property could not be divided or sold during the lifetimes of his daughters, Mrs. Elizabeth Van Ness and Miss Sarah B. Hayes. They were to enjoy the income from it and upon their deaths, it was to go to the three children of Mrs. Van Ness. In 1859, William H. Briant (1827-1912) became the caretaker of the Hayes Estate. He was the son of Aaron Briant, who had farmed the area before him, and the great-great-grandson of Cornelius Briant who settled the family in Springfield in 1717.

Briant Park is an Olmsted-designed pastoral park with a pond as its major attraction. *October 4, 2009.*

William Briant built the first dam creating a 12-acre spring-fed lake then known as Spring Lake. Below the dam he ran a mill which had a huge wheel to grind wheat, rye, corn, and buckwheat. The pond was used for its ice and two large icehouses were built on the property. This pond provided the area with ice for iceboxes and skaters spent many hours there each winter. A boathouse provided a place to rent rowboats and a picnic grove was open to all, free of charge, for many years. The dam was washed out by a flood in 1888 and rebuilt in 1889. However, it was rebuilt lower, which reduced the size of the pond to seven acres. The dam that stands today at the east end of the pond was built by Works Progress Administration laborers in 1938.

In 1896, Miss Hayes filed a petition to annul the portion of the will that prohibited the sale of the property. The courts had previously approved the sale of portions of the property over the years. There remained about 150 acres, practically all of which was still wooded. At some point William Briant took ownership of the property or a part of it, but no records have been found to support the details of this transaction. In 1930 the estate of Mr. Briant sold the remaining property, including the ten-bedroom home, to the Union County Park Commission. Briant, who had been a Union County Freeholder, had apparently specified this transaction in his will.[1]

Because Briant Park was initially developed as a small section of a parkway connected to the Rahway River parkway, many of the earlier plans drafted involved the roadways. The following Olmsted Brothers company employees developed the plans for this park: Percival Gallagher, William Lyman Phillips, Edwin M. Prellwitz, and J. Harry Scott. The topographical maps in the files at the Frederick Law Olmsted Historic Site in Brookline are dated October 1926. One showed the section from Shunpike Road to Springfield Avenue and another showed the area from Watchung Reservation to Shunpike Road. Percival Gallagher produced several study plans, one being over six feet long. In December 1926, Edwin M. Prellwitz developed the study for the connection of Briant Pond Parkway to the Rahway River Parkway, which is approximately one mile to the east. In January 1927, the firm created study plans for the roads and pond. The preliminary general plan for the parkway was

Olmsted designs call for distinct and varied borders around large masses of water and land. Here is the landscaped edge of Briant Park's pond. *October 4, 2009.*

The trail in Briant Park takes a visitor into a dense wooded area where there is a variety of flora including saplings, moss, and ferns. *October 4, 2009.*

produced in March 1927. The parkway was shown from the Watchung Reservation to the Rahway River parkway, but this parkway never was completed. Despite the designing efforts expended, the only park that was built was the 30-acre Briant Pond Park.

In June 1930, the firm produced a study plan for the proposed park situated in Springfield and Summit. In July 1930, Edwin M. Prellwitz created the study plan of Briant Pond with play areas in cross sections and details. A copy of this plan is located at the Union County Division of Park Planning and Maintenance. The plan shows a main entryway at the corner of Morris Avenue (now Springfield Avenue) and Briant Parkway, a field house on the banks of the pond, the original wooded section covering most of the southeast section, and meandering paths skirting various playfields. Another plan was created to present an alternative scheme for the spillway and brook. The 1930 Commission Report indicated that the pond restoration had been completed. The field house was never constructed.

Unfortunately, construction on the park came to a halt during the Depression and only resumed with funding from the Works Project Administration in 1938. The dam had burst and emergency funding was used to rebuild it. New plans were drawn in-house for the Union County Park Commission. The positions of the paths were in different locations than on the 1930 plan and no roadway was built as suggested by the Olmsted plan. By and large, the larger elements of the park, such as the wooded and open sections, and the shape of the pond were based on the Olmsted plan. In 1947, a curved retaining wall was constructed to allow the formation of a flat area for a baseball diamond. While the wall remains as the prominent man-made feature in the park, the baseball diamond has since been removed.[2]

In 1947, the Union County Park Commission wrote, "older residents familiar with the area requested the Commission to restore the old pond to its former glory and for that reason special consideration was given to the waterside view. Huge weeping willows hang low over the pond and trees and shrubs blend into the landscape."[3]

Momentum is now building for refurbishing Briant Park led by the East Summit Association and Briant Park Olmsted Conservancy. A master plan was produced in November 2009 by Rhodeside & Harwell. The focus is to return to the park more characteristic elements from the original Olmsted design. Meetings were held during July 2010 with the Union County Board of Freeholders and Green Acres officials, and an application has been submitted for Green Acres funding, a program under the auspices of the state Department of Environmental Protection. Masur Engineering, hired by the county, had already done a lot of preparation by completing an engineering plan. The first step is dredging the pond. Plans also call for rebuilding the bridge closest to Shunpike Road, providing another access to the hiking paths. Van Winkle Brook, which flows into the pond, also needs to be cleaned. It is also hoped that the Rails to Trails program could potentially use the dormant Rahway Valley Railroad right-of-way to link Briant Park with Hidden Valley Park, which already connects to the Watchung Reservation, adding more than 2,100 acres of parkland to Briant Park users.[4]

In Briant Park, a large pastoral lawn is edged by a small forest. *October 4, 2009.*

At the edge of the open lawn in Briant Park, newly planted trees create shade circles. *October 4, 2009.*

Endnotes for Briant Park:

[1]Edmund B. Raftis. *Summit, New Jersey; From Poverty Hill to The Hill City.* (Seattle, Washington: Great Swamp Press, 1996).
[2]*Briant Pond Park Master Plan.* Rhodeside & Harwell, November 2009.
[3]Union County Park Commission**.** *Twenty-five Year Report of the Union County Park Commission 1921-1946*; p. 23.
[4]"Summit's Briant Park on board for new 'old' look," published on September 1, 2010 on NJ.com.

Chapter 34
Woodbridge Park: Woodbridge (1928)

The Olmsted Brothers designed one park in Middlesex County. This is an engineered park, Woodbridge Park (or Heard's Brook Park). It is a long and narrow municipal park winding along both banks of Heard's Brook as it traverses four five blocks through the center of Woodbridge Township. It is located between North Park Drive on the north; Pearl Street on the east; South Park Drive on the south; and Mobile Avenue on the west. In the 1920s, the Township was compelled to find a solution to the flooding along Heard's Brook and included it as one of the municipality's building campaigns.[1] The narrow park lands and curving roadways flank the channeled waterway. There are four bridges carrying cross traffic over the brook.

In the late 1920s, Woodbridge Township engaged the services of the Olmsted Brothers and the topographical maps arrived at the company's Brookline offices in April 1928. Five employees worked to plan the park; they were James D. Graham, Lyle L. Blundell, Edward D. Rando, Carlton M. Archibald, and Joseph Bannon. The undated preliminary plan shows roadways along greens, stream, and lake. In July 1928, Lyle L. Blundell produced two preliminary study schemes. In August 1928, James D. Graham made a grading plan of the area that intersects Elmwood Avenue, Middlesex Avenue, Amboy Avenue, School Street, and which extends to Pearl Street from Peyser Street (now Mobile Avenue). The playground area with wading pool was bordered by Pearl Street, Brook Street, School Street, and Park Avenue. Blundell created the cross sections to go with Graham's plans. In August, typical cross sections of the brook and profiles for the parkway drives to accompany the plan were made but not signed. In September 1928, Lyle L. Blundell created the planting plans for the entire length of the park.

A 1931 aerial photograph of Woodbridge shows that the work of grading, planting, and roadway-building was complete, but only on the eastern half of the park. The ponds on the west half of the park were developed later and can be seen in the 1940 aerial photograph.[2] This project transformed open fields into a park and tamed Heard's Brook

watercourse through the center of Woodbridge. Over the following decades, residential neighborhoods would cover the subdivided land on both sides of the park.

Olmsted Brothers employee Lyle L. Blundell developed the planting plan including this semicircle of pine trees for the park along Heard's Brook in Woodbridge. *October 21, 2009.*

The banks of Heard's Brook in the western section of Woodbridge Park have more vegetation than the eastern section. The plants create a natural-looking bank at this concrete channeled watercourse. *August 1, 2009.*

Endnotes for Woodbridge Park:

[1]Virginia Bergen Troeger and Robert J. McEwen. *Woodbridge, New Jersey; New Jersey's Oldest Township.* (Charleston, South Carolina: Arcadia Publishing, 2002).
[2]United States Department of Agriculture. Aerial photographs of Middlesex County, New Jersey, 1931 and 1940.

Chapter 35
Brookdale Park: Montclair and Bloomfield (1930)

Brookdale Park is an Essex County park shared by two municipalities, Montclair and Bloomfield. It is located in the northeast part of Essex County roughly bounded by Bellevue Avenue on the north; Newell Drive and Overlook Avenue on the east; Watchung Avenue on the south; and Grove Street on the west. It is the third largest park in the Essex County system, consisting of 121 acres. The land was originally a gathering place of the Lenape Indians. During the 17th century, Dutch settlers moved into the area and transformed it into farming and grazing land. The fields were known as Stonehouse Plains, which is what the area was called until the late 1800s, when the location was to get a post office. It was then decided that Stonehouse Plains was too long, so it was shortened to Brookdale. In 1928, the Essex County Park Commission began purchasing land for the park.[1]

A photograph taken by Herman G. Cuthbert in Brookdale Park on July 3, 1935 shows men cultivating newly-planted trees and shrubs in the southern part near Watchung Avenue, Bloomfield. *Courtesy of the Essex County Department of Parks, Recreation, and Cultural Affairs.*

Brookdale Park is a 121-acre oasis of green during the spring and summer for many residents who live in the surrounding early 20th century suburban developments. *May 31, 2009.*

The design and construction of Brookdale Park began in 1930. The following Olmsted Brothers employees worked on this design: William Lyman Phillips; Lyle L. Blundell; John B. Moseley; Benjamin G. Donovan; Sen Yu; John J. Sullivan; George T. Lenehan; Percival Gallagher; Jacob Sloet; Edward D. Rando; Henry McLaren; Edwin M. Prellwitz; Joseph Bannon; Carlton M. Archibald; Hans J. Koehler; and Edward Clarke Whiting.

The Olmsted Brothers received the topographical maps drawn by a local surveyor in January 1930. In February 1930, William Lyman Phillips and John B. Moseley created a grading plan, which would be revised a year later. In May 1930, Lyle L. Blundell created the preliminary study, a preliminary plan, and a preliminary grading study for the southwest portion of the park. In July 1930, Benjamin G. Donovan produced the general plan of the park. Moseley developed a grading plan for the vicinity of the casino and bandstand in June 1930. In August 1930, Sen Yu created a study plan with elevations for a field house near the track. In October 1930, the firm changed the grade on the east drive and Moseley revised the grading plan profiles. In December 1930, Blundell created a study plan for the service building and yard.

In March 1931, Phillips produced a grading plan for the roads and in April 1931, Sen Yu produced elevations, plans, and sections for a casino. In May 1931, John J. Sullivan prepared a sketch plan of the proposed park connection with a street plan for the area west of the park. After conducting field visits, Percival Gallagher modified the study plans. In June 1931, George T. Lenehan created cross sections to accompany a plan showing the vicinity of the track and Blundell created a study for the entrance from Grove Street. Blundell also revised a grading plan in the vicinity of the track. Sen Yu worked on the grading plan for the widening of Bellevue Avenue and John J. Sullivan made cross sections to accompany it. In July 1931, Sullivan made plans creating a parkway along Yantacaw Brook north of the park and John B. Moseley worked on a study plan for the Parkview Road entrance. William Lyman Phillips made a grading plan for the drive entrance off Grove Street. In August 1931, Edward D. Rando created a cross section of the running track. In September 1931, Henry McLaren drew up the general plan of the park and Jacob Sloet produced the planting plan. The staff also produced a grading plan showing the revised road and border mound grades. In October 1931, Moseley made a study plan for treatment of the concert grove.

An area with specimen trees and groves in the western half give way to two open fields in the east half of Brookdale Park. *May 31, 2009.*

A sycamore tree along the East Park Drive in Brookdale Park. This park was designed for automobile access and the separation between walkways and roads is very distinct. *May 31, 2009.*

In March 1932, John B. Moseley made a grading plan for the area around the grandstand. In July 1932, Edwin M. Prellwitz produced the study plan for the border mound in the north corner. In January 1933, planting plans were produced for the areas around the bandstand, ball fields, and tennis courts. In May 1933, Prellwitz created a study plan for additional boundary planting in the north corner. In February 1934, Hans J. Koehler produced several study plans and grading plans for the rock garden. Carlton M. Archibald designed the revised grading plan for the pond. In March 1936, Joseph Bannon prepared a grading plan for the rock garden area and Koehler produced a planting plan for the section west of the pond. In July 1936, Edward Clarke Whiting and Koehler made several study plans of an outlook plateau wall. In February and March 1937, Koehler worked on cross sections, plans, and profiles of a watercourse in the rock garden area.

The initial work was underway by 1930. When the Depression hit, the work that was originally estimated to take only a few years was extended to many years. Construction became dependent upon labor available from the Works Progress Administration. Although residents had used various sections of the park as they were finished, Brookdale Park officially opened on January 1, 1937; however, there was no ceremony. The 1937 Annual Report from the Essex County Park Commission stated: In 1937, the work at Brookdale Park continued toward completion. This included grading and top soiling; lawn seeding and planting (491 trees and 3,660 shrubs were planted), completion of road paving and curb work, construction of three tennis courts, and the construction of a reinforced concrete grandstand seating 3,200 at the athletic field.[2]

This small open field ringed with trees in the northern part of Brookdale Park is set aside for archery. *May 31, 2009.*

Not part of the original design, a rose garden was established in 1959 by the North Jersey Rose Society with a donation of 750 rose bushes. The garden has grown to include 1,500 rose bushes in 29 separate beds. Because of cutbacks, the County discontinued its paid staff to the garden and the Rose Society stopped their association with it. The garden languished until the newly formed Essex County Master Gardeners, under the leadership of Jonathan Forsell, took over the care and restoration of the Rose Garden as a community project beginning in 1997.[3] It is one of the major attractions in this heavily used neighborhood park, especially in June.

The rose garden in full bloom at Brookdale Park. *May 31, 2009.*

Endnotes for Chapter 35: Brookdale Park

[1]Essex County Department of Parks, Recreation, and Cultural Affairs: http://www.essex-countynj.org/p/index.php?section=af/system.
[2] *Thirty-ninth Report of the Park Commission of Essex County 1936-1937.* (Newark, N. J.: Essex County Park Commission, 1938): p. 8.
[3]Master Gardeners of Essex County web site: http://www.mgessex.org/cms/index.php?page=rose-garden

Chapter 36
Ivy Hill Park: Newark (1930)

Ivy Hill Park is a 19-acre neighborhood park in Newark run by the Essex County Park Commission. It is the green open space surrounded by high rise apartments, Seton Hall University, and urban residential streets. On the Newark-South Orange border, the park is roughly bounded by Mt. Vernon Place on the south and west, Seton Hall University to the north; and Tuxedo Parkway to the east. It was designed by the Olmsted Brothers firm in the 1930s after land was secured from the City of Newark in 1927. It was established to meet the recreational needs of the residents in this rapidly developing section of Newark, South Orange, and Irvington. The original tract of land measured 18 acres, which was enlarged by one acre to its current size in 1938. The first eleven years of development are credited to the Works Progress Administration laborers. An aerial photograph from 1931 shows the land as an open field with a scattering of trees.[1]

The following Olmsted Brothers employees worked on this park's design: Lyle L. Blundell; Percival Gallagher; Hans J. Koehler; Joseph F. Bannon; and Lawrence A. Enerson. In December 1929, the topographic maps produced by W. N. Brown, Inc., which showed the sizes and locations of existing trees and pre-existing roads were received at the Brookline office. In October 1930, an unsigned preliminary grading plan indicating main recreational features and paths had been created and Percival Gallagher drew up a foliage outline. In December 1930, an unsigned plan with proposed revised grades and a preliminary grading plan were prepared.

The simple planting plan for Ivy Hill Park included incorporating preexisting trees into the groves. The trees dwarf the field house built in the 1930s. *October 11, 2009.*

In December 1935, Hans J. Koehler and Joseph F. Bannon produced a planting list for planting around the field house. Notes indicate the Olmsted Brothers left the scheme undecided for planting until a pergola was built. The plan had additional notes about planting around the tennis courts. The grading plan for the field house was also produced in December 1935. Hans J. Koehler created the final planting plan for the field house in January 1936. In April 1937, Lawrence A. Enerson created a study plan for a bowling green and courts. The plan showed the courts, paths, tree locations, and a field house.

According to the Essex County Park Commission's annual reports, on November 12, 1935, work began on Ivy Hill Park. It consisted of the stripping and placing of topsoil and supplying and grading dirt from outside sources. A tool house was also built. By 1936, work was progressing more rapidly. The field house was built and the plantings were partially complete. Footpaths were laid out and four tennis courts were constructed. In the autumn, 2,500 trees and shrubs were planted. In 1937, the shelter at the children's playground was built and some concrete walkways were laid out. By 1938, the work consisted of completing the planting, installing the equipment at the playground, and completing the concrete sidewalks along Mt. Vernon Place.[2]

Under the terms of a 1986 agreement with Seton Hall University, the County has a 25-year, no-cost lease for one acre of University property that has six tennis courts. This land is contiguous with the park and brings the total number of courts in the park to ten. In exchange, the County rehabilitated the tennis courts and allowed Seton Hall University use of the park's facilities. Other improvements included redesign of the field area for football, soccer, baseball, and softball, and improvements to the existing basketball court and playground, along with general site work.

Recent improvements include: the installation of rubberized safety surface in the playground completed in 2003; modernization of three softball/baseball fields and installation of two new basketball courts completed in 2005. The park has a community memorial garden completed in 2008. It is to commemorate three murder victims, Terrance Aeriel, Dashon Harvey, and Iofemi Hightower, and to honor the bravery of survivor Natasha Aeriel. These four Newark students were shot in the Mount Vernon School playground in August 2007. Essex County Executive Joseph DiVincenzo spoke at the dedication ceremony. "This beautiful garden will provide current residents and future generations with a place to reflect and find solace. We hope this will become a revered place that will have a positive effect on the neighborhood and influence other young people to steer clear of gangs and violence, and to follow a productive path."[3]

Ivy Hill Park's border mound along Mt. Vernon Place can be seen in the background. This view shows the early autumn foliage of the grouped sycamore trees near the tennis courts. *October 11, 2009.*

Endnotes for Chapter 36: Ivy Hill Park

[1] Essex County Department of Parks, Recreation, and Cultural Affairs: http://www.essex-countynj.org/p/index.php?section=af/system.
[2] Essex County Park Commission Annual Reports for 1935, 1936, 1937, and 1938.

[3] April 7, 2008 press release located on the Essex County website: www.essex-countynj.org/index.php?section=pr/print/040708

Passaic County Parks and Garret Mountain Reservation: Paterson and West Paterson (1930)

Garret Mountain Reservation is the largest of four Passaic County parks designed by the Olmsted Brothers firm. The others include Goffle Brook Park in Hawthorne and Weasel Brook Park in Clifton (discussed in the next chapters), and Preakness Valley Park in Wayne, which is now a golf course and not included in this book. The movement to establish the Passaic County Park Commission began in 1925. One year later, sixteen prominent citizens petitioned the New Jersey Supreme Court for the appointment of a preliminary park commission, which was sworn in on July 3, 1926. The preliminary commission was charged to conduct a survey of possible land for parks, and to prepare a comprehensive plan for their acquisition, development, and maintenance. Following the lead of the neighboring Essex County, the Passaic County Park Commission selected the Olmsted Brothers firm to prepare a Master Plan. The firm submitted their plan on July 9, 1927. On November 8, 1927, the voters of Passaic County approved a referendum for the creation of a permanent park commission.[1]

Garret Mountain Reservation, a 568-acre recreational area situated more than 500 feet above sea level, provides sweeping views of northern New Jersey and the New York City skyline. The dramatic landscape is composed of the First Watchung Mountain. Overlooking the City of Paterson, the Passaic County Park Commission acquired the Lambert Castle property and over 500 of the adjacent acres in 1928.

The Lenape Indians first occupied this area. They used to drive deer off the cliffs of Garret Mountain. The area east of Paterson was settled by the Dutch starting around 1679. Due to the influence of Alexander Hamilton, Paterson became the first planned industrial city in the United States utilizing the powerful Great Falls. Later it became known as Silk City, due to the many silk manufactories located here. Garret Mountain got its name sometime after 1812. Local history indicates that members of a fraternal organization, the "Garret Society," named from the group's habit of holding secret meeting in attics or garrets, lugged an artillery piece up to the top of the mountain and set it off on the Fourth of July, waking the entire city. Another story is that the Jersey Dutch language had the term "Gebarrack" meaning "at the mountain" and that was changed into "Garret."[2]

The castle built by Catholina Lambert in 1892 is now the headquarters for both the Park System and the Passaic County Historical Society. "Belle Vista" was constructed of sandstone, much of it quarried from Garret Mountain. The interior of the Castle was organized around a three-story open atrium called the court. It was here that Lambert displayed many of his prized European and American paintings. In 1914, financial problems forced Lambert to mortgage his estate and sell his art collection. Lambert died in 1923, a few weeks shy of his 89th birthday. His son and heir, Walter, inherited the Castle and sold the furnishings and later the Castle itself for $125,000 to the City of Paterson. For several years, it was used as a fresh air camp for disadvantaged children. In 1934, the Passaic County Park Commission purchased the castle and renovated it for park system use. The Passaic County Historical Society established its museum and library in the Castle. The building is listed on the state and National Registers of Historic Places. Lambert Castle was extensively restored and rehabilitated over a five-year period by the Board of Chosen Freeholders, with the assistance of federal and state grants. The Castle was rededicated in September of 2000.[3]

This postcard shows the dramatic Garret Rock at the north end of Garret Mountain Reservation overlooking the City of Paterson in Passaic County.

The following Olmsted Brothers employees worked on the design of Garret Mountain Reservation: Edwin M. Prellwitz, Jack E. Pulver, Carroll A. Towne, Russell N. Barnes, Dana W. Clarke, Sen Yu, John B. Moseley, Henry McLaren, Percival Gallagher, Walter Clarke, James A. Britton, Benjamin S. Pray, and James Sturgis Pray.

The initial maps were received in offices of the Olmsted Brothers in December 1929 for the area around Lambert Castle. Edwin M. Prellwitz and Jack E. Pulver made a study for development of the region near the Castle. The plan includes the Lambert Castle with administration buildings, terrace, garden, swimming pool, and bathhouse. The grounds also include parking, the tower, Valley Road, Mill Street, and the bordering railroad with railroad station. In April 1930, Prellwitz created a plan that included the property line, roads, and a proposed shelter. In July 1930, Carroll A. Towne produced a preliminary plan for a shelter and Pulver drew the details for its construction. In October 1930 Prellwitz created a study for development and in April 1931 drafted the road and grading plan. Dana W. Clarke drew the road profiles for the same area.

Based on the Olmsted plans, the Passaic County Parks Commission produced a set of contract drawings for the construction of the main roadway through the Reservation. The detailed drawings show both the profile and plans of the curving roadway and the bridges and culverts. The original surface is shown and, in several places, the ledge rock needed to be removed.[4]

The basalt rocks in Garret Mountain Reservation. *October 8, 2009.*

The Stony Brook picnic shelter is located at the southern end of Barbour's Pond in Garret Mountain Reservation. *October 8, 2009.*

In March 1931, Russell N. Barnes drew a study for planting plan for the section between Lambert Castle and the Delaware, Lackawanna & Western Railroad underpass. That month, plans were generated for trails and the area surrounding the tower, as well as the planting plan for the area between the Old Quarry and Garret Rock. Edwin M. Prellwitz also designed a pergola with benches and a railing for the tower. In November 1931, the Olmsted Brothers staff produced the plan for grading the automobile lookout. In December 1931, Sen Yu drew the grading plan for the region about the tower and the approach to the castle. In January 1932, Prellwitz created a diagram for possible arrangement of swimming pool area and John B. Moseley revised the grading plan for the auto overlook. In February 1932, Benjamin S. Pray made a revised study for region about the castle. In March 1932, Russell N. Barnes developed the planting plan for the auto overlook that included the Benson Monument.

In 1935, the Passaic County Park Commission proposed projects to be paid for by the Works Progress Administration (WPA). Commission plans show a new parking area near Barbour's Pond and the creation of a series of winding footpaths and bridle paths. Certain areas of the Reservation woods were to be cleared of underbrush and dead wood turned into mulch. The large, terraced parking lot with stone walls was built by WPA laborers based on the Commission plans drawn in 1936. The stairs at the auto overlook and pergolas at the southern end of Barbour's pond were also built from Olmsted designs.

During World War Two, the fire tower built in 1911 on Garret Mountain was used as an early aircraft warning station. Barracks were also built. On top of the mountain is the 70-foot Lambert Tower, used as an observatory and summerhouse. In 1980, John Evans Architect and Planners drew a set of plans for a variety of improvements including tennis courts, boat docks, and a horse stable. Garret Mountain Reservation continues to offer park visitors a wide range of recreational activities and facilities. These facilities include an equestrian center, athletic fields, fishing, picnic grounds, jogging paths, and trails for cross country skiing, hiking and running. At the Garret Mountain Equestrian Center, residents can take horseback riding lessons or ride on the park's bridle paths.

These steps were designed by the Olmsted Brothers and built by Works Progress Administration laborers in the 1930s using locally found materials. *October 8, 2009.*

The Benson monument was included in the Olmsted Brothers' plan for the auto overlook at Garret Mountain Reservation. Robert Dix Benson was the first president of the Passaic County Park Commission. *December 9, 2010.*

Endnotes for Chapter 37: Garret Mountain

[1]From the Goffle Brook National Register Nomination written by Mary Delaney Krugman Associates in 2005.

[2]Charles A. Shriner. *Four Chapters of Paterson History*. (Paterson, N. J.: Lont & Overkamp Publishing Co., 1919): pp. 69-70

[3]Passaic County Park Commission website at: http://www. passaiccountynj.org/countyparks.htm

[4]The Passaic County Park Commission plans including those created by the Olmsted Brothers firm are on file at the Passaic County Engineering Office in Paterson.

Chapter 38
Goffle Brook Park: Hawthorne (1931)

Goffle Brook Park is a long and meandering park that traverses north to south following the course of its namesake Goffle Brook. This small creek flows through a portion of Hawthorne Borough in Passaic County. The park is run by the Passaic County Parks Commission and in 2002, was listed in the New Jersey and National Register of Historic Places. The 103-acre park is roughly bordered by Goffle Road on the west and north, several residential streets including May Street, Brookside Avenue, Bamford Avenue, and First Avenue to the east, and an industrial zone and Thomas Avenue to the south. There are four roadways carried by bridges over the brook: Goffle Hill Road, Rea Avenue, Warburton Avenue, and Diamond Bridge Avenue.

The Olmsted Brothers 1927 master plan for the Passaic County Park Commission suggested that the area along Goffle Brook was appropriate for a "Broad Open Meadow Park," which is similar to many others in New Jersey.[1]

This postcard view from Diamond Bridge Avenue shows the still pastoral setting of the banks of Goffle Brook. The card, postmarked in 1945, also shows on the right, a portion of a 1931 bridge that has recently been replaced.

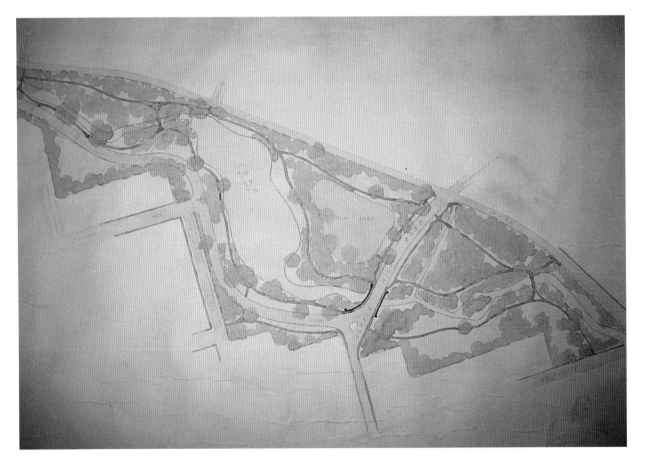

Detail from the Olmsted Brothers preliminary plan for Goffle Brook Park showing the northernmost pond. Edwin Prellwitz drew the plan with ink and watercolors in June 1931. *Courtesy of the Passaic County Office of the Engineer.*

The following Olmsted Brothers employees worked on the designs for Goffle Brook Park: Carroll A. Towne; A. W. Phillips; Joseph Bannon; Percival Gallagher; Edwin M. Prellwitz; Frank W. Sherman; John B. Moseley; Benjamin S. Pray; and Walter Clarke.

The Olmsted Brothers firm received the topographical maps in November 1929. The plan of the park is 28 inches wide and 103 inches long. Due to this extreme linearity, the land was divided into multiple sections defined by the cross streets. In June 1930, Carroll A. Towne produced a study for a bridge. Percival Gallagher conducted site visits and wrote field notes in March 1931. In July 1931, A. W. Phillips made a study for a bridge at Diamond Bridge Avenue and a grading study and cross sections. In March 1931, the plan for the proposed road was created. Edwin M. Prellwitz produced the preliminary grading plan for the entire park in June 1931, which included the locations of the roads, paths, pond,

meadow, and baseball playfield.[2] Prellwitz also conducted field visits and included his field notes in August 1931.

In September 1931, Walter Clarke and Prellwitz produced sections and profiles to accompany the preliminary grading plan. In October 1931, Frank W. Sherman produced a study of the vicinity of the pond. In December 1931, John B. Moseley produced a study of the pond and a plan for the southern portion and Sherman created a study of the change in road line between Diamond Bridge Avenue and South Avenue. In January 1932, Sherman produced a grading plan and cross sections for the southern section from Maitland Ave to Diamond Bridge Avenue and Benjamin S. Pray made a study for the development of school lands in relation to the parkway. Moseley produced the road profiles for the road to the field house and pond in January 1932. In February 1932, Carroll A. Towne produced study drawings with a side elevation and cross section for a footbridge and a sketch for a concrete highway bridge in Park Drive.

The Van Winkle Pond in the northern section of Goffle Brook Park. The Arnold Dam was built anew in 1936 by a Works Progress Administration construction crew. *June 13, 2009.*

In 1931, the Diamond Bridge Avenue bridge was rebuilt two feet higher to allow a footpath to follow the bank of the brook. Although the plans were created by 1932, the work of landscaping the park was largely carried out later by laborers in the Works Progress Administration (WPA) program during the 1930s' Depression. In 1935, WPA Project 1-188 named the "General Development of Goffle Brook Park" included road grading, brook relocation, grading of footpaths and general grading, excavation for a lake, (which was subsequently filled in), and reconstruction of the Arnold Dam at Van Winkle's Pond. The work was completed by December 1936. In subsequent years, several other WPA work projects furthered the park's development until it was complete in 1939. There are only a few aspects of the Olmsted Brothers' plans that were never executed due to financial constraints, such as the field house designed by John Moseley. In large part the plans were carried out and this park retains the gentle slopes and plantings envisioned by the firm. In 1982-1984, parts of the park were rehabilitated.[3]

On a rainy day, you virtually have the park to yourself. Here the lush greensward of the southern section with its gently slopes is topped by a memorial surrounded by hedges. *June 13, 2009.*

Goffle Brook Park in Hawthorne. The rain was heavy at times and made for a challenging photographic experience. In the distance is an historic footbridge carrying a path over Goffle Brook. *June 13, 2009.*

A sign at the footbridge indicates this is a truss bridge relocated from Ringwood. Historic preservation of engineered structures is as important as preservation of historic houses and parks. *March 15, 2009.*

Endnotes for Chapter 38: Goffle Brook Park

[1] All the information about the history of the park came from the National Register nomination written by Mary Delaney Krugman Associates in 2002. It is on file at the National Park Service in Washington, D.C.

[2] The original Olmsted Brothers preliminary plan is on file at the Passaic County Engineering Office in Paterson.

[3] All this information about the history of the park came from the National Register nomination written by Mary Delaney Krugman Associates in 2002. It is on file at the National Park Service in Washington, D.C.

Chapter 39
Weasel Brook Park: Clifton (1931)

This twenty-acre urban park is located in the City of Clifton. The neighborhood park is run by the Passaic County Parks Department and is roughly bounded on the north by Clinton Avenue; on the east by Third Street; on the south by Home Place; and on the west by Paulison Avenue. Long before it was a park, the land was owned by Gysbert Vanderhoef, who, in the early 1700s, built a house, a sawmill, and a grist mill. The mills were operated continuously for over 160 years.[1] In the early 20th century, the Martin Dairy Farm was located on this land.[2]

In the early 1930s, the Olmsted Brothers worked on planning this 20-acre park as part of the same project as a playground along Weasel Brook in a different section of Clifton (between Lexington and Central Avenues). That playground is no longer in existence. The grading plan for the larger park off Paulinson Avenue is on file at the Passaic County Engineering Office. This plan, #18, is a large grading study drawn by Edwin Prellwitz dated October 8, 1931. It included the topography and shows how the Olmsted Brothers changed the course of the creek, added ponds on both sides of a new curving road that connected Jewett Avenue to Gregory Avenue carried over the brook by a bridge. Other plans at the Frederick Law Olmsted Historic Site in Brookline include the topographical map, a plan for a fieldhouse, the foliage plan to accompany plan #18, and cross sections and profiles of the new roadway to accompany plan #18.

In the 1930s, this small pond was created with this semicircular weir at Weasel Brook Park in Clifton. The weeping willow trees located at the pond's edge are very characteristic of an Olmsted Brothers planting plan. *June 13, 2009.*

The rugged stone arch bridge itself was designed in 1935 by the Passaic County Park Commission as a Civil Works Administration project. The staff at the Office of County Engineers also designed the playground, footbridge, and the semi-circular masonry weir for the Passaic County Park Commission. The drawings were approved by County Engineer and Superintendent, Frederick W. Loede. Works Progress Administration laborers constructed the bridge in 1935 and 1936.

In 1937, a site plan of the Vanderhoof House located on the north side of the brook was drawn as part of the Historic American Buildings Survey. The plan shows the new park, the curving road, new bridge, and semi-circular weir forming the pond. The park has a pastoral lawn with a ring of trees and the main feature of the brook, which bisects the park. One of its unique features is its regulation horseshoe pits. They are one of the very few in the tri-state area and are often the site of professional horseshoe tournaments and championships.[3]

Weasel Brook Park in Clifton has at its center, a flowing stream that was redirected and deepened following the Olmsted Brothers plans. Works Progress Administration laborers built the stone arch bridge in 1935 and 1936. *June 13, 2009.*

Endnotes for Chapter 39: Weasel Brook Park

[1]David L. VanDillen. "Commerce and Industry," in Elvira Hessler, David L. VanDillen, and William J. Wurst, *A Clifton Sampler*. (Clifton, New Jersey: Clifton Public Library, 1991); p. 61.
[2]Sandra L. Giordano. *Clifton.* (Charleston, South Carolina: Arcadia Publishing, 2008); p. 13.
[3]From the Passaic County Department of Parks website:www. passaiccountynj/parkshistoricalparks/weaselbrookpark.html

Chapter 40

Parvin State Park: Pittsgrove (1931)

Parvin State Park is the Olmsted Brothers' park that is the furthest south in the state. It is a 1,137-acre park near Millville and Olivet in Salem County. Bounded by Almond Road on the north, Parvin Mill Road to the east, Morton Avenue to the south and Centerton Road to the west, aerial views show this is largely a heavily wooded property surrounded by vast tracts of farmland. A thousand years ago, the Lenape hunted and fished in the stream named Muddy Run, the stream that feeds Parvin Lake. What is now Parvin Sate Park was included in 2,928 acres of land purchased from the Proprietors of West New Jersey in 1742 by John Estaugh, which he later passed to Captain Richard Parker who sold the property to Lemuel Parvin in 1796.

Parvin Lake is a man-made lake. Around 1783, the Muddy Run was dammed to create a lake to power a sawmill. The mill and property remained in the Parvin family for many generations and in 1847, Lemuel Parvin replaced the old mill with a new one. When Lemuel's oldest child, Jane, married in 1849, he turned the mill over to his new son-in-law Coombs Ackley. The mill subsequently became

known as the Coombs Ackley Mill, and probably carried that identity for the remainder of its existence into the 1930s. Coombs Ackley also built the house at the southeast corner of Almond and Parvin Mill Road, where he and his family lived. Today, although not open to the public, the house is the oldest remaining building in the park, and provides a visible connection with the Parvin family, for whom the park was named.

In the late 1800s, Coombs Ackley sold the property, which later became Parvin State Park, to a man named Smith, who reportedly was the first to create recreational facilities around the lake, then known as Union Grove Lake. Smith established the beach and, about a mile upstream, the picnic area at Second Landing. Also on the north side of the lake near the main beach was a boat livery, concession stand, and caretaker's house. Bungalows were available for vacationers to rent and organized groups could rent the Community House. In the 1920s after overseeing Union Grove Lake for about 20 years, Smith left the property to his son. In 1930, the State purchased 918 acres of land and

This postcard view of Parvin State Park's beach at Parvin Lake was created after the new bathhouse was completed in 1938.

The lake reflecting the sunset light at Parvin State Park. The semi-circular, poured concrete spillway was built shortly after a flood destroyed the old dam in September 1940. *July 22, 2009.*

the 108-acre lake. On September 12, 1931, the property was dedicated as Parvin State Park.[1]

In 1931, the Olmsted Brothers were hired to provide a design for this new state park. The following employees worked on the plans: Walter Clarke; Edward D. Rando; William Lyman Phillips; James G. Langdon; James A. Britton; and Joseph F. Bannon.

Mr. Wilber of the Salem County Engineer's office drew maps showing the area of the state park lands including the former owners, boundaries of the options, and existing buildings. They were received at the Olmsted Brothers in Brookline in 1931. In September 1931, James G. Langdon worked on a study for arrangement of bathhouse lockers.

A preliminary study for the bathhouse showed the location of the water supply plant, the sewage treatment facility, road locations, and a park building. The proposal called for the county road to be relocated further from the shore of the lake in order to accommodate the bathhouse. The general plan and planting plan were produced in October 1931, showing the new bathhouse, parking lots, refectory, and recreational facilities and a replacement of some older buildings. James G. Langdon drew sketches of the bathhouse elevations and the plans for the bathhouse were drawn by James A. Britton. In January 1932, Joseph F. Bannon drew the revised general plan with new park improvements.

Similar to Highpoint State Park in Sussex County, Parvin Park was developed during the height of the 1930s' Great Depression by Civilian Conservation Corps laborers. In October 1933, Company 1225 was formed and assigned to the Parvin State Park Project. The workers moved into a camp located about one mile west of the main beach at Parvin State Park. The Army ran the camp in quasi-military fashion and there were barracks, a mess hall, and a recreation hall. The young men received $30 per month, $25 of which was to be sent home to their families.

Company 1225 remained at Parvin State Park until 1937. The laborers cleared portions of the forest for campsites, created trails and roadways, and constructed the gates, campsite markers, tent platforms, and pavilions. These pavilions survive at Jagger's Point, Island Point, and at Second Landing. Company 1225 also built the main beach complex including an enlarged beach, the brick buildings at the beach entrance, and the parking lot across the road. They built several bridges across the Muddy Run and dug the southern branch to the lake transforming the peninsula at the northeast corner of the lake into an island, which they then connected to the mainland by constructing a bridge. The island is now known as Flag Island for the American Flag the Scouts displayed there. One of Company 1225's biggest and most difficult tasks was the removal of fallen trees and digging out the muck from the swamp that would be transformed into Thundergust Lake.

After October 1937, the newly formed Company 2227V, comprised of World War One veterans, was stationed at Parvin Park. These skilled workers put the finishing touches on Thundergust Lake, built the adjoining picnic area, and completed the landscaping throughout the Park. They constructed all the rental cabins and the caretaker's cabin, most of which are still in use. They also replaced the southerly bridge to Flag Island with what is known today as White Bridge.

The 1938-1939 report of the Board of Conservation and Development, the agency in charge of state parks, stated that the new brick bathhouse completed in 1938, could accommodate 2,200 bathers. This new building replaced the previously inadequate one. Parking for 700 cars was also completed.[2]

Joseph Truncer was the first superintendent and he served from 1932 to 1947. He was succeeded by J. Ira Kolb, who was at the Park until 1957. Next was John Broshkevitch, who was succeeded by J. William Bailey in 1961. In 1971, Joe R. Reed took over and remained until 1998, when he was succeeded by W. Scott Mauger, who remained until 2003. The superintendent in 2006 was Dean Cramer. Today, Parvin State Park is known throughout New Jersey and many other states as an exceptional recreation and natural area, and is enjoyed by people from many parts of the United States.[3]

Thundergust Lake at Parvin State Park is a manmade lake created by the Civilian Conservation Corps in the 1930s. *July 22, 2009.*

Flower garden near the Olmsted Brothers designed bathhouse at Parvin State Park. These plantings attract butterflies. *July 22, 2009.*

Endnotes for Chapter 40: Parvin State Park

[1]Herbert G. Wegner, Parvin State Park Appreciation Committee. "A History of Parvin State Park," August 2006. On the website at www. friendsofparvin.org.

[2]Board of Conservation and Development. *Report of the Board of Conservation and Development.* (Trenton, New Jersey: The Board, 1938-1939); p. 27.

[3]Herbert G. Wegner, Parvin State Park Appreciation Committee. "A History of Parvin State Park," August 2006. On the website at www. friendsofparvin.org.

Chapter 41

Mills Reservation: Cedar Grove and Montclair (1958)

Mills Reservation is a 157-acre reservation located in Cedar Grove and Montclair. It is bordered by Reservoir Drive on the west, Normal Avenue on the north, Highland Avenue to the east, and Mountainside Park, a Montclair Township park, on the south. In 1954, the Essex County Park Commission received a gift of 119 acres from the Davella Mills Foundation. Additional acreage was acquired in a land exchange for some County property in Branch Brook Park that went to Newark for Barringer High School. Even more acreage purchased in 1962 and 1967 completed Mills Reservation. The stipulation of the original gift was that the land be preserved in its natural state. In an earlier 1915 report, the Olmsted Brothers recommended that Essex County develop a Crest Parkway Project (that included this tract of land on Watchung Mountain known as "The Crest") that would be a high view-commanding parkway not to be equaled in the eastern Atlantic states, except for the Palisades along the Hudson River."[1]

The stone piers have plaques marking the southern entryway into Mills Reservation. *October 22, 2009.*

In March 1955, the Olmsted Brothers received the topographical maps from Essex County. In September 1958 the firm created a preliminary plan showing the roads, areas of trees, buildings, parking, and overlooks. A preliminary study plan, created in April 1961, included the additional land purchased from City of Newark and picnic areas, paths, and shelters. In May 1961, revised plans included a playground and a fence, contours, roads, and fences. The only development actually undertaken on this land was a small parking area and a system of walking trails, which gives the public access to the interior. This minimal design by the Olmsted Brother firm represents the last association between the company and the Essex County Park Commission.

This woodland always attracts hikers and bird watchers, who observe migratory birds, such as warblers in the spring and hawks in the fall. The outcrop at Quarry Point provides a scenic lookout.[2] Although the Olmsted Brothers company was involved, the plans were never carried out. There is too little landscape architectural development to distinguish this reservation as anything but a planned suburban wilderness.

The view through autumn foliage is looking east toward New York City from Mills Reservation. *October 22, 2009.*

Endnotes for Chapter 41: Mills Reservation

[1] Resolution for Mountaintop Park adopted by the Town of Montclair Planning Board on May 4, 1953. In the files of the Essex County Parks Department.
[2] Essex County Department of Parks, Recreation, and Cultural Affairs: http://www.essex-countynj.org/p/index.php?section=af/system.

Chapter 42

Lenape Park: Springfield, Union, Cranford, Kenilworth, and Westfield (1962)

Lenape Park is the youngest park in New Jersey that was designed with input from an Olmsted named company. Located at the intersection of five municipalities in Union County, it is roughly bounded by Kenilworth Avenue on the south; the Rahway River on the east; Diamond Road on the north; and County Park Road on the west. It connects Echo Lake Park with Nomahegan Park and Black Brook Park. It is a 450-acre natural area and part of a green chain of Union County parks that follows along the course of the Rahway River as it traverses the county. The new East Coast Greenway passes through this park. Within the heavily wooded parkland, Normahiggin and Black Brooks join the north branch of the Rahway River as it flows south through various municipalities, eventually emptying into the Arthur Kill, the tidal strait that separates New Jersey from Staten Island.

The land comprising Lenape Park was acquired by Union County in the 1920s. It consists mostly of forested wetland but also includes various developed and managed features. The main entrance is a landscaped median (Nomahegan Boulevard) located at the Park's southeastern border. This entrance terminates at a small parking lot bounded by a managed bluebird habitat, a small field house built in 1927, and a shooting range. A second entrance for pedestrians only is located off Nomahegan Drive and leads to a pond.[1]

In the fall of 1962, the Park Commission retained the Olmsted Associates to prepare a preliminary development plan for the area and to recommend the most desirable use of this area for the people of Union County. The preliminary development plan shows a network of connected walkways and roads circulating through the land with arboretums and meadows. The landscape architects determined that this area offered more potential for free play recreational needs rather than for sports and organized recreational activities. The Park Commission set aside $50,000 to start the development. In October 1963, the Commission began work in this area and began clearing work in the section across from Echo Lake Park and extending down along Normahiggin Brook for about 1,000 feet.[2]

In 1961, the company made planimeter readings and one year later produced a key map of the area. The topographic maps were produced for the area between Kenilworth Boulevard, Echo Lake Park, Route 22, and Black Brook Park in March 1963. The firm also received an overlay map showing areas prone to flooding. The preliminary plans of the west and east sections were drawn up in May 1963. A third plan showed baseball field, picnic areas, a flood spillway, an observation tower and a skeet shooting range. The firm produced flood plain diagrams and a preliminary development plan for a report and a study for the proposed park roadway from Springfield Avenue.

The Olmsted Brothers created a pond in the south portion of Lenape Park just off Kenilworth Boulevard. This contoured pond has native plantings along its banks. *May 17, 2009.*

The firm produced a study of a roadway and water channel for the preliminary developmental plan. The areas covered included the layout and grades near Manitou circle, the boating area, the arboretum, and observation tower. Later, they worked on the layout for the picnic area and game field, made revisions to the roads in the east section and in the west section, and made changes to the roads and notes on plantings. In July 1963, study plans were created showing the profiles of the estimated cuts and fills. The schematic circulation layouts were produced this month as well. In July 1963, the firm created the general park plan and a grading plan for a pond excavation along Normahiggin Brook in November 1963. An aerial photograph from 1964 shows the two ponds; one in the western section and the second near Kenilworth Boulevard, and series of trails though the heavily wooded park.

In the 1970s, the Army Corps of Engineers changed the appearance of the park with their Rahway River flood control project. The course of the Normahiggin Brook was altered and a berm topped with an asphalt path was built between 1979 and 1987 to contain flood waters to the park. By far, the land of Lenape Park has remained undeveloped. The Olmsted Associates firm recommended a naturalistic approach that combined conservation of habitat with rural pastimes. However, most of the Olmsted suggestions for buildings, roads, and landscaped areas were never implemented and the woodland habitat remains the predominant one here.[3] Lenape Park remains an important linking park along the Rahway River corridor within the Union County Park system.

Lenape Park also is significant as the last work by an Olmsted-named landscape architectural firm in the state of New Jersey. It is hoped that the Olmsted legacy is one of great historic importance to be treasured and protected for future generations.

The largely natural Lenape Park is home to many species of flora and fauna, including white tailed deer. *May 17, 2009.*

Lenape Park features a fishing pond near the park entrance at Nomahegan Drive. *May 17, 2009.*

Endnotes for Chapter 42: Lenape Park

[1] Lenape Park Bio-Blitz: http://www.kean.edu/~scodella/BioBlitz05/Lenape.html
[2] Union County Park Commission. *Report of the Union County Park Commission 1958-1963*; n.p.
[3] Lenape Park Bio-Blitz: http://www.kean.edu/~scodella/BioBlitz05/Lenape.html

Chapter 43
Olmsted Brothers Employees

Aldrich, Raymond W: He was employed from 1931 to 1952. He was a member of the American Society of Landscape Architects beginning in 1908 and in the 1920s, was Secretary of the Boston Chapter. He worked on South Mountain Reservation and Wheeler Park.

Andrews, Wolcott E.: He was an employee from 1930-1948 and worked on Mattano Park and Wheeler Park.

Archibald, Carlton M.: He was an employee from 1929 to 1942. He worked on South Mountain Reservation (1933), Rahway River Park, Watchung Reservation, Cedar Brook Park, Echo Lake Park, Warinanco Park, Wheeler Park, Woodbridge Park, and Brookdale Park.

Auten, Andrew: He graduated from Oberlin College in 1896 and became a member of the American Society of Landscape Architects in 1904. He worked on Weequahic Park in 1902.

Bannon, Joseph F.: He was an employee from 1918 to 1925. He worked on Vailsburg Park (1920), Green Brook Park, Maplewood Park, Rahway River Park, Cedar Brook Park, Echo Lake Park, Wheeler Park (1926), Parvin Park (1931) Verona Park (1931), South Mountain Reservation (1933), Woodbridge Park, Brookdale Park, Goffle Brook Park, Ivy Hill Park (1935), and Branch Brook Park (1937).

Barnes, Russell N.: He was an employee from 1927 to 1936. He worked on Watsessing Park, Rahway River Park, Watchung Reservation, Warinanco Park, Mattano Park (1929), Wheeler Park, and Garret Mountain Reservation (1931).

Blossom, Henry Hill: He became a junior member of the American Society of Landscape Architects in 1914. He worked on Watsessing Park, Irvington Park, and South Mountain Reservation.

Blundell, Lyle L.: An employee from 1924-1934, in 1931, he became a Professor of Horticulture at the University of Massachusetts at Amherst. He worked on Branch Brook Park (1924), Echo Lake Park (1924-25), Riverbank Park (1927), Woodbridge Park (1928), South Mountain Reservation

(1929), Eagle Rock Reservation (1929), Eastside Park, Orange Park, Brookdale Park (1930-31), Irvington Park, Glenfield and Wheeler Park in 1931, Ivy Hill Park, Verona Park, Rahway River Park, Watchung Reservation, and Cedar Brook Park.

Bourne, Frank A.: Trained as an architectural draftsman, he worked on Branch Brook Park, South Mountain Reservation (the pumping station) in 1898, and Eagle Rock Reservation in 1898.

Bradley, George: Employed in 1924, he worked on Rahway River Park, Watchung Reservation, Cedar Brook Park, and Echo Lake Park.

Britton, James A.: He was an architecture student who graduated from Syracuse University in 1925 and was employed at the Olmsted Brothers firm from 1925 to 1933. He designed the bandstand at Green Brook Park in 1926 and the Parvin Park's bathhouse in 1931. He also worked on Wheeler Park and Garret Mountain Reservation.

Canning, Hubert M.: Employed in 1919, he worked on Westside Park and Branch Brook Park.

Carpenter, Thomas E.: Employed by the Olmsted Brothers from 1918 to 1930, and went on to have a long career with the National Park Service. He worked on South Mountain Reservation, Westside Park (1921), Riverbank Park, Vailsburg Park (1921), Cedar Brook Park (1924), Echo Lake Park (1924-25), Warinanco Park (1924), Green Brook Park (1926), Maplewood Park, Rahway River Park, Watchung Reservation, Verona Park and Wheeler Park (1926), and Mattano Park (1927).

Clark, Dana W.: Employed from 1929 to 1932, he worked on Verona Park (1931) and Garret Mountain Reservation.

Clarke, Walter F.: He worked on South Mountain Reservation (1927), Branch Brook Park (1927, 1931) Mattano Park (1927), Wheeler Park (1929) and Eagle Rock Reservation (1932). He joined the United States Army Corps of Engineers at the start of World War II and remained with the Corps following the war.

Clarke, Walter J.: He worked on South Mountain Reservation in 1902 and Irvington Park in 1909.

Clarke, Arthur: Employed from 1918 to 1954, he worked on Branch Brook Park, Eagle Rock Reservation, Weequahic Park, Watsessing Park, Irvington Park, Rahway River Park, Cedar Brook Park, Warinanco Park, Elizabeth River Park, Wheeler Park, Garret Mountain Reservation, Goffle Brook Park, Ivy Hill Park, and Parvin Park.

Clune, John J.: Employed from 1913 to 1928, he worked on South Mountain Reservation (1913) and Yantacaw Park.

Comerford, A.: He worked on Branch Brook Park, Eagle Rock Reservation, Watsessing Park (1908), Irvington Park, and Riverbank Park.

Cook, Wilber David Jr., (1869-1938): He was employed circa 1898 to 1906. He became a member of the American Society of Landscape Architects in 1906 and a Fellow in 1910. He worked on Branch Brook Park (1898-1899, 1903), Eagle Rock Reservation (1899), Orange Park, South Mountain Reservation (1898), Weequahic Park (1902), Eastside Park, Westside Park, and Anderson Park.

Culham, Gordon J.: An employee from 1926-1930, he worked on Warinanco Park and Wheeler Park.

Dall, Marcus H.: He worked on Branch Brook Park in 1899 and Watsessing Park in 1912.

Dawson, James Frederick (1874 –1941): Dawson studied agriculture and horticulture at Harvard and graduated in 1896. He began work in the Olmsted Brothers firm, becoming an expert in landscape design and plant material. In 1904, John Charles Olmsted and Frederick Law Olmsted, Jr. chose Dawson to be the first associate partner. Dawson would spend his entire career with the firm. He became a junior member of the American Society of Landscape Architects beginning in 1905 and was named a Fellow in 1914. He worked on Branch Brook Park (1899-1903), Eagle Rock Reservation, Orange Park, Weequahic Park (1900), Westside Park, Watsessing Park, and Anderson Park.

De Forest, Alling Stephen (1875-1957): Trained as a draftsman at the Taylor Business College, he would be employed at the Olmsted Brothers firm beginning in 1897 and again from 1899 to 1900. He was a Fellow in the American Society of Landscape Architects beginning in 1908. He worked on Branch Brook Park (1900) and Orange Park.

Donovan, Benjamin G.: He worked on South Mountain Reservation (1914-1922), Weequahic Park, Vailsburg Park (1920), Green Brook Park (1923), Rahway River Park, Watchung Reservation, High Point Park, Warinanco Park, Brookdale Park (1930), and Eagle Rock Reservation (1931).

Dorr, P. W.: He worked on Weequahic Park, (1910), Westside Park, Watsessing Park (1911), Irvington Park (1912), Riverbank Park (1912), Glenfield Park (1910), Yantacaw Park (1913), Grover Cleveland Park (1915), and Vailsburg Park (1920).

Douglas, Edward A.: He was employed from 1908 to 1933. He worked on Branch Brook Park (1899-1900), Weequahic Park, Westside Park (1900), Green Brook Park (1923), and Watchung Reservation.

Doyle, J. Louis: He worked on Branch Brook Park, Eagle Rock Reservation (1901), and Vailsburg Park (1920).

Edmunds, J. S.: He worked on South Mountain Reservation (1898), Branch Brook Park (1899), Weequahic Park (1900), and Watsessing Park (1900).

Eliot, Charles W. (1899-1993): Named after his uncle Charles Eliot, who had been a partner in the firm Olmsted, Olmsted & Eliot, Charles W. Eliot was a student at Harvard College in 1917, took leave to participate in World War One, returned to college and graduated in 1920. He received a master's degree in 1923 from the School of Landscape Architecture. He apprenticed with the Olmsted Brothers firm and worked on Vailsburg Park, Verona Park, and Green Brook Park (1922).

Enerson, Lawrence A.: An employee from 1935 to 1939, he worked on Brookdale Park and Ivy Hill Park (1935).

French, Prentiss (b. 1894): He earned a Master's Degree in Landscape Architecture from Harvard in 1921 and worked for the Olmsted Brothers from 1921 to 1924. He worked on Weequahic Park and Green Brook Park (1922).

Gallagher, Percival R. (1874-1934): One of the most important employees for the New Jersey parks, he studied horticulture at Harvard's Bussey Institute and took classes in the Fine Arts program where he met Frederick Law Olmsted, Jr. Graduating in 1894, Gallagher joined firm of Olmsted, Olmsted, & Eliot. His projects there included restoration of the plants on the U. S. Capitol Grounds in Washington, D.C. In 1904, he attempted to open a firm with landscape architect James Sturgis Pray. Gallagher was not very proficient running a firm and he returned to the Olmsted Brothers company after two years. He became a junior member of the American Society of Landscape Architects in 1904 and was named a Fellow in 1910. In 1914, he joined the executive committee. In 1927, he became a full partner at Olmsted Brothers, Landscape Architects. He worked on South Mountain Reservation (1899), Eagle Rock Reservation (1901-1902), Watsessing Park (1911), Weequahic Park (1914, 1918), Yantacaw Park, Grover Cleveland Park (1915), Belleville Park (1915-17), Verona Park, Green Brook Park (1922), Rahway River Park, Branch Brook Park (1924), Watchung Reservation, Cedar Brook Park (1924, 1927, 1932), Library Square in Plainfield (1924), Echo Lake Park, Warinanco Park, Wheeler Park (1925), Briant Park, Brookdale Park, Garret Mountain Reservation, Goffle Brook Park, Ivy Hill Park, and Mattano Park (1927).

Glover, Benjamin F.: An employee from 1921 to 1926, he worked on Echo Lake Park and Warinanco Park.

Graham, James D.: An employee from 1926 to 1930, he worked on Branch Brook Park (1926), Eagle Rock Reservation, Watsessing Park, Rahway River Park, Cedar Brook Park, Echo Lake Park, Elizabeth River Park, and Woodbridge Park (1928).

Greenleaf, James L. (1857-1933): Greenleaf graduated from the Columbia School of Mines and after practicing as a civil engineer in the late 1890s, turned to landscape architecture. He was a Fellow in the ASLA beginning in 1904 and was ASLA President from 1922-1927. He was on the National Commission of Fine Arts from 1918-1927. After World War I, he supervised the landscaping of cemeteries of the American dead in France. He also had much to do with landscaping the grounds about the Lincoln Memorial in Washington. He worked on Verona Park (1922) and Mattano Park.

Halfenstein, A. John: He worked on Eagle Rock (1919), Weequahic Park (1922), and Warinanco Park (1923).

Herbst, J. B.: He worked in Branch Brook Park, Eagle Rock Reservation (1899), Watsessing Park (1900), and Anderson Park.

Hubbard, Henry Vincent (1875-1947): Hubbard graduated Harvard School 1897. He was employed in the Olmsted Brothers firm from 1901-1906 before assuming a teaching post at Harvard University where he became known for his innovative use of actual design problems in the classroom. He was a member of the American Society for Landscape Architects beginning 1905 and became a fellow in 1910. He served as ASLA president from 1931-1935. He worked on Branch Brook Park (1901-1903).

Humans, William M.: He worked on Branch Brook Park (1905), South Mountain Reservation, and Anderson Park.

Jackson, Robert Fuller (b. 1875): He graduated from Massachusetts Institute of Technology in 1903 and was employed by the Olmsted Brothers firm as an architectural draftsman beginning in 1909. He worked on Branch Brook Park (1909), Weequahic Park, Grover Cleveland Park (1915), and Cedar Brook Park (1924).

Jeffers, T. C.: He worked on Anderson Park, Riverbank Park (1912), Glenfield Park, and Yantacaw Park (1912).

Jones, Percy R.: Employed from 1886 to 1927, and Chief Assistant in 1910, he worked on Cadwalader Park, Branch Brook Park (1898 –1904, 1920, 1924), Eagle Rock Reservation (1899-1901, 1909, 1911), South Mountain Reservation (1902, 1924), Weequahic Park (1901, 1910, 1924), Watsessing Park (1908), Westside Park, Anderson Park, Irvington Park (1908), Riverbank Park (1908), Glenfield Park, Yantacaw Park (1912), Vailsburg Park (1920), Verona Park (1921-22), Green Brook Park (1924), Maplewood Park, Rahway River Park, Watchung Reservation, Cedar Brook Park (1924), Echo Lake Park (1924-25), Warinanco Park (1923), Mattano Park (1927), Wheeler Park, and Elizabeth River Park.

Keeling, Edward L.: He worked on Weequahic Park (1910), Westside Park, Irvington Park (1910), Glenfield Park, Watsessing Park (1915), Yantacaw Park, and Grover Cleveland Park.

Kellaway, Herbert J. (1867–1947): A major figure among landscape architects in the United States, Kellaway learned his art and craft in Frederick Law Olmsted's office. He began to practice independently in 1906, and was elected a Fellow of the American Society of Landscape Architects in 1912. Expert in laying out home plantings, he published a book *How to Lay Out Suburban Home Grounds* in 1907. He worked on Branch Brook Park (1899), Eagle Rock Reservation (1899), Orange Park (1900), Weequahic Park, and Watsessing Park (1901).

Koehler, Hans J.: He was an employee from 1890 to 1945 and a tree expert. The Olmsted Brothers published his book *A List of Common Names for Trees*, in 1915. He worked on Branch Brook Park (1903), Eagle Rock Reservation (1910), Eastside Park, South Mountain Reservation (1909-1927), Weequahic Park (1922), Irvington Park, Riverbank Park, Green Brook Park (1922), Verona Park (1931), Brookdale Park (1930-1937), and Ivy Hill Park.

Langdon, James G.: He was employed from 1925-1935. He became a Fellow in the American Society of Landscape Architects beginning 1918. He worked on Parvin Park in (1931).

Larsen, Johan Selmer (1876-1967): Born in Norway in 1876, he joined his grandfather's coppersmith business, which was engaged in adorning public buildings. Larsen followed his dreams to the United States and landed a job with the Olmsted office in Brookline. He was an employee from 1917-1921 and worked on Echo Lake Park.

LaVallee, L. Palmer: Graduated from Worcester Academy in 1916, he was an employee from 1925-1935. He worked on Rahway River Park and Cedar Brook Park.

Lenehan, George T.: He was an employee from 1931 to 1945 and worked on Brookdale Park (1931) and Garret Mountain Reservation.

Malley, Frank H.: He was an employee from 1924 to 1937 and worked on Branch Brook Park and Echo Lake Park.

Manning, A. Chandler: He was an employee from 1910 to 1934. He was a member of the American Society of Landscape Architects beginning in 1921. He worked on Weequahic Park, Watsessing Park, and Grover Cleveland Park.

Manning, Warren H.: He was president of the American Society of Landscape Architects from 1913-1914. He worked on Watsessing Park (1915).

Marquis, William Bell (1887-1978): Graduated from Harvard in 1912 with a Masters degree in Landscape Architecture, he became a Member of the American Society of Landscape Architects in 1920. He was an employee from 1919 to 1962 and became a partner in 1937. He worked on Branch Brook Park, Green Brook Park (1922), and Echo Lake Park.

McLaren, Henry: He was an employee from 1930 to 1933 and worked on Branch Brook Park, Brookdale Park, and Garret Mountain Reservation.

Millard, Herbert E.: He graduated Harvard, class of 1898. He was an employee from 1909 to 1944. He worked on Branch Brook Park (1912), Orange Park, Weequahic Park, Glenfield Park (1910), and Westside Park (1912).

Mische, Emanuel Tillman (1870-1934): He was a world class horticulturist who worked at the Olmsted Brothers firm for eight years. He became a member of the American Society of Landscape Architects in 1905 and was named a Fellow in 1918. He worked on Branch Brook Park (1899-1901), Eagle Rock Reservation (1899), Orange Park, and Weequahic Park (1901).

Moseley, John B.: He was an employee in the 1930s. He worked on Branch Brook Park, Eagle Rock Reservation, Brookdale Park (1930-31), Garret Mountain Reservation (1932), and Goffle Brook Park.

Munroe, William H.: He became a member of the American Society of Landscape Architects in 1919. He worked on Weequahic Park, Westside Park (1900), Eagle Rock Reservation (1901), South Mountain Reservation (1902), Orange Park, and Watsessing Park.

Nicolesco, Theodore: He worked on Orange Park and Branch Brook Park in 1899.

Nye, Henry C.: He was an employee in the 1930s and was the chief landscape architect for the 1939 World's Fair in New York City. He worked on Verona Park, Rahway River Park, Cedar Brook Park, Echo Lake Park, Warinanco Park, and Wheeler Park.

Olmsted, Frederick Law, Senior (1822-1903): Best known as the landscape architect that designed Central Park in New York. He studied engineering and chemical and physical science in their relation to agriculture at Yale, then engaged himself to a farmer as a common laborer with a view of learning the practical details of farming. When the Central Park Commission was created in New York City in 1856, he was awarded the highest premium for his plans for the park, competing with thirty-four others. The following year he was appointed landscape architect and superintendent of the Park. During the early part of the Civil War, he served as secretary to the United States Sanitary Commission. In association with his partners he designed, besides the parks for New York, those of Brooklyn, Boston, Montreal, Chicago, and other cities as well as the grounds and terraces of the Capitol at Washington and the Columbian Exposition in Chicago. He designed Cadwalader Park in Trenton (1891).

Olmsted, Frederick Law, Junior (1870-1957): The son of Frederick Law Olmsted, Senior. He was a graduate of Harvard University (1894) and a founding partner of the Olmsted Brothers landscaping firm, along with his stepbrother, John Charles Olmsted. By 1920 his projects included metropolitan park systems and greenways throughout the country. He was a founding member of the

American Society of Landscape Architects. In New Jersey, he worked on Eagle Rock Reservation (1899) and Verona Park.

Olmsted, John Charles (1852-1920): The nephew and stepson of Frederick Law Olmsted, Sr., John Charles Olmsted was a graduate of Yale's Sheffield Scientific School. With his stepbrother, Frederick Law Olmsted, Jr., he founded Olmsted Brothers, a landscape architectural firm in Brookline, Massachusetts. The Olmsted Brothers company continued the landscape design work begun by his stepfather. The firm designed many urban parks, park systems, grounds of private estates, and college campuses in the 20th century. In 1899, John Olmsted was a founding member and first president of the American Society of Landscape Architects. He worked on the following parks and reservations in New Jersey: West Side Park, Branch Brook Park (1898-1899), Orange Park (1898), Eagle Rock Reservation (1899), South Mountain Reservation (1898-1901), Weequahic Park (1899-1900, 1908), Anderson Park (1903), Irvington Park, Riverbank Park (1908), and Glenfield Park (1910).

Parker, Carl Rust (1882-1966): He graduated from Phillips Academy in 1901, which provided him his only landscape architecture training. He was employed in the Olmsted Brothers firm from 1901-1910 and 1919-1961 as a draftsman, planting designer, and supervisor of construction. He was a member of the ASLA, beginning in 1908, and became a Fellow in 1915. In 1950, Parker became a partner of the Olmsted Brothers where he remained until his retirement in 1961 at age seventy-nine. He worked on Branch Brook Park (1904), South Mountain Reservation, Weequahic Park, Watsessing Park (1910), Anderson Park, Irvington Park, Riverbank Park, Cedar Brook Park, Echo Lake Park, and Warinanco Park (1924).

Phillips, William Lyman (d. 1966): In 1910, he graduated with honors from Harvard and the next year joined the Olmsted Brothers firm where he was employed until 1949. He was a member of the ASLA beginning 1912. During World War I, he built cantonments in the United States for the Quartermaster Corps and was later in charge of landscaping American military cemeteries in France. He worked on South Mountain Reservation, Anderson Park, Rahway River Park, Briant Park, Brookdale Park (1930-31), Garret Mountain Reservation, and Parvin Park.

Phillips, A. W.: He worked on South Mountain Reservation (1928), Rahway River Park, Goffle Brook Park, and Branch Brook Park (1928).

Platt, Clarence Deforest: Graduated from Harvard University with a Masters in Landscape Architecture in

1925, he was employed from 1925 to 1928. He worked on Watchung Reservation.

Pray, Benjamin S.: He was the son of James Sturgis Pray. He attended the Harvard University School of Landscape Architecture in the 1920s. He was employed by the Olmsted Brothers in 1929 and worked on Garret Mountain Reservation and Goffle Brook Park.

Pray, James Sturgis (1871-1929): A native of Boston and a graduate of Harvard in 1898, he worked in the Olmsted Brothers office from 1898 to 1903. He became a member of the American Society of Landscape Architects in 1903, a Fellow in 1906, and he served as president from 1915 to 1920. He worked on Orange Park.

Pree, Henry: He worked on Weequahic Park (1914), Westside Park, Vailsburg Park (1920), Verona Park (1922), Green Brook Park, and Maplewood Park.

Prellwitz, Edwin M.: He worked on South Mountain Reservation (1920), Rahway River Park, Cedar Brook Park, Library Square in Plainfield (1924), Echo Lake Park (1925), Wheeler Park (1925), Mattano Park (1927-29), Briant Pond Park (1930), Brookdale Park (1930-33), Weasel Brook Park (1931), Eagle Rock Reservation (1932), Garret Mountain Reservation, and Goffle Brook Park.

Price, Thomas D.: A graduate of Ohio State University and Harvard University, he was employed from 1927 to 1932. He worked on Eastside Park, Rahway River Park, and Watchung Reservation.

Pulver, Jack E.: He worked on Rahway River Park, Warinanco Park, and Garret Mountain Reservation (1930).

Rando, Edward D.: He worked on Branch Brook Park (1927), Riverbank Park (1927), Verona (1927), Eagle Rock Reservation (1931), Rahway River Park, Cedar Brook Park, Mattano Park (1929), Woodbridge Park, Brookdale Park, and Parvin Park.

Richmond, H. P.: Trained as an architectural draftsman at the Massachusetts Institute of Technology, he worked on Orange Park (1898), Branch Brook Park (1899), South Mountain Reservation, Weequahic Park (1900), and Westside Park.

Sawyer, Ralph Eldon: A 1908 graduate of Harvard, he worked on Branch Brook Park (1902-1904), South Mountain Reservation, Weequahic park (1910), Watsessing Park, Anderson Park, Riverbank Park, and Glenfield Park (1912).

Scholtes, A. G.: He worked on Echo Lake Park, Cedar Brook Park (1943), and Warinanco Park.

Scott, J. Harry: He worked on Echo Lake Park (1925), Verona Park (1926), Branch Brook Park (1927), South Mountain Reservation (1928, 1933), Green Brook Park, Maplewood Park, Rahway River Park, Cedar Brook Park, Warinanco Park, and Briant Park.

Sherman, Milton F.: He worked on Branch Brook Park, South Mountain Reservation (1927), Cedar Brook Park, Echo Lake Park, and Goffle Brook Park.

Sloet, Jacob H.: He worked on South Mountain Reservation, Weequahic Park (1924), Cedar Brook Park (1924), and Brookdale Park.

Smith, Faris B.: He worked on High Point Park in 1923.

Smith, Alfred J.: He worked on Branch Brook Park, Eagle Rock Reservation, Weequahic Park (1900), Watsessing Park, Warinanco Park, and Cedar Brook Park.

Smith, William G.: He drew the plan of South Mountain Reservation in 1902.

Spooner, Arthur E.: He worked on Branch Brook Park and Grover Cleveland Park.

Sturgis, Edward: He graduated from Harvard in 1890 and worked on Branch Brook Park (1899, 1902), Eagle Rock Reservation (1899), Orange Park (1898), and Westside Park.

Sullivan, John J.: He worked on Eagle Rock Reservation, Glenfield Park, Verona Park (1932), and Brookdale Park (1931).

Towne, Carroll A.: He worked on Riverbank Park (1929-31), Mattano Park, Goffle Brook Park, and Garret Mountain Reservation (1930).

Vinal, Arthur H. (1854-1923): He was an architectural draftsman and worked on Branch Brook Park (1898-1901), Orange Park, Westside Park (1899), and Weequahic Park (1900).

Wait, C. R.: An architectural draftsman, he worked on Branch Brook Park (1899), Watsessing Park (1908), Eagle Rock Reservation (1909), Riverbank Park (1908), Westside Park, Watsessing Park (1908), Yantacaw Park, and Grover Cleveland Park.

White, Stanley Hart (1891-1979): He graduated from Harvard with a Masters of Landscape Architecture in 1915 and was an Olmsted Brothers employee from 1916 to 1920, becoming a Member of the American Society of Landscape Architects in 1921. He became known as one of the most important educators of landscape architecture during his 37-year career at the University of Illinois. He worked on Branch Brook Park, Weequahic Park (1918), Westside Park, and Watsessing Park.

Whiting, Edward Clarke (1881-1962): Graduated from Harvard in 1903 and joined the firm in 1905. Whiting became a partner in 1920 and he spent his entire professional career with the Olmsted Brothers firm until 1959. He became a Member of the American Society of Landscape Architects in 1912. He worked on Cadwalader Park, Branch Brook Park, Weequahic Park (1922), Anderson Park, Vailsburg Park (1922), Rahway River Park, and Brookdale Park (1936).

Wood, Paul E.: He worked on Branch Brook Park (1899, 1921), Weequahic Park, Vailsburg Park (1920), Green Brook Park (1922), and Warinanco Park.

Woodberry, Gordon: He worked on Branch Brook Park (1928), Rahway River Park, Echo Lake Park, Warinanco Park, and Mattano Park (1929).

Woolner, William C.: He worked on Branch Brook Park (1899), Eagle Rock Reservation (1899), South Mountain Reservation (1900), Orange Park, Weequahic Park (1899-1901), Westside Park, and Watsessing Park (1901).

Wyman, Alanson Phelps (1870-1947): He was employed from 1899 to 1902. He became a member of the American Society of Landscape Architects in 1905 and a Fellow in 1912. He worked on Branch Brook Park and Weequahic Park in 1901.

Yu, Sen: He was an architectural draftsman. He worked on Mattano Park, Brookdale Park (1930), Weasel Brook Park (1931), and Garret Mountain Reservation (1931).

Zach, Leon H.: He worked on Green Brook Park (1922) and Echo Lake Park.

Bibliography

Allen, David Grayson. *The Olmsted National Historic Site and the Growth of Historic Landscape Preservation.* Hanover, N. H.: University Press of New England, 2007.

Barber, Alfred N. *John A. Roebling: An Account of the Ceremonies at the Unveiling of a Monument to His Memory*. Trenton, New Jersey: Roebling Press, 1908.

Beveridge, Charles E. "The Seven S's of Olmsted Design," January 1986 posted on the National Association of Olmsted Parks' website.

Birnbaum, Charles A. and Robin Karson**.** *Pioneers of American Landscape Design*. New York: McGraw-Hill, 2000.

Board of Conservation and Development. *Report of the Board of Conservation and Development.* Trenton, New Jersey: The Board, 1938-1939.

Demmer, John. *Nutley.* Charleston, South Carolina: Arcadia Publishing, 1997 reprinted 2002.

Briant Pond Park Master Plan. Rhodeside & Harwell. Prepared for the Briant Park Olmsted Conservancy, November 2009.

Dickson, William B. Letter to Montclair Town Clerk in June 1905. On file at the Montclair Public Library, Montclair, New Jersey.

Dorflinger, Don and Marietta. *Orange: A Postcard Guide to Its Past.* Charleston, South Carolina: Arcadia Publishing, 1999.

Dupont, Ronald J. and Kevin Wright. *High Point of the Blue Mountains*. Newton, New Jersey: Sussex County Historical Society, 1990.

Essex County Department of Parks. *Fourth Annual Report of the Board of Commissioners,1898-99.* Newark, New Jersey: Grover Bros.,1900.

Essex County Department of Parks. *Twenty-fifth Annual Report of the Board of Commissioners, 1920.* Newark, New Jersey: The W. H. Shurts Co., Printers, 1921.

Essex County Department of Parks. *Twenty-seventh Annual Report of the Board of Commissioners, 1922.* Newark, N.J.: Colyer Printing Co. 1923.

Essex County Department of Parks. *Thirty-third Annual Report of the Essex County Park Commission*, 1928.

Essex County Department of Parks. *Forty-seventh Annual Report of the Essex County Park Commission*, 1945.

Fagan, Joseph. *Eagle Rock Reservation.* Charleston, South Carolina: Arcadia Publishing, 2002.

Federal Writers' Project. *New Jersey, a Guide to Its Present and Past.* New York: The Viking Press, 1939.

Forty-third Annual Report of the Park Commission of Essex County, 1941. Newark, N.J.: Essex County Park Commission,1942.

Giordano, Sandra L. *Clifton*. Charleston, South Carolina: Arcadia Publishing, 2008.

Hessler, Elvira, David L. VanDillen, and William J. Wurst. *A Clifton Sampler*. Clifton, New Jersey: Clifton Public Library, 1991.

"History of the Union County Park System; Special Feature, Warinanco Park." Warinanco Park Tour Committee: Elizabeth, New Jersey, 2010.

Kelsey, Frederick W. *The First County Park System; A Complete History of the Inception and Development of the Essex County Parks of New Jersey.* New York, New York: J.S. Ogilvie Publishing Company, 1905.

Lurie, Maxine N. and Marc Mappen, eds. *Encyclopedia of New Jersey.* New Brunswick, New Jersey: Rutgers University Press, 2004.

Mann, William A. *Landscape Architecture: An Illustrated History in Timelines, Site Plans, and Biography*. New York, New York: John Wiley & Sons, Inc., 1993.

Manual of the Park Commission of the City of Trenton. Trenton, N.J.: Naar, Day & Naar, Printers, 1893.

Modica, Glenn R. *Cadwalader Heights; The History of an Olmsted Neighborhood, Trenton, New Jersey*. Newtown, Pennsylvania: Bucks Digital Printing, 2007.

National Association for Olmsted Parks. *The Master List of Design Projects of the Olmsted Firm 1857-1979*. Lucy Lawliss, Caroline Loughlin, Lauren Meier, eds. Second Edition, Washington, D.C.: National Association for Olmsted Parks, 2008.

Olmsted Brothers, Landscape Architects. "High Point Park, New Jersey; A Report Concerning Its Development." Brookline, Massachusetts; Olmsted Brothers, November 7, 1923.

Olmsted Brothers, Landscape Architects. "Report to the Union County Park Commission." Brookline, Massachusetts, July 5, 1921

Osborne, Peter. *High Point State Park and the Civilian Conservation Corps.* Charleston, South Carolina: Arcadia Publishing, 2002.

Paulsson, Martin. "Franklin Murphy," *Encyclopedia of New Jersey*. Eds. Maxine N. Lurie and Marc Mappen. New Brunswick, New Jersey: Rutgers University Press, 2004.

Shriner, Charles A. *Four Chapters of Paterson History*. Paterson, N.J.: Lont & Overkamp Publishing Co., 1919.

Siegel, Alan A. *Irvington*. Charleston, South Carolina: Arcadia Publishing, Inc., 1997.

Stevenson, Elizabeth. *Parkmaker: A Life of Frederick Law Olmsted*. Reprint edition, New Brunswick, N.J.: Transaction Publishers, 2000.

Troeger, Virginia Bergen and Robert J. McEwen. *Woodbridge, New Jersey; New Jersey's Oldest Township*. Charleston, South Carolina: Arcadia Publishing, 2002.

Union County Park Commission, "Echo Lake Park; Mountainside and Westfield," brochure circa 1950.

Union County Park Commission. *Report of the Union County Park Commission 1926-1927-1928*.

Union County Park Commission. *Report of the Union County Park Commission 1928-1929-1930.*

Union County Park Commission. *Report of the Union County Park Commission, New Jersey 1947-1957.* 1958.

Union County Park Commission. Report of the Union County Park Commission 1958-1963

The Union County Park Commission. *Twenty-Five Year Report of The Union County Park Commission 1921-1946.*

Urquhart, Frank John. *A History of The City of Newark, New Jersey Embracing Practically Two and A Half Centuries 1666-1913*. Volume 2. New York, New York: Lewis Historical Publishing Company, 1915.

Wack, Henry Wellington and the Committee of One Hundred. *Official guide and manual of the 250th anniversary celebration of the founding of the city of Newark, New Jersey 1666-1916.* Newark, New Jersey: Publicity Committee, 1916.

Yeats, Lauren Pancurak. *Linden, New Jersey*. Charleston, South Carolina: Arcadia Publishing, 2002.

Zatz, Arline. *New Jersey's Great Gardens: A Four-Season Guide to 125 Public Gardens, Parks, and Arboretums*. Woodstock, Vermont: The Countryman Press, 1999.

NEWSPAPER ARTICLES:

Childe, Cromwell. "A Chain of Beautiful Parks" *New York Times*, 6 April 1902.

Ermino, Vinessa "Neighborhood Snapshot," *Star-Ledger*. 22 November 2007.

The Orange Chronicle. "Park Supplement; Map and views of the Essex County park system." Orange, New Jersey, 9 April 1898.

"Summit's Briant Park on board for new 'old' look," published on September 1, 2010 on NJ.com.

Torrey, Raymond H. "Jersey County Parks Extend Their Bounds; Union Follows Essex in Developing a System of Open Tracts That are Readily Accessible to Its Large Centers of Population," *New York Times*, 21 November 1926.

PERSONAL CORRESPONDENCE

Stefel, April M. E-mail communication, 17 December 2010.

Streeter, Cathy Bird. Personal correspondence. 16 March 2009.

WEBSITES

Essex County Department of Parks, Recreation, and Cultural Affairs: http://www.essex-countynj.org/p/index.php?section=af/system

McGann, Mary Ann. "South Mountain High; A look at South Mountain Reservation." Matters Magazine on the internet at www.maplewoodonline.com/southmountain, 2009.

Save Outdoor Sculpture! database on the Smithsonian Institution Research Information System (SIRIS) at the Smithsonian American Art Museum: http://americanart.si.edu/research/programs/sos/.

Trenton Historical Society newspaper articles of the George Washington statue at www.trentonnhistory.org/Records/Statue.html.

Friends of Anderson Park website. http://www.friendsofandersonpark.com/

Friends of Riverbank Park website http://www.newarkhistory.com/riverbank.html

Grover Cleveland Park Conservancy: http://www.groverclevelandpark.org/Thepark/history.html

Union County Department of Parks and Community Renewal: http://ucnj.org/community/Parks-Community-Renewal/parks-facilities/parks

Plainfield Public Library website at: www.plainfieldlibrary.info/AboutUs/History.html.

Index